Key Concepts in E-Commerce

Alan Charlesworth

palgrave
macmillan

First published 2007 by
PALGRAVE MACMILLAN
Houndmills, Basingstoke, Hampshire RG21 6XS and
175 Fifth Avenue, New York, N.Y. 10010
Companies and representatives throughout the world

PALGRAVE MACMILLAN is the global academic imprint of the Palgrave Macmillan division of St. Martin's Press, LLC and of Palgrave Macmillan Ltd. Macmillan® is a registered trademark in the United States, United Kingdom and other countries. Palgrave is a registered trademark in the European Union and other countries.

ISBN-13: 978 0–230–51671–7
ISBN-10: 0–230–51671–8

This book is printed on paper suitable for recycling and made from fully managed and sustained forest sources. Logging, pulping and manufacturing processes are expected to conform to the environmental regulatons of the country of origin.

A catalogue record for this book is available from the British Library.

Library of Congress Cataloging-in-Publication Data
Charlesworth, Alan, 1956–
    Key concepts in e-commerce / Alan Charlesworth.
      p. cm. – (Palgrave key concepts)
    Includes bibliographical references and index.
    ISBN-13: 978–0–230–51671–7 (pbk.)
    ISBN-10: 0–230–51671–8 (pbk.)
      1. Electronic commerce–Dictionaries. 2. Internet. I. Title.

    HF5548.32.C47238 2007
    381'.14203–dc22   2006052751

10 9 8 7 6 5 4 3 2
16 15 14 13 12 11 10 09 08 07

Printed and bound in China

To Julia, always

Contents

Acknowledgements

To all at Palgrave Macmillan who made this publication possible, with particular thanks to Suzannah Burywood and Karen Griffiths.

To the book's copy-editor, Juanita Bullough. I consider my grammar skills to be reasonably good, but Juanita puts me in a rather dark shade. Thanks to Juanita, the presentation of the content is far better than my original draft, and I am now an expert on (among other things) use of the compound adjective.

To Andy Wynd. Sadly, Andy lost his fight with cancer in 2000 – but not before he taught me the basics of e-commerce technology. Quite an achievement, given that at the time I usually struggled to simply find the switch to turn on a PC. You are missed, Andy.

Key Concepts in E-Commerce – online

In the Internet age a textbook is expected to have a web site – so a book about e-commerce would be particularly remiss if it too didn't have its own web presence.

The web site for *Key Concepts in E-Commerce* is, however, no gesture towards conformity – it is a resource all readers of the book should visit on a regular basis.

A significant problem the author faced when writing this book was that e-commerce is, by its very nature, dynamic. In the time it took to write them, some terms required updating – with others needing to be deleted altogether because they had been superseded or fallen out of common usage. Furthermore, new terms come into use on a regular basis – fresh additions were being added to the glossary right up the last date for submission to the publisher. It is this state of affairs that the book's web site seeks to address.

If any of the terms in this book requires updating, it will be on the web site. If technology renders a term obsolete, its replacement will be there, and – perhaps most importantly – any new terms that emerge between this and the next edition of the book will be on the web site also.

Visit the *Key Concepts in E-Commerce* web site at:

www.palgrave.com/keyconceptse-commerce

Introduction

This is a book about e-commerce written from a business perspective, rather than a book on information technology (IT). Any technical terms are simplified and included only because an understanding of them would be an advantage in a business context. It is, predominantly, a book for students and practitioners of any aspect of business that involves the use of the Internet. If there are any IT practitioners or students who wish to learn about the online business applications of the technology they work with, it is for them also.

The structure of the glossary

While every effort has been made to include all of the key concepts in e-commerce, the phenomenon is that e-commerce is still evolving as a discipline – it being only around a decade old – and it is changing at a pace never before experienced in a business environment. As a result of this a number of significant difficulties arise, namely that:

- new concepts will have surfaced since this book was written;
- concepts popular at the time of writing lose favour or are superseded; or
- many practices are known by different names – for example, the terms *search engine* spam, *link* spam and *web* spam are all used to describe the same practice.

(Note that the book's web site will feature new terms which might emerge after publication.)

In other cases, the *unregulated* nature of the Internet as a medium for communication has caused the origins of definitions to become obscured – with various terms being exposed or promoted in the medium itself, with no check being necessary to support the validity of comments made in connection to them. This is exemplified by the abbreviation 'RSS'. For the more technically minded, this stands for *RDF Site Summary* or possibly *Rich Site Summary*. However, when the technology became commonly used it also came to be known by the definition that, for the less technically minded, more closely describes what the technology does – *Really Simple Syndication*. Another problem is the phenomenon of the so-called backronym. A portmanteau of *back* and *acronym*, a backronym is where a term begins life as an ordinary word but is later converted into an acronym. Spam and PING are two examples of this practice.

For the reasons listed above, the definition or description of some terms may be disputed by some. Such disputes might arise because (a) the author is wrong, or (b) the reader is wrong. More likely, however, is that either the author's or the reader's sources of reference are wrong. While every effort has been made to verify the terms used in this book, the very nature of the way and speed in which e-commerce has developed makes this an inexact science. An example of such ambiguity is the term URL, standing for *uniform resource locator*. So common is the mistake of identifying the first word as *universal* (even in academic papers and texts), that people will argue that *universal* is correct, citing its use in (incorrect) publications to support their argument.

While the book concentrates on words, terms and phrases used in e-commerce, a number of more generic Internet-related entries have been added – *avatar*, for example. These are included to help the readers develop an understanding of the culture of both the Internet and its users – essentially, the environment in which e-commerce is conducted.

Throughout the book some terms are listed under their acronym or abbreviation, while others are presented in full. The listing decision is based on whether readers are more likely to come across the abbreviation or the full phrase. Hence, HTML is listed as such, with the full term (hypertext mark-up language) in brackets, while the reverse is the case for *clickthrough rate*, where only a specialist publication might use the abbreviation (CTR).

The key concepts have been arranged alphabetically in order to ensure that the reader can quickly find the term or entry of immediate interest. Such is the integrated nature of e-commerce that many of the terms listed are affected by, or themselves affect, others. To address this, each entry has its own definition, with any reference to another key concept term or phrase within that definition being highlighted in **bold** – thus enabling readers to investigate related terms.

Glossary terms – a guide

The book avoids promotion of specific brands or products. There are instances, however, when to make this resolution absolute would be to the detriment of the content. An obvious example is Google. The brand now has so many applications that an e-commerce glossary without reference to the brand would be incomplete – it is now even considered to be a verb (to *google*). Similarly, PageRank is part of the Google search algorithm (and is trademarked as such), but to exclude it would be to miss out a valuable element of online marketing. Another exception is where products or services are available without charge, often in *open source* – the Bobby web-compliance tool fits into this category. Mention of any product or brand should not be considered as an endorsement, nor should any omission be considered to be a rebuke or dismissal.

There are a number of entries that cover only the online, or e-commerce, application of that practice or concept. This is deliberate. Any attempt to cover in full the offline version of terms would make this book both lacking in focus and somewhat unwieldy. An example of this is *behavioural targeting*. Marketers in particular will recognize the concept as it will have significant coverage in any marketing text. In this book, however, only the online application is addressed. It is expected that the reader will have at least *some* knowledge of business and so be familiar with such concepts in their offline manifestation. Those readers who are not familiar with any (offline) concepts or practices are advised to use the companion books in the Palgrave Key Concepts series.

In a similar vein, there are terms from non-business disciplines that have e-commerce connotations or applications. In these cases only the e-commerce-related description is offered. For example, an *algorithm* is a mathematical or computational procedure, but if the e-commerce student or practitioner were to come across the word at all, it would be in relation to search engines. Therefore, in this glossary, the term defined is *search engine algorithm*.

There are a limited number of legal terms included in the book. Readers should note that any definitions offered are only *general* descriptions of the terms and how they relate to the e-commerce practitioner and should not be considered to be legal advice.

Prior to using the book the reader is advised to review a number of terms included in the text – an understanding of which will help in appreciating much of the other content of the glossary. Those terms are: e-business, 'e' (as a prefix), cyber (as a prefix) and online (as a prefix).

A/B testing

An offline concept that is practised in an e-commerce environment when testing web site or email performance. The basic premise is that an equal number of users are exposed to an email or web page – or combination of the two – that has been developed in two formats (that is, A and B). In the test, equal quantities of **traffic** are directed to each (by either period-based changes or using a **traffic splitter code**) and results recorded to measure which works best. Things that can be tested using an A/B split include headlines, copy, graphical images, banner ads, PPC ads, button colours – indeed, anything where there is the potential to improve the response and be able to measure the improvements.

See also **web site analytics, KPIs, micro-improvements** and **persuasion architecture.**

Above the fold

Originally a expression used in newspaper publishing, above the fold is a reference to full-size newspapers being folded in half by the majority of readers. The term refers to the top half of the front page – above the fold – which is where the most important and/or eye-catching content will be. The phrase has been adapted by web publishers in a very similar context; the online phrase referring to that part of the web site that is visible in the user's **browser** without them **scrolling** down. For the **web publisher** that part of the web page that is visible as soon as it downloads is just as valuable as its newspaper equivalent

See also **viewable area.**

Access control

Any kind of device that determines who can have access to a network resource. The requirement for a **log-in** and **password** is the norm.

See also **encryption.**

Access provider

See Internet service provider.

Accessibility

See web site accessibility.

Accountable marketing

A term used to describe **pay per click** advertising, the nature of which facilitates easy cost vs results analysis. This is in contrast to the unaccountable nature of corporate marketing – branding, for example. Finance departments like the pay per click model as each ad is accountable in that it costs no money if it is not successful in its objective (that is, if no one clicks on it, it costs no money). This concept is contrary to the well-used maxim that half of all advertising spend is wasted, but you never know which half (historians can't agree whether the phrase should be attributed to US department store owner, John Wanamaker, or soap magnate Lord Leverhulme). In accountable marketing, however, no money is wasted – unless you are the victim of **click fraud**.

Active content

Any content on a web site that is either interactive or dynamic – effectively, anything that moves on the web page. Because the term dates back to time when movement on a web page was unusual, it is rarely used these days. Note that the term should not be confused with an **active server page**.

Active server page (ASP)

A dynamically created web page that uses **software** which is processed on the web **browser** before being served to the user. Used mostly for online query forms, an active server page can be identified by the .asp suffix on a page's **URL**.

See also **dynamic web pages**.

Active token

An electronic device that can generate passwords on a one-off basis as part of a security system. The unique password is normally presented to the user as an **image** (rather than text) so that it must then be physically typed into the **browser**. An active token increases security by preventing any kind of software from *reading* and copying the text automatically.

Active window

That part of a web site that is seen by the user at any given time, making it the prime real estate on a computer screen.

See also **viewable area** and **above the fold**.

ActiveX

A Microsoft-developed independent program which can be safely downloaded to a computer and immediately run without fear of viruses or other harm to the computer or its files, ActiveX makes it possible for web pages to include functions such as animations and calculators. Note, however, that a similar definition can be found for **Java**, ActiveX being Microsoft's version of a program with the same function.

Ad

A common abbreviation for advert, which is in turn an abbreviation of advertisement. For no apparent reason, it has become common practice to use *ad* when referring to any kind of advertisement in an online context.

Ad aggregators

See **online advertising network**.

Ad banner

See **banner**.

Ad-blocker

See **pop-up blocker**.

AdCenter

The trade name of MSN's **pay per click** advertising system.

See also **AdWords** and **Yahoo! search marketing**.

A

Ad network

See online advertising network.

Address Verification System (AVS)

Software that automatically checks a user's address held on file against that entered on an online form. It is normally used by banks and credit-card companies to detect fraudulent transactions.

Ad-gaming

See advergaming.

Ad impression

A **metric** used in **web site analytics**, this is the number of times a **banner** ad is **downloaded** during a specific period of time. Note that because the ad has been downloaded does not necessarily mean the user has even seen it, never mind taken any notice of it. There is also the issue of whether or not the ad has actually downloaded onto the **browser** screen before the user clicks on a **link** and moves off of the page, particularly if it is not in the **viewable area**.

See also impression.

Ad inventory

Used for the purposes of invoicing, ad inventory is the number of **ad impressions** that a web site sells over a period of time, normally a month.

Adlab (the adCenter Incubation Lab)

A Microsoft research and development unit that looks specifically at increasing income through ad sales.

Ad listing

The textual content that a user sees when a sponsored ad appears on a **search engine return page** – the *listing*. The ad listing is made up of a title and a short description of the product or service being promoted. The composition of the listing is important in that it will be the difference between a user clicking on it or not, and so best practice is to include a **call to action**.

Ad rotation (also known as *dynamic* rotation)

It is rare for web sites to display the same ads continuously, primarily because more revenue can be earned by changing them on a frequent basis – or *rotating* them. There are a number of methods of rotation: (a) by **user session** – where the same ads are displayed while a user is on the site, (b) by page **download** – each time a user opens a page on the site a different ad from a series is displayed, or (c) by user profile (see **contextual and behavioural targeting**).

See also **adsense, surround sessions** and **dayparts**.

Ad scheduling

See **dayparting**.

AdSense

A method of web site ad distribution from the Google organization. Ads (from Google) that are related to a page's content, or matching the characteristics and interests of visitors, are automatically posted on publishers' sites, so earning revenue for the site's publisher. Technically advanced, the system is based on the offline concept of **contextual and behavioural targeting** and the technology involved is sometimes referred to as **collaborative filtering**.

Ad server

A third-party **server** (3PAS) that stores ads and delivers them to web site visitors, normally used by an **online advertising network**. Having ads on a separate server allows publishers to feature ads on their site(s) without having to store those ads on their own servers. They also allow ad networks to control the distribution of the ads they are handling for clients. **Adware** is normally used to record ad server activity. Publishers should be aware, however, that an ad server is running slowly, or the ads are too large, the downloading ads could cause the web site itself to download slowly also. Users can see if a web site is running adware by looking at the **status bar** at the foot of their browser. This shows the **URL** of where content is being downloaded from. Normally this will be the URL of the web site itself, but it could also feature the URL of the ad server distributing the ads – for example, something like www.adserverspecialistcompany.com/aparticularadvert.

A

ADSL

See **digital subscriber line**.

Ad space

The area of a web site designated to carry **banner ads**. The space could be filled with banners designated by the publisher of the site, or the space could display ads hosted on a third-party **ad server**. Banner sizes are one of the few things that are standard throughout web site design and publishing – probably because they are the only source of income for many web sites. Convention also dictates where on the web page banners are hosted – normally across the top, down the right-hand side and along the bottom.

Ad sponsor

See **sponsored listing**.

Adult web site

Although normally a euphemism for a web site that has pornographic – *adult* – content, the phrase can also refer to gambling or any other sites not deemed suitable for children.

Advergaming (also known as ad-gaming)

Although advergaming makes use of computer games as a medium for advertising, this is a simplified description of the concept. Using a similar concept to **viral marketing**, advergaming relies on a viral element for its success – with users passing games on to other users on the web. Advergames vary from being a sponsored web page where users visit and play arcade-type games online to more sophisticated **alternate-reality gaming**. That most games require some kind of registration betrays the fact that advergaming has multiple marketing objectives, with user data being used for research and/or target marketing agendas.

Advertising copy

The textual content of an **ad**. The term *copy* is used because the words should encourage the viewer to take an action that will help the ad meet its objective(s). Often ad copy will consist of little more than a call to action.

See also **content (2)**.

A

Advertorial

Also known as infomercials, advertorials are ads that are presented in the form of editorial content. The concept is to offer content that is stimulating to the reader while at the same time delivering a marketing message. Although they are used successfully in offline media, advertorials carry a certain *commercial* stigma and online application is rare. Those web sites that do use the model tend to list it under various euphemisms such as *special advertising section, special promotional feature* or *integrated content* to make them more attractive to web users. In some instances the difference between an advertorial (content written by the advertiser) and sponsored content (paid for by the sponsor but written by the publisher) is narrow – and not readily apparent to the reader.

Ad view

See **ad impression**.

Adware

A type of **spyware** that collects information about web **users** in order to display targeted ads in that user's **browser** window. Exhibited ads are based on the user's browsing patterns – see **contextual and behavioural targeting**. Those advertisers who seek to gain commercial advantage by less scrupulous means can use adware that has the ability to deliver competitive ads next to or over the top of a site's existing ads without the user's knowledge or the publisher's permission.

AdWords

Google's **pay per click** advertising system. Ads can be placed as **sponsored ads** on a Google **search engine results page** (and on any site that is part of Google's 'content network' as part of their **AdSense** service). Recognizing how complex their ad systems have become, in April 2006 Google introduced its AdWords Editor, a free downloadable account-management tool. Such is the popularity of Google that AdWords is often used as the generic term for the practice, even though the other major search engines have their own versions – **Yahoo! search marketing** and **MSN adCenter**.

A

Affiliate

See **affiliate marketing**.

Affiliate management

In a normal state of affairs only major web site publishers can handle their own **affiliate marketing** programmes, as sourcing and negotiating with multiple advertisers is a complex and time-consuming exercise. It is far more common for publishers (particularly of small web sites) to use third-party affiliate-management services to facilitate transactions.

Affiliate marketing

Although affiliate marketing is a close relative of **online advertising**, the use of affiliates to increase sales is a partnership between advertisers and publishers which goes beyond mere advertising. The concept is for business A to have other businesses sell their product or service for them – though not in the same way as a manufacturer would use wholesalers and retailers. Affiliate marketing is, essentially, a referral programme with partners in the affiliation agreeing to a fee that is paid when a referred customer completes a transaction. An offline example would be a car-hire firm that rewards a hotel for referring clients. Online, this means that the publisher of the web site that hosts the affiliate ad will benefit financially if a user follows a link from their site to the advertiser's site and subsequently makes a purchase. However, ad **banners** are passive, sitting on the web page waiting for the user to click on them, whereas for an affiliate programme to be successful, the affiliated organization (the one publishing the site containing the links) must be proactive – vigorously promoting the product or service that is on offer. Successful affiliate marketing is very much a partnership between advertiser and publisher, and so should be of benefit to both parties. The epitome of good affiliate practice is Amazon, who built its business using affiliates to promote – and sell – books on behalf of the online bookseller. However, being an affiliate also produces a form of direct income, in much the same way that selling advertising space on a web site does. It is estimated that around 20 per cent of online retail sales originate with affiliates.

A

Affiliate programme

The terms and operating procedures for both parties in **affiliate marketing**.

Agent

In an e-commerce environment, this is a software program that performs a specific information-gathering or processing task. Naturally, individuals and entities that act as agents in the offline definition can use the Internet to conduct their business – though this is one practice that has not succumbed to the 'e' prefix – that is, e-agents.

Aggregation of products

Essentially, the role of a retailer in the distribution chain – that is, bringing to one place a variety of products that will appeal to a large number of customers – aggregation of products is the identification, sourcing, ordering, receiving, storage and display of goods for sale. Such activities represent a significant expense for ·a **bricks-and-mortar** retailer, but for the online retailer much of this cost is reduced, particularly those that operate as a **virtual business**. Amazon, for example, does not have to carry the stock of books as do offline book stores.

Aggregation services

See **content aggregator.**

AIDA (Attention, Interest, Desire, Action)

A model of direct sales dating back to the 1890s when salesman St Elmo Lewis introduced the concept, and which has been developed constantly since then – notably in 1925 when E. K. Strong included it in his 1925 book, *The Psychology of Selling*. The online concept requires the marketer to ask: did the ad grab attention, arouse an interest, stimulate desire and provide a call for action? It is included here because the AIDA model is highly pertinent for both web sites and emails. Some contemporary authors (and practitioners) have added an 'S' to the acronym, standing for *satisfaction*. While this does *close the loop* in the action-cycle, the original concept was intended for advertising, whose action-cycle would end at their response to the ad, at which point sales procedures would take over. To add 'satisfaction' to the AIDA model suggests that the customer jumps from the call to action straight to post-purchase, missing out a number of stages in the sales process. Even online – where the 'S' has been added most prominently – the customer would have to go through an online buying procedure, and then take delivery of the goods before *satisfaction* was determined. Both of these events (purchase and delivery) are fraught with complications that may cause the user to fall out of the **conversion funnel**. As previously mentioned, the AIDA concept belongs to a time long before most modern media – let alone the Internet – existed. While the model is still

A

valid, attempts have been made to bring it into the Internet age by renaming the process. Although some work well (for example the *scent trail* from grokdotcom.com), all follow the basic principles of AIDA. An element in the **online buying cycle**, AIDA is also the basis for **persuasion architecture**.

AJAX (Asynchronous JavaScript and XML)

A web site development tool used to create applications that are interactive. The purpose of the AJAX technology is to move much of the computation to the user's computer so that web pages do not have to reload completely when an interactive application is used. This means that speed and interactivity are increased. Search engine marketers should take care, however. Unless administered judiciously, AJAX can cause problems in any **search engine optimization** for sites that use the technology.

Algorithm

See **search engine algorithm**.

Alt tags

See **alt text**.

Alternate reality gaming

A development of **advergaming**, the concept of alternate reality gaming was pioneered commercially by online campaigns for products such as the film *AI* and the game Halo 2, which combined reality and fantasy using the Internet. Alternate reality gaming efforts can blend computer game play, hoax web sites and unfolding online mysteries with offline activities such as phone messages and other sinister-seeming intrusions into gamers' real-world lives. In e-commerce terms, the concept can be used as a promotion or as a medium for carrying ads.

Alt text

A **tag** used in **HTML** to describe an **image** on a web site – that is, *alternative text* that should describe the image. Sadly, too few designers use the facility to actually *describe* the image, often simply putting in the file name instead. Non-**broadband** surfers often use the web with their **browser**'s image facility turned off so that pages download more

A

quickly. In these circumstances the alt text tag would describe the image (for example, 'picture of Humberston church'). More important is the tag's use by visually impaired surfers, for whom the alt text would be spoken by their text-reader software – for them 'image 1234.jpg' would mean nothing, whereas 'picture of Humberston church' gives them a description of what the sighted user is viewing. Also important is that search engine algorithms take notice of alt text tags. In the example above, someone searching on the term 'Humberston church', or simply 'Humberston' would be likely to find that image – or the page it is on – featured in the **search engine results page**.

Analogue

Media-related devices can be described or represented in one of two forms; analogue or digital. The principal feature of analogue representations is that they are continuous. In contrast, digital representations consist of values measured at discrete intervals. Generally, analogue services (for example radio, TV, mobile telephones) are inferior to their digital equivalent. When used in a computing environment, the term *digital* is most commonly used to describe the conversion of real-world information to a binary format, as in digital radio, etc. For this reason, digital has become a familiar prefix to denote the *online* application of an *offline* subject.

See also **e** and **online (as a prefix)**.

Anchor tag

The HTML instruction for text or an image to be a **link**. For this reason a word, sentence, phrase or paragraph on a web page that includes a link to another page or site might be referred to as the anchor text. The page to which the link takes the user is the **target page.**

A

Animated GIF

A format for saving **graphics** that allows several images to be saved at once and then displayed by web browsers one after another – so creating the illusion of movement (as with cartoons). It was one of the first forms of *movement* used on the web, and is still popular today. Used mostly in **banner** ads, its popularity stems from the fact that each image can be small (in data-transmission terms), and so the images download and play quickly.

Anonymous FTP

See **FTP**.

Applet

A software component that runs within another **application**. In an e-commerce context, that application is the web **browser**. Unlike a **program**, an applet cannot run independently. Applets are very small, secure, and work with a number of **platforms**, making them ideal for Internet application. A popular application is in **Java**.

Application

Another way to say computer – or **software** – program, this term is most likely to be used by **techies**.

Application Service Provider (ASP) (or **Application Software Provider**)

A third-party entity that uses a central data centre to manage and distribute software-based services to customers. In an e-commerce environment, a business may use an ASP to host web sites, provide online shopping facilities or facilitate credit-card transactions.

See also **utility computing**.

Archie

Generally accepted as the first Internet search engine (note: *Internet*, not *web*). Developed by student Alan Emtage in the early 1990s, Archie was designed to help academics find documents in Internet-linked archives.

See also **WWW Wanderer** and **SMART**.

ARPANET (Advanced Research Projects Agency Network)

The forerunner of the **Internet**, ARPANET was developed in the late 1960s and early 1970s by the US Department of Defense as an experiment in wide-area networking. The objective was to develop a communications system that would survive a nuclear explosion that had rendered all other methods of communication inoperable.

See also **packet**.

A

ASCII (American Standard Code for Information Interchange)

The worldwide standard for the code numbers used by computers to represent all the upper- and lower-case Latin letters, numbers, punctuation, etc. There are 128 standard ASCII codes, each of which can be represented by a seven-digit binary number: from 0000000 to 1111111. ASCII is not normally something an e-commerce practitioner would need to know about, but it is frequently referred to by **techies**.

ASP

See application service provider.

Asymmetric digital subscriber line (ADSL)

See digital subscriber line.

Atomic phrases

See cue words.

Attachment

A file which is attached to, and then sent along with, an email message. Any kind of file can be attached – text, graphics, sound, for example – but some attachments are too large to be accepted by the service provider. As most **viruses** are spread using attachments, using them in **email marketing** is not advisable, as recipients will be reluctant to open them and worse, assume the email is malicious.

Auction

See online auction.

A

Authentication

The process by which the identity of a person is verified as being that which they claim. Although a password can be a form of authentication, it would normally be a **digital certificate** or **digital signature**.

Authentication codes

These are used by **Internet service providers** to tell their inbound servers whether or not the sender is authorized to send emails from the

IP address and that the sender is who they claim to be. Authentication codes are part of **spam**-prevention measures.

Authentication tagging

In order to help legitimate emails pass through **spam filters**, data (in the form of **tags**) are embedded into each email to identify the sending organization. These enable receiving **Internet Service Providers** to verify that senders are actually who they say they are, making it virtually impossible for **spammers** and **phishers** to hide their identities.

See also **email delivery protocol standards**.

Autoresponder

Sometimes known as a *mailbot*, an autoresponder is an automated email reply system that responds to incoming email. While a common use is to inform senders that the receiver is out of the office at that time and when they will return, autorespond-emails are also useful as sales tools when used in response to sales orders. For example, an autorespond-email confirming a flight or holiday booking could include details of a special offer on airport car-parking. However, out of office-type autorespond messages do have a drawback. Should a **spam** message receive a reply from an autoresponder it is telling the spammer that the email account is live, and so they will target the address with even more spam messages.

Avatars

Animated computer characters meant to represent a *virtual* person. That they invariably display human-like behaviour perhaps betrays the origin of the term – a Hindu bodily manifestation of an Immortal, or the Ultimate, Being. Widespread use of the term has diluted its meaning over time, with avatar being used to describe anything from *character* images as personal identifiers on forums and chat rooms to the *talking head*-type representations used on some web sites as a way of presenting verbal messages.

A

B2–

For the traditional (that is, offline) business, trading with end users is known as *consumer* marketing and trading with other businesses is referred to as *industrial* marketing. On the Internet these have been replaced by the terms *business-to-consumer* and *business-to-business* trading, with each being more commonly known by the abbreviations B2C and B2B, respectively. The apparent logic of these descriptions has seen them generally replace the terms *consumer* and *industrial*, particularly among the new generation of business students and practitioners. B2B and B2C are not, however, the limit to the B2 range of trading. Others include B2E (business-to-employee) and B2G (business-to-government).

See also **C2B** and **C2C**.

B2B e-marketplaces

Based on the offline notion that is the *market* (a place where buyers and sellers come together), and applying the concept of **aggregation of products**, an e-marketplace has numerous sellers feeding goods/services into an online facility where multiple buyers can source goods. In the concept, the virtual marketplace is run – as a business model – by a third party who facilitates trade between the various buyers and sellers, taking a percentage of transactions or a fixed fee for the service. The concept is also known as the *butterfly model* – a concept that originated in the late 1990s – because a pictorial representation of multiple buyers and sellers surrounding a virtual marketplace resembles a butterfly's wings around its body.

B2B portal

See **portal**.

B2C business-to-consumer

See **B2-**.

B2E business-to-employee

See **B2-**.

B2G business-to-government

See **B2-**.

Backbone

A high-speed line or series of connections that form a major pathway within a **network** – the human bone-structure analogy being particularly apt, as failure of the backbone invariably causes problems with all associated bones. In an e-commerce context, the most common application of the term is when it refers to the main connection with the Internet as used by **Internet service providers**, with users coming across the term when web connections are not working due to 'problems with the backbone'.

Back end (operations)

See **back office**.

Backlinks

See **link**.

Back office (operations)

Although programmers might beg to differ, in e-commerce terms *back end* and *back office* effectively mean the same thing – with *office* being more pertinent to the business community. The term has technical origins, where the element of a software application that interfaces with end users referred to as the front end, and the **server** element, the back end. Offline, however, it has always been common practice to refer to staff who deal with customers as *front office* and those who have no contact with customers as *back office*. In e-commerce the two come together. Front office refers to those elements of the **web presence** with which users (customers) interact, and back office those elements of the business that support customer transactions. For example, on an online shop the front-office operations would be everything from the customer arriving on the site – **usability**, **navigation**, **graphics**, **sales copy**, and so on – up to the point where they confirm a purchase. Anything that supports the **fulfilment** of that online sale is deemed back-office operations. This would include such things as inventory management, purchasing (from suppliers), payment processing, storage, packaging and delivery.

B

BackRub

The project that brought together Google founders Larry Page and Sergey Brin, and which was the foundation stone of **PageRank**, which differentiated Google from other search engines. Simply put, BackRub was a tool to track where a web site's inbound **links** came from – rather than simply where outbound links went.

Bait piece

A concept that has existed offline for decades, the term describes an article or editorial that attracts the interest of consumers – hence *bait* – but also acts as a promotion for a product or service offered by the producer of the bait piece. Online, free information is offered as bait to generate sales leads (see **lead generation**). The free offer might be an article that tells readers how to solve a particular problem. To work best, the free article should be associated to the product or service for which that article is bait. For example, a **search engine marketing** (SEM) company might offer an article entitled 'the beginner's guide to optimizing a web page for search engines'. By downloading the free article the user has identified themselves as a **prospect** for the SEM company. Online, the free article is often referred to as a **white paper**, and so the concept has become known by that term.

See also **bait and switch.**

Bait and switch

The basic premise of this practice, which originates offline, is that potential customers, or **prospects**, are tempted by an offer in an ad or shop-window display for a product – but when they speak to a salesperson they are *switched* to another (usually more expensive) substitute product. Although the practice can be illegal (advertising goods that do not exist, for example), and perhaps always morally dubious, it is common practice in sales environments. If the sales person has the skill to **up sell** the buyer to the more expensive product by convincing the customer it is better suited to their needs, then the customer may well overlook the fact that they were enticed by a *bait* ad. Online the practice is (a) easier to perform – an ad needing the user to simply click on the bait ('click here for cheap goods'), but also (b) easier to reject – users clicking on the back button. Note that a bait and switch strategy can cause harm to any organization or brand that uses it and so should be practised with care.

See also **clicker's remorse.**

B

Bandwidth

The rate at which data is transmitted – in e-commerce terms, how much content can be sent through an Internet connection in a fixed amount of time. Bandwidth is normally measured in bits per second (bps) or megabits per second (Mbps) – often referred to as *megs* – or even in its singular form, as in 4 meg. **Download time** is partially determined by bandwidth, and so is important to e-commerce practitioners.

See also **broadband.**

Banned

Although the term has a myriad of offline applications, in an e-commerce environment it normally refers to web pages being removed – *banned* – from a search engine's **index** because they have broken the search engine's guidelines or the site is guilty of **spamming**. Although the term is commonly used in this way, being banned from a search engine is most usually referred to as being **de-listed**.

See also **reinclusion request.**

Banner (banner ad)

The first format of ad to appear online – around 1994; *see* **Hotwired** – banners are still the most popular form of online advertising. Banner ads are normally described by their sizes, which are fixed in order for web developers to design-in spaces for ads. Banner sizes (in pixels) include:

- 468 × 60 – the most common, and so **de facto standard**, size;
- 234 × 60 – the *half*-banner;
- 120 × 60 and 125 × 125 – *button* size;
- 120 × 600 and 160 × 600 – *skyscrapers*, which appear down the side of a web page.

Banner sizes are not universal across all **ad servers**, however. For example, Google's **AdSense** uses 728 × 90 *leaderboards* and 300 × 250 *inline rectangles* that are unique to that service.

In order to show some movement – and so attract attention – some banners use **animated GIFs**. Although the term banner is normally associated with fixed-position ads, **pop-up ads** are also sometimes described as banners. More recently, other types of banner have been added. These include:

- The expandable banner – where an ordinary banner (normally 468 × 60) expands to three or four times its size as a mouse is

B

moved over it, and collapses back to a banner size when the mouse is moved away.

- The margin landscape banner – this takes advantage of the fact that many web sites are designed for smaller screens than are being used by some surfers. For example, a common width for web pages is 800 pixels, yet some users will have a screen that will accommodate 1024 – leaving 'blank' screen down the side. The margin landscape banner takes advantage of this empty margin by filling it with an ad that appears like scenic background, not moving when the user scrolls down the page.
- The full-scale takeover banner – as its name suggests, this banner covers the entire page content for a limited, specified time before disappearing. It has a transparent background so only its images and content are visible over the host page's content.
- The full-scale landscape banner – a rarely used application that works best on pages that not only have white backgrounds, but plenty of **white space**. The ad, normally a branding imprint, appears *behind* the content of the page and can only be seen through the transparent content, rather like a scenic background image. It does not move when the user scrolls down the page.
- The sticky banner – this can vary in size, but is usually relatively small (for example 88 × 31) and *sticks* to the screen as the user scrolls down the page, meaning it is always in view.
- **Search&display** banners – allow searches to take place within the banner.

Banner advertising

The use of **banners** on web pages to promote a product or service. By clicking on the banner the visitor is normally taken to the advertiser's own web site – preferably a **landing page**. Because the user can react to the ad immediately, banner advertising is considered to be an element of interactive marketing.

Banner exchange

The practice of two or more organizations exchanging – *swapping* – the placement of banners on each other's web site. Although it can be beneficial (a neighbouring hotel and restaurant, for example), it is rarely practised with discretion and is most commonly used in an attempt to increase search engine ratings; *see* **link popularity**.

B

Banner farm

A web site that consists solely of banner ads. Originally, the objective of these sites was to generate revenue through advertising and **affiliate-marketing** income, which then developed into selling banners to web site publishers who wanted to increase links to their site with the aim of improving search engine ranking. Success at either is rare, as search engines recognize and penalize the practice.

Banner swapping

See **banner exchange**.

BCC (blind carbon copy)

See **CC/BCC**.

Behavioural targeting

See **contextual and behavioural targeting**.

Benchmark

A predetermined standard against which performance can be measured. It is included here because the fast-evolving nature of e-commerce has resulted in there being few *online* benchmarks that stand any test of time before technology – or better practice – supersedes them. Having no dependable benchmark makes objective assessment of any practice – an **online advertising** campaign, for example – difficult, if not impossible. Similarly, there is no benchmark for good, or effective, web site design.

B

Beta

A term used to describe an early release (the *beta* release) of a product – particularly software – to a limited group of users (*beta* testers) in order to perfect the product. The phrase *in beta* is used to identify something that is at this test stage of its development. While the original concept was to test the product, it has become common for beta testing to be used to test the market for a new product. Google, for example, labelled its search engine to be in beta for the early years of its availability. This added to its attraction for **geeks** and early adopters, and prompted its spread virally (see **viral marketing**) amongst academics and journalists before breaking into the mainstream marketplace.

Beta testing

See **beta**.

Bid gap

Although this could refer to any gap between bids, in an auction or **online tender**, for example, in e-commerce the term is normally associated with the gap between two advertisers who are competing for the top positions on a **paid placement** search engine.

Bid jamming

A tactic used in competitive bidding for **keywords** for **paid placement** on search engines, bid jamming keeps a bid marginally below that of a chosen competitor, so requiring them to pay the highest possible cost-per-click (CPC) value to maintain a particular position. In other words, you do not win the highest placement, but you do force up competitor's costs. Manual practice of such a tactic is virtually impossible, utilization of **bid-management software** being the norm. Bid jamming might be considered to be the converse to **bid shadowing**.

Bid-management software

Software, normally run by third parties, that manages an advertiser's **ad listings** on **PPC** search engines. When looking to win the auction for popular keywords in competitive markets, simply making a single bid and sitting back is no longer an option. As the name suggests, bid-management software allows users to manage bidding by systematically updating bids to maintain specific bid positions, move bid positions up and down to achieve specified objectives and enable advertisers to compete in *bid wars*. Such software can provide competitive advantage in strongly contested markets. See also **bid jamming**, **bid surfing**, **time-based bidding**, **return bidding** and **bid shadowing**. Note also that the major search engines are introducing new features to their ad programmes on a regular basis, making bid management an even more specialized occupation. Google has recognized this and in April 2006 introduced its AdWords Editor, a free downloadable account management tool, with other players in the industry expected to follow suit.

B

Bid shadowing

A tactic used in competitive bidding for **keywords** for **paid placement** on search engines, bid shadowing involves maintaining a bid position slightly above a specified competitor's bid. By shadowing bids in this way, bidding profiles can be matched (competitor moves up, you move up, competitor moves down, you move down), therefore ensuring that bids are always winning, but never significantly higher than they need to be. Manual practice of such a tactic is virtually impossible, utilization of **bid-management software** being the norm.

> See also **bid jamming**.

Big Red Switch (BRS)

A phrase used predominantly by **techies** to describe the immediate shutdown of a system using the main or emergency power switch. The term is believed to have its origins in older IBM machines which had, as an off button, a big red switch. In an e-commerce environment the term is often used to describe a total shutdown, whether deliberate or not.

Bit

An abbreviation of *binary digit*, a bit is the smallest unit of information on a computer. A single bit can hold only one of two values: 0 or 1 – therefore they are rarely used on their own. To be of value, bits are combined into larger units, the smallest of which is a **byte**, made up of 8 bits.

Bitmap

A type of digital picture made up of **pixels**, each of which is a separate colour. Although they present clearer images, bitmap files normally take up more **memory** than other image files, and so are rarely used online as they will slow the **download time**.

B

Blackberry

The registered trade mark (that is, Blackberry®) that has become synonymous with wireless devices that are an all-in-one mobile phone, email device, web browser and organizer. The email facility is useful in that it is always connected, with the network *pushing* email to the device without the user having to dial up to collect it.

Black Friday

> See **Cyber Monday**.

Black-hat hacker

See hacker.

Black-hat search engine optimization

A description given to the practice of those who seek to gain high **search engine listings** by nefarious means. The term is based on the old cowboy axiom of good guys wearing white hats and the bad guys, black.

See also cloaking, IP spoofing and search engine optimization.

Black Monday

See Cyber Monday.

Blended threat

A security threat that is a combination of **viruses**, **worms**, **Trojan horses** or any other malicious code that exploits Internet vulnerabilities.

Blind (advertising) network

See online advertising network.

Blog (blogging)

A blog, short for *web log*, is an individual's online personal journal. Typically updated daily, blogs normally reflect the personality of the author, and are an element of **consumer-generated media**. Although the term *weblog* was first used in 1997, with the *blog* being introduced in 1999, the practice dates back to the early 1990s when individuals who surfed the web listed (or *logged*) web sites that they found interesting, often with their own review of the sites. In the days of few web sites and no search engines, the blogger's web sites became the starting point for **surfers** looking for new sites. Blogs have a significance as a marketing tool in that they use a push technology (**RSS**) to take their content to the reader, rather than waiting for the reader to visit a web site. As with 'e' and 'cyber', *blog* is also becoming a common prefix when used to describe blog-related practices. For example; information retrieval expert Dr Edel Garcia has coined the terms 'blogonomy' (the dissemination of false knowledge through electronic forums) and 'blogorrhea' (the intentional dissemination of that false knowledge for a profit or commercial interests).

See also commercial blog, boss blog and flog.

B

Blogger

Someone who writes a **blog**.

Blogma

Described by some as being a *blogger's blog*, perhaps the most appropriate definition of blogma is that on blogma.com: 'a special portal designed to highlight the most popular technology topics discussed throughout the expanding universe of Web logs'.

Blog monitoring tools

Software that helps organizations – and brands – track what consumers are saying about them in blogs more frequently, easily and inexpensively.

See also **consumer-generated media** and **online reputation management**.

Blogonomy

See **blog**.

Blogorrhea

See **blog**.

Blogosphere (also blogsphere)

The universe in which blogs reside. The interconnecting nature of blogs means that few (if any) blogs exist in isolation, rather as part of a **virtual community** or – depending on their subject – social **networks**. Although there is an element of tangibility about a blog in that it appears in a browser window, like the world wide web itself which exists in cyberspace, blogs also exist in a virtual environment – their own sphere or world. The term Blogosphere was first used by Brad L. Graham on his own blog (www.bradlands.com) in September 1999.

Blogreader

See **RSS tracker**.

Blogroll

A blogger's list of their favourite **blogs** and **bloggers** – as in *roll* of honour. Although these may have started as gestures of tribute to fellow bloggers, their significance rocketed when the major search engines identified the cross-linking as signs of expert content, and so rewarded them with higher rankings.

Blog spam

Messages left on blogs that have the single purpose of gaining an incoming link to a site with the intention of increasing that site's **search engine rank**. Each message will include the **URL** of the target site – so creating the link – but nothing relevant to the subject of the original blog. Like other types of **spam**, blog spam is an annoyance to those on its receiving end. It can be prevented by using some method of **pre-moderation**.

Bluetooth

A short-range radio technology that facilitates wireless communication between suitably enabled devices. Common examples are wireless keyboards and mice. Bluetooth headsets for mobile phones and **smart phones** mean the devices can be used hands-free.

Bobby

A free online tool which allows a site to be checked for compliance against the **W3C** disability accessibility guidelines for compliance. Sites that pass these tests are allowed to display a *Bobby Approved* logo. It should be noted, however, that the Bobby application only tests for conformity, and does not correct or rewrite any element of the web site being assessed. Arguably, all sites should be accessible to disabled users, so the Bobby test should be part of any web site's development. Displaying the logo will obviously attract those with disabilities but might also be seen by some as representing a *caring* organization. See also **Disability Discrimination Act**, **Pas 78** and **web site accessibility**. The Bobby web site can be found on http://webxact.watchfire. com. Note that in the UK all web sites should, by law, be accessible to the disabled.

B

Bookmark

The practice of saving the **URL** of a web site so that the site can be revisited in the future. A link to the site is saved in the user's web **browser**, normally in a storage facility that allows sites to be catalogued in folders with personal annotations added. In some browsers, bookmarks are known as favourites.

Boolean search

Based on Boolean logic, this kind of search allows the inclusion – or exclusion – of documents containing specific words through the use of instructions like 'AND', 'NOT' and 'OR'. For example – 'Athens NOT Georgia' if you are searching for information on the capital of Greece. Classic logic holds that all statements can be expressed in binary terms (yes or no, right or wrong, black or white), so the search for Athens should be 'Athens AND Greece', thus excluding all web sites for the Athens in Georgia, USA. Boolean logic accepts that there may be grey areas in many issues – in the example given, that there is more than one Athens. Fuzzy logic goes a step further by accepting that there are degrees of truth in most *real-life* situations – in linguistic terms, allowing for imprecise notions such as *slightly* and *very*. Classic search, for example, could not cope with degrees of temperature; it would have to be hot, not *very* hot or *fairly* hot. Search engines allow Boolean and fuzzy search in order to best help the user find what they are looking for – be that a specific search, or something more general. The nature of fuzzy search is that it will find matches even when words are only partially spelled or misspelled. Fuzzy logic is also behind the *tilde search*, where the searcher uses the tilde (~) to instruct the search to also consider synonyms preceding or following the word specific to the keyword as well as to reveal phrases with alternative beginnings or endings, for example, hotshot/shot/shotgun.

Boot

A term used to describe the start-up of a computer. Turning a computer off then immediately on again – perhaps to clear a problem – is commonly known as *re*booting.

Boss blog

As the name suggests, this is a **blog** written by someone within the organization who has some, if not total, authority – they are a boss. Like all **commercial blogs**, these must be developed with care. This type of blog is best suited to organizations and/or brands that [already] have a good relationship with their customers and whose customers are passionate about the product or service offered.

Bot

See **spider**.

Bounce

See **email bounce** and **web site bounce**.

Bow tie theory

A result of research conducted by AltaVista, Compaq and IBM in 2000, the bow tie theory of the Internet focuses on the importance of **links** on the Internet. The theory is that the Internet can be defined as being made up of four types of site:

1 The *core* is made up of sites that share links and traffic (about 30 per cent).
2 *Origination* sites that direct people into the core (about 20 per cent).
3 *Termination* sites that have links from the core but few back in (about 20 per cent).
4 *Isolated* sites that have few links and little traffic (about 30 per cent).

While the theory is sound, quite why it was called the bow tie theory escapes this author – a bow tie having a centre and two *wings*, the theory having a centre (core) and three *wings*.

Bozo filter

A **spam**-reducing feature offered by many **email clients**. It allows users to block (filter) messages from specific email addresses, the list of blocked addresses being dubbed a *bozo* list.

Bps (bits-per-second)

A measurement of how fast data is moved from one place to another in an online environment. Bps is normally used as the unit to indicate a particular systems speed. For example, a 28.8 **modem** can move 28,800 **bits** per second.

Branded keyword

When purchasing keywords for search engine advertising or paid place-ment, they are considered to be *branded* if they are associated with the names, trademarks or slogans of particular companies. After legal

B

action in the USA, most search engines refuse the purchase of keywords that are trademarks.

Branding

See **online branding.**

Breadcrumbs

A navigational aid that appears (normally) at the top of a web page to show the user where they are and where they have been on the site – the final entry being the current page. Each page or section visited is listed in order, rather like a running index. For example, on a tourism site the breadcrumb might read:

Europe > Greece > Athens > Syntagma Square > Accommodation > Hotels > Grand Bretagne Hotel

Clicking on any of the previous pages listed in the breadcrumb list takes the user back to that page. Breadcrumbs are particularly useful for very big sites where the visitor might delve *deep* into the content.

Bricks-and-clicks (traders)

A term used to describe a business which trades both offline and online.

Bricks-and-mortar (traders)

A term used to describe a business which trades offline – that is, in a building made from *bricks and mortar*, as opposed to a **virtual business**.

Broadband

Technically, a type of digital data transmission in which each medium (wire) carries multiple signals, or channels, simultaneously. However, because broadband connections allow a higher rate of data transmission, the term has become synonymous with *fast* Internet access. Speeds of 256 kilobits per second (kbit/s) and greater are commonly considered to be *broadband* – this is reflected in the way such services are marketed. The expansion of broadband networks was (and still is) seen as a seminal event in the development of the web. Those who have used a contemporary broadband connection to access the web would find it hard to believe just what surfing the web was like in the mid to late 1990s with a low **Bps** dial-up modem connection. The analogy (popular at that time) that modems were dirt tracks and broadband represented six-lane motorways on the **information superhighway** is still good today. Without broadband, many of the online applications common on today's web – radio and video, for example – simply do not work. Note however, that broadband provider's offers of (for example) up to 8 Mbps (megabytes per second) is misleading. In reality data-delivery rates are reliant on variables such as the quality of the receiver's connection, the distance from the local exchange and even whether or not the user has installed and maintained their **router** correctly. 2Mbps is generally acknowledged as sufficient to cope with current Internet applications, including **streaming** media.

Broadband fixed wireless access (BFWA)

A method of receiving **broadband** over wireless networks, normally via an aerial on the roof of the user's premises.

Brochureware

The original use of the term was a derogatory description for a web site made up of content taken directly from offline promotional literature with no attempt adapt it to an online context. As that practice has declined (though not completely disappeared), it has become a more general description of *static* sites that offer no interactivity. Although viewed by some in a negative way as they do not make use of the inter-active nature of Internet technology, brochureware sites – online brochures – can meet the online objectives of many companies, partic-ularly SMEs, although it is advisable for textual content to be contextu-alized for the Internet (see **content contextualization**). Brochureware sites are sometimes referred to as **white van web sites**.

Broken image

The term used to describe an **image** that has not downloaded on to a user's **browser**. The fault is normally one in the **HTML** or other **source code** of the page. It is also possible that the user is surfing with their browser's image facility turned off (so pages **download** quicker). A broken image is replaced by the browser with its own image which informs the user that something is wrong.

Broken link

A web site **link** that, when clicked on, does not take users where they were supposed – and hoped – to go. Often, they lead to a dead-end **404**

B

message that says the requested page could not be found. Pages at the end of a broken link are sometimes described as **orphan pages**.

Browser (1)

A **client** program that provides access to the web – Internet Explorer, Netscape or Firefox, for example. It should be noted that the presentation of a web site's content can differ when viewed in different browsers – or even different versions of the same browser (see **browser compatibility**). While web designers and technicians tend to write off those who cannot read their sites, marketers should always question a policy that excludes any customers (see also **rule of one**). In layperson's terms, it is the browser that sends out a *request* for a page on the web as identified by the user (by typing in a **URL** or clicking on a **link**). When the request is received by the **server** that is hosting the page, the elements of that page (text, images, etc.) are then sent – *served* – to the requesting browser.

See also **cache**.

Browser (2)

A person who navigates through and reads (*browses*) the web.

See also **user**.

Browser compatibility

Although there is much communality between them, not all browsers read web site **source code** in the same way. This means that if a web site is designed specifically for one browser – say Internet Explorer (IE) – it will not appear on a Firefox, Netscape or Mac browser in precisely the same format as on IE. Although the number of web sites affected by lack of compatibility is relatively small – estimates suggest less than 10 per cent – in an offline-trading environment no trader would knowingly exclude 10 per cent of potential customers. Yet online, this is common practice.

BRS

See **big red switch**.

B

Bug

Although offline the term has many applications, in an online environment *bug* means any fault, glitch, mistake or problem that interferes
with the smooth running of a program, computer system or web site.

Bulletin board system/service (BBS)

A computerized online meeting and announcement system that allows
people to carry on discussions, download files and make announcements without all the participants being connected to the system at the
same time.

See also **consumer-generated media.**

Business blog (b-blog)

See **commercial blog.**

Butterfly model

See **B2B e-marketplaces.**

Buying funnel

See **purchase funnel.**

Buyer behaviour

See **online buyer behaviour.**

Buy-side e-marketplace

As the name suggests, *buy-side* considers business transactions from the
point of view of the buyer – and is used primarily when referring to
procurement transactions within a supply chain in a B2B context.

See also **e-procurement** and **e-marketplace.**

Buzz marketing

See **viral marketing.**

B

Byte

An abbreviation of *binary term*, a byte is a unit of storage and is made up of a set of **bits** that represent a single character – there are 8 bits in a byte. Larger storage (memory) is measured in kilobytes (1,024 bytes), megabytes (1,048,576 bytes) and gigabytes (1,073,741,824 bytes). As the prefixes to these terms suggest, the number of bytes is often rounded down to 1,000, 1,000,000, and 1,000,000,000, respectively. A thousand gigabytes is a terabyte.

B

C2C (consumer-to-consumer (trading))

The term used to describe the practice of individuals *trading* with other individuals. While this has been common practice over the years (car-boot and yard sales, for example), the Internet has opened up whole new markets for individuals who wish to buy from or sell to other individuals. Auction sites such as eBay thrive on this trade (though for many product categories on eBay, the sellers are actually businesses), and it is this concept for which **Napster** became famous when it allowed individuals to sell, swap or give music files to other individuals.

C2B (consumer-to-business (trading))

Although it exists as an e-commerce model, the concept of C2B trading is rare in practice. In theory any individual can seek to sell products or services to a business. However, if that individual does so with any frequency, or seeks to make a profit from it, they would be deemed to be a business themselves – making the transaction **B2B**. Another facet to the C2B model that makes use of the **e-marketplace** is that of the customer posting a message on a web site that invites businesses to bid on products or services that the consumer needs. This has few practical applications in anything but very specialized markets, often where the consumer is buying something that is normally considered a B2B product or service – building services for a private house extension, for example.

Cache

A name given to temporary storage space on a computer. Web pages accessed previously are stored in the computer browser's cache directory (on the hard drive). When the user returns to a web site that has been recently accessed, the browser calls it up from the cache rather than the original **server**. Caches can also be held at **ISP**s and large organizations that operate their own servers.

Call to action

A word or phrase on a web site that invokes an action from the user. In a marketing context the action would be that desired by the marketer. Online, the call to action is an integral part of **conversion**, **navigation** and **information architecture**. A call to action could be to have the user:

- make a purchase online;
- complete an online order form;
- contact an organization by telephone;
- contact an organization by email;
- complete a contact form;
- subscribe to a newsletter;
- join an online forum;
- download a file, e.g. a White Paper;
- forward a viral marketing message;
- apply for the membership of a club or association.

The call to action is a part of the copy (see **content 2**) of a web site, and if it is to be effective, its development is best left to experts.

Campaign conversion

A **metric** that tracks all the **conversions** that have taken place in the period that a specific marketing or promotional campaign has run. For example, how many new customers were gained over the six weeks a **paid placement** ad was included on specific **keywords**.

CAN-SPAM Act 2003 (Controlling the Assault of Non-Solicited Pornography and Marketing Act)

A US law enforced by the Federal Trade Commission (FTC) which was intended to address the issue of **spam** on the Internet. Critics argue that it not only fails to prevent spam, but actually endorses its use. Non-US traders should be aware of the details of the Act as it can be applied to email *received* in America – no matter where it originates.

Cascading Style Sheets (CSS)

An application of **HTML** that gives web site developers more control over how web pages are displayed. CSS helps designers create sites where all pages conform to the same design principles. However, the use of CSS can, if not used judiciously, cause problems for **search engine optimization** of pages created using it.

Case sensitive

Where upper-case *CHARACTERS* are distinguished from lower-case *characters*.

Cashback shopping sites

Web sites that offer users small rewards for visiting online shops linked from them. The concept is a kind of amalgam of **affiliate marketing**, **pay per click** advertising and offline reward cards. The idea is that all parties gain. The cashback site host gets income from sending traffic to the shopping sites, the online shop gains in visitor numbers and the user can collect reward points or cash. More popular in the USA than Europe, two examples are rpoints.com and linemypocket.com.

Catalogue services

In an e-commerce context, these are web sites where a number of suppliers present their wares in an **e-marketplace**-type environment. The goods can be listed by supplier, but the more successful will list all associated products from all suppliers together on the same web pages. Complex software ensures the orders for the various products go to the right suppliers. The site's publisher will normally take a periodic fixed fee or percentage of any exchanges. Although the early days of the web saw a number of B2C catalogues appear online, the development and availability of easy-to-use online checkout facilities allowed vendors to sell goods on their own sites. The contemporary application is normally in **B2B** trading, where businesses (particularly **SME**s) have the opportunity to promote their wares on a well-visited, normally industry-specific site. Such sites often serve as **portals** for industries or specific markets.

Cause-related marketing

An extension of ethical marketing, cause-related marketing is where the organization actively supports a chosen cause and seeks to gain competitive advantage from the show of support. Its significance in e-commerce is that the Internet provides a relatively inexpensive platform for individuals or micro-businesses to express their concern for a cause in a commercial environment.

Cc/bcc (carbon copy/blind carbon copy)

The facility on an email to send the same message to multiple recipients. If the email is *cc-ed* then all those who receive the message will be able to see the email addresses of all intended recipients. In a closed environment this will not be a problem – for example, all members of a department within an organization. However, in a marketing environment this might not be acceptable. For example, a vendor sending an email promoting a special offer to six valued customers would be telling each of them which other customers are being offered the promotion. Or, perhaps worse, the email addresses of the *cc-ed* recipients might be used for **spam** purposes by third parties. In these cases the recipients should be *bcc-ed – blind* copied – so that other people on the address list cannot be seen by all recipients. Although it is a cheap method of **email marketing**, using the bcc facility is not considered good practice in that discipline.

ccTLD (country code Top Level Domain)

See **DNS**.

Cease and desist letter

Although not exclusive to e-commerce, many online entities have been sent these letters from lawyers (it is an American term). Essentially, the letter requests that a person or organization stop any activity mentioned in the letter to prevent legal action. Common reasons for receiving an e-commerce-related cease and desist letter are (a) the unauthorized use of copyrighted content, (b) use of a disputed domain name, (c) the use of a trademark in keyword advertising or (d) libellous content, particularly on sites containing **consumer-generated media**.

Cellular

Communications systems that divide a geographic region into sections, called cells – as in cellphones.

CGI (Common Gateway Interface)

The rules that describe how a **web server** communicates with another piece of software on the same machine, and vice versa. A common application for CGI on web sites is that of online forms, where a CGI program can process the form's data once it is submitted by the user.

CGI-bin

The common name of a directory on a **web server** in which CGI programs are stored. The *bin* part of cgi-bin is a shorthand version of binary.

CGM

See **consumer-generated media.**

Channel conflict

In situations where a manufacturer has the option of different channels of distribution through which to reach the consumer there is the potential for conflict between those channels. In the early days of the Internet such conflict was touted as being a significant problem in two scenarios: (a) external to the organization, and (b) internal to the organization. In the first scenario the Internet was seen as being a way of taking intermediaries out of the distribution chain. The manufacturer would simply sell directly to the consumer through a web site. While this is true of a small minority of products, the value of the intermediary – developed over many years – was soon acknowledged and the web was adopted by manufactures for promotion, branding and the provision of after-sales services only. The second scenario saw many retailers being reluctant to use the web for online sales as they thought it would cannibalize their offline sales. Again, these fears were proved to be unfounded. Indeed, forward-thinking organizations soon realized that strategic use of the Internet can complement and improve, rather than harm, offline sales.

See also **disintermediation.**

Chat

The term used to describe a *real-time* keyboard conversation on the Internet. Chatting takes place in a *chat* room – a virtual meeting-place. The term originates from the definition of chat – informal conversation – and the first online chats were mainly **techies** seeking help or giving advice on computing matters. Now there is hardly a subject that doesn't have someone, somewhere, chatting about it.

See also **newsgroup** and **consumer-generated media.**

Chat room

See **chat.**

Check box (noun) or check a box (verb)

A small box that users can click their mouse in to confirm a choice. The boxes are normally square – with a click creating a *tick* in that box, as is the practice for paper forms – or a circle that is filled by a dot to signify that it has been *checked*. Check boxes are used extensively online as a selector (for example, clicking the box for a required product, colour and size) or as a confirmation (for example, clicking the box to confirm **terms and conditions** have been read). Online market research questionnaires are also a common application, where there parameters of the form can make it so that only one, or multiple, boxes can be checked.

Check out

See **shopping cart.**

cHTML (compact HTML)

A reduced version of **HTML** for use on small devices such as mobile phones that have hardware restrictions such as small memory capacity.

Churn

A term used to describe the loss of customers over a period of time expressed as a percentage of lost customers out of total customers. It is normally seen as an element of e-commerce analytics.

Citizen cinema

A term accredited to the *Los Angeles Times* that describes online archives of short amateur video clips, ranging from a few seconds up to ten minutes in length. The clips – often filmed on mobile-phone cameras – are mainly a collection of the boring (someone eating a meal) or the funny (someone dancing badly) that are only of any real interest to friends and family of those in the clips. However, such is the nature of the Internet that surfers visit citizen-cinema sites in their thousands – particularly the one that was instrumental in launching the phenomenon, YouTube.com (motto: broadcast yourself). A third group of clips is that which features copyrighted material – both images and music. Although the owners of such content (mostly short extracts of shows copied from other media) sometimes threaten legal action, most realize that such sites were actually promoting the programmes or films from which the clips were taken and relented. Marketers have taken the concept to heart and use it as part of viral marketing campaigns, releasing *sneak peeks* of new shows or ads. Critics refer to those who film themselves as iVideots (video idiots). Citizen cinema is an aspect of **consumer-generated media.**

Citizen journalism/journalist (also known as civilian journalism/journalist)

The concept that citizens can play an active role in collecting, reporting, analyzing and disseminating news and information – activities that prior to the introduction of the web as a medium of communication were the domain of professional reporters only. Although there is a significant difference in the dictionary definition of journalist and publisher, in this context it is not unusual for citizen journalist and citizen publisher to be interchangeable.

See also **blog** and **consumer-generated media**.

Citizen publisher

See **citizen journalist**.

Classic logic/search

See **Boolean search**.

Clear GIF

See **web bug**.

Click (1) verb

Users *click* on a mouse button to instruct their computer to carry out a command.

Click (2) noun

As used in the phrase 'competition is only a click away', meaning that a customer need only make one click of the mouse to move from a web site to that of a competitor.

Click fraud

A general term applied to any **pay per click** campaign where a **click-through** is not made by a genuine customer. While all are not maliciously fraudulent – student-type pranks or genuine mistakes, for example – businesses are most worried by multiple clickthroughs that are deliberate attempts to defraud the advertiser.

C

In business models where the publisher of a web site that carries ads is paid for every click on those ads there is the opportunity for abuse. Annoying, but not a major problem, is where a competitor might click on another business's ads, so increasing that company's advertising costs. More serious, however, is the *pay per click scam*, which works in this way. In this scenario, Business A is either the site's publisher, or more likely, an agency that handles advertising accounts. Business B is the advertiser. Business A makes money every time a particular ad for business B is clicked because business B will pay business A for every clickthrough. For this example, the fee business B pays is 10p for every click on an ad that takes the user to their web site. The corrupt agency or publisher – business A – then hires surfers – so-called *paid to read* rings – to click on the ads, paying them 2p every time they do so (software can be used to make bogus clicks, but it is easier to detect). The result is 8p profit on every click for the unscrupulous business A. Not only does this mean a direct loss of money for business B – 10p per fraudulent click – but any metrics of that ad campaign will be flawed and so of no use for analysis. More sophisticated scammers will actually set up their own *bogus* sites, register with **AdSense** (for example), then have the phantom clickers visit the site and click on the links. Opportunists should note, however, that the search engines are constantly upgrading their software to detect and prevent such scams.

Clicker's remorse

Perhaps rather self-explanatory, this term describes a user's state of mind when they follow a certain online route (by clicking on links) only to find that resulting web sites do not meet their needs. The relevance for e-commerce is that if the user follows a link from a web page and the result is clicker's remorse, then they lose faith in not only the advertiser, but the web site that hosts the link or ad. Examples might include (a) clicking on a link on a **search engine results page** only to find the resulting page does not match the search query, or (b) an ad that turns out to be a form **bait and switch**.

Clickpath

See **clickstream**.

Clicks-and-bricks

See **clicks-and-mortar**.

Clicks-and-mortar

Businesses that trade both online and offline. The term derives from the concept that the business uses *clicks* (of the mouse) and *mortar* (referring to physical buildings) in its methods of trading in both consumer and industrial markets. Clicks-and-mortar businesses must have e-commerce-enabled web sites so that sales and/or orders can be completed online. A business that uses the web only as a medium for promotion or customer service is not considered to be such.

See also bricks and mortar, pure online business and virtual business.

Clicks-and-mortar retailers

See clicks-and-mortar.

Clickstream

Also known as a *clickpath*, this is the route a visitor takes through a web site. Such information is used in **web site analytics** and also to assess **persuasion architecture**. The term is sometimes used in a wider context to represent a user's path through the web itself – that is, multiple web sites rather than just one – sometimes referred to as being a user's digital footprint.

Clickstream-based email marketing

An email message or campaign based on users' **clickstream** data. Although many organizations will email customers with messages or offers based on a customer's purchase history – because you bought A, we think you will like B – clickstream-based emails feature offers based on the web pages a user has visited recently – but from which they have not made a purchase. On a holiday web site, for example, a customer might have spent time looking at hotels in, and flights to, Paris – so any email offer will feature that city.

Clickthrough

The term used to describe the action of clicking on a **link**, that is, you *click through* to the next web page. Although it refers to any link, clickthrough is most commonly used in assessing online advertising.

See clickthrough rate.

c

Clickthrough rate (CTR)

The percentage of **clickthroughs** to the total number of times the **link** is **downloaded**. For example, if a banner ad has 100 **impressions** and 20 users click on that banner, the clickthrough rate is 20 per cent. The clickthrough rate is often the **metric** by which an ad campaign is judged. Practitioners in both **online advertising** and **email marketing** will use recognized industry-specific clickthrough rates as a guide. These rates will vary, but for many email campaigns a clickthrough rate of single percentage figures is the norm, for some industries less than one percent being acceptable. This is compatible to offline direct marketing, where promotional messages sent by post – *junk mail* – have traditionally had a poor response rate.

Click to call

The technology that facilitates **pay per call** advertising, click to call – as the name suggests – is when a user clicks on an ad (or web site link) in order to have the advertiser ring the user. Naturally the user must enter their telephone number on a form, and it is also normal for the user to stipulate when they expect the call – immediately, in ten minutes or in an hour, for example. The main advantage of the system is that each click to call response represents genuine **lead generation**. Although the main application is to have users respond to an online ad, the technology can be used as part of **persuasive momentum** or part of the sales conversion process. For example, if **web site analytics** show that users might leave a purchase process at a certain point – perhaps an issue of size of the product – then they can be prompted to click to call, so allowing the telesales staff to close the deal. Note, however, that offering global coverage for click to call is problematic not only with regard to time zones, but also that the organization must employ multi-lingual sales staff.

C

Click-wrap

Also known as *shrink* wrap, this is where a customer must complete an action before they can continue with an online process – usually filling in a form or confirming terms and/or conditions in order to continue with a transaction. The phrase comes from the original practice where the user would have to scroll down the click-wrapped content to get to the **link** to the next page, so continuing the process. More recently, however, the scrolling has been replaced by simply **checking a box** to confirm (whatever), the user being prevented from moving on to the next page in the process until a box is checked. It is the online method of having people agree that they have read the small print (even if they haven't actually done so), and is most commonly used for **terms and conditions** or **disclaimers**. It can also be used outside actual transactions, but this is not common as it might hinder any **persuasion architecture** of the site.

Client

A software program that is used to contact and obtain data from a server software program on another computer; in layperson's terms, a computer that is connected to the **server** on a **network**. A **web browser** is commonly referred to as a client.

Cloaking

See **search engine cloaking**.

Closed-loop reporting

An **e-metric** that measures the effectiveness of an online ad by tracking users who have viewed a specific ad to see if they responded to the objective of the ad – make a purchase, for example – that is, the loop is closed from first view to final response.

Clustering

A search engine's practice of grouping pages from a web site into one entry on the **search engine results page** (SERP) rather than having one organization fill the SERP with a multitude of pages from the same site. This is generally useful to the search engine user – in early searches the first twenty or more returns would commonly all be different pages from the same web site.

CMS

See **content management software**.

Collaborative filtering

With close associations to **contextual targeting**, and based on the concept of **segmentation**, collaborative filtering is the term used to describe a technical aspect of that concept. Software is used to analyse customer data, apply formulas acquired from behavioural sciences and then predict the products or services that customer might purchase to satisfy their needs. Any predictions made based on individual customers' profiles can then be applied to groups of customers – *segments* – with similar profiles.

Collaborative web site

Sometimes known as a cooperative web site, this is a site that is developed and published by more than one entity – though more than two is rare. An extension of the concept of co-branding, the idea is that by combining the offering of two businesses customer needs will be better met. An example might be two small businesses that manufacturer and/or supply specialist equipment aimed at a specific market segment, where one product will complement the other. A collaborative web site could be developed as a **portal** in order to attract more visitors.

Commercial blog

This is a **blog** that is developed by an organization rather than an individual, normally as part of a branding strategy. Done properly, such an undertaking can be a definite advantage in developing consumer relationships. Done badly, the contrary will be true. False blogging (**flogging**) is easily spotted, and the results can be the absolute opposite of what is desired.

See also **boss blog**.

Commercial network

See **networks (commercial and social)**.

Commodity content

Web site **content** that is generic in nature and freely available to anyone who might wish to use it. Such content is normally found on non-commercial sites and is often advisory in nature – it is common on non-commercial **portals** and in **consumer-generated media**.

Common Gateway Interface

See **CGI**.

Common short codes (CSCs)

Sometimes referred to as simply *short codes*, these are mobile phone numbers that are made up of significantly fewer numbers – usually four or five – than normal. CSC numbers are frequently used in after-sales promotions or applications such as charity donations, competition entries or voting in association with a TV programme. CSC is included here as the numbers can be used in association with e-commerce promotions or initiatives, particularly to the **MySpace generation**.

Community web site

See **virtual community**.

Comparison advertising

Not as common in Europe as in the USA, comparison advertising can appear online in **paid placement** advertising on search engines. This is where an advertiser selects **keywords** that are synonymous with their competitors, so that when users search on those keywords with the objective of finding the web site of the company associated with that phrase, they get the ad for the company practising comparison advertising. For example, company A is known for its tag line 'the best yagahit there is'. Company B, a competitor, buys the keyword listing for the phrase line 'the best yagahit there is'. The opportunity for comparison advertising now arises for company B. Having achieved high listings in the **search engine results page** (SERP), company B can make the descriptive text in the **ad listing** either non-complimentary to company B, or outright derogatory (ours is smaller/bigger/slower/faster than theirs). There is an additional consideration, however. Search engines do not accept bids on **branded keywords**. As well as there being legal constraints where trademarks are involved, it would not go down too well with major ad revenue spenders if, when their product was entered as a search term, a derogatory web site was listed top of the SERP.

Comparison search

See **shopping comparison site**.

Comparison site

Whereas **shopping comparison sites** seek out and compare prices for specified products, comparison sites make purchase comparisons for

C

users based on personal data inputted by those users. Common applications include utility supply. For example, the customer inputs details of their gas and electricity use over a calendar year and the comparison site calculates which supplier would provide best value for money in those circumstances. The comparison site generates income from the businesses to which it refers customers.

Compatibility

In computing terms, compatibility refers to the ability of **hardware** or **software** to work with versions that are older (backwards compatibility) or newer (forwards compatibility).

Compression

The reduction of a file that takes up a lot of **memory** to one that takes up much less. It is used to reduce the size of files being sent by email. Compressed files are commonly known as **zip files**.

Conceptual search

A search for documents based on the concept of the search term rather than the specific words in the term. Rather than simply matching key words or phrases, conceptual search attempts to analyse a document for *meaning*. Entering a phrase (or even an entire document) will return all documents that address related topics – even if they do not share the keywords with the query. For example, if the search is for a key *legal* phrase, the conceptual search will return all documents that refer to legal cases that pertain to the search term.

Confirmation page

At the end of a purchase transaction or an online registration the user should be presented with a page confirming the completion of the process – the confirmation page. Like many utilitarian web pages, the confirmation page – like the **autoresponder** – is an excellent vehicle for a marketing message, though the opportunity is often ignored.

Consumer-controlled advertising

A concept which suggests that, using contemporary technology, the advertising that consumers actually see can be decided by those

C

consumers – rather than being *pushed* at them, as with traditional media. The forerunner of this concept is online search, where the user decides the keywords on which they are going to search and so, effectively, dictates the ads they will be presented with on the **search engine results page**. Naturally, the marketer has matched ads with keywords in preparation for searchers using those terms, but nevertheless the delivery of those ads is determined by the consumer.

Consumer-generated media (CGM)

Also sometimes referred to as **user-generated content (UGC)**, this is the contemporary, and online, version of **conversational media**. In an e-commerce context, CGM refers to web sites that exist for, and thrive on, the public's comments. For some users, it is such content that makes the web attractive. Research from the Edelman Trust Barometer (www.edelman.com) published in January 2006 found that in the US 'a person like me' was considered to be a more credible source of information about a company than doctors and academic experts. In this case, 'a person like me' is someone who completes a product review – or similar – online. CGM is arguably the most significant effect the Internet has on marketing, it being a key element in the concept of **helping the buyer to buy**. The online manifestation of CGM comes in a number of public comment sites. Concentrating on how they impact on e-commerce, these include:

- Consumer protection sites – although normally published or promoted by a consumer protection organization, there may be elements of CGM on those sites. Any consumer input is likely, however, to be used as an example (of complaints, or a case study that is then followed up by the publishing organization), and so will be vetted before publication.
- Consumer review sites – sites set up as consumer review forums where consumers are encouraged to comment on goods and services they have purchased. Review sites are very popular in the travel, computing and electrical goods industries. Some consumer review sites actually advocate that companies use the sites for consumer research and invite replies to customer complaints. It is common for these sites to include other content on the subject covered and so be considered to be **portals**.
- **Chat rooms** – although chat rooms may seem to be simply that – chitchat – the participants frequently chat about a product or service they have used or experienced. Even 'social' chat can be useful to marketers; comments about a movie or TV show, for example.

C

- **Bulletin boards** – rather like chat rooms, the comments left on bulletin boards may not be overtly about products, services or brands, but that does not mean that those messages might not provide information useful to commercial organizations.
- **Blogs** – almost by definition, people who write blogs are outgoing by nature. Blogs could be specifically about products or services, or it could just be that the blogger has had a good or bad experience with a product or service and wants to tell the world about it. Blogs are particularly significant because many are picked up by search engines for their indexes. This means that a customer's rant about a brand on their own rather obscure blog could be picked up by the search engines and appear in their listings when someone searches on that brand name.
- **Cyberbashing** sites – by their very nature these sites are made up of criticism from unsatisfied customers – some of them very inflammatory, even libellous.
- **Virtual community** web sites – where, on part of the site, members might comment on a particular product or service that is relevant to that community's shared interest.
- **Online social shopping** – where like-minded individuals give opinions and tips to fellow shoppers.

Such is the nature of the web that one site – perhaps a **portal** – could address more than one of those features listed above.

Organizations should constantly monitor CGM sites both as part of an **online reputation management** strategy and as market research – perhaps as part of a marketing information system. Also significant for the online marketer is the use of CGM sites for hosting advertising. That many sites – or pages within them – are subject-specific makes them excellent for targeted advertising.

See also **citizen cinema.**

Consumer Protection (Distance Selling) Regulations 2000 (DSRs)

Significant to e-commerce because these EU regulations apply to any organization that sells goods or services to consumers through an organized distance-selling scheme where there is no face-to-face contact between the business and the consumer – which includes the Internet. Although online auctions are not covered by the DSRs, fixed-price sales through 'buy-now' features on auction sites (as used on eBay) are not exempt because the sale is not concluded by process of auction. The DSRs applies only to B2C transactions, and B2B trading is not covered.

See also **Electronic Commerce (EC Directive) regulations 2002 (ECRs).**

Consumer protection sites

See **consumer-generated media.**

Consumer review sites

See **consumer-generated media.**

Content (1)

All the text, pictures, sound and other data on a web site.

Content (2)

Specifically, the textual content of a web site – as opposed to **graphics**. There is an important difference between textual *content* and *copy*, and for that reason the two are addressed together in this section. The textual content of a web site is that part of the site that the publisher wishes the user to read. Content would include such things as contact details, articles, **FAQ** lists, company details (about us), shipping details and privacy policies. Content should answer customers' questions and solve problems. Copy, on the other hand, is text that persuades the reader to do something that will meet the objectives of the site – place an order, for example. That it is often called *sales* copy betrays its origins. The most obvious copy is the **call to action**, but this could encourage users to go and read (more) content – privacy or company details, for example – that will add to the user's confidence in the web site. However, the line between content and copy is often blurred, and the distinction may vary from site to site. For example, a product description could be part content (description), part copy (order now, few in stock). That many web site developers do not recognize where the distinction lies is a clear indication that both content and copy writing are specialist occupations. In the early days of the web, content and copy were largely ignored as an important element of e-commerce – and for many sites this is still the case, though successful e-commerce practitioners assigning significance to both is prompting many web site publishers to give them more credence. Note that an email that is part of an **email marketing** campaign will also contain both content and copy, though because of its nature – direct marketing – it is likely to contain more of the latter.

See also **content contextualization, fascinations** and **false logic.**

Content aggregation services

See **content aggregator.**

Content aggregator

A software application that retrieves content from web sites for publication on another. Web site publishers can run the software themselves or employ *aggregation services* to undertake the task. Note that this is not theft of copyrighted work because the supplier will have authorized its syndication – a fee might be involved. The most common type of information to be aggregated is news, so allowing a web site to have up-to-date news reports on its web pages without having to gather and report that news. **Blogs** are another common source of content.

Content contextualization

In an e-commerce environment this refers to the writing (or rewriting) of content so that it is in context with the media in which it will be read – that is, online. It is common practice, though not *good* practice, for a web site's content to be taken *verbatim* from literature prepared for another medium. The content in printed brochures, for example, is not written in a way that readers can interact with it – as is possible using **links** online. Grammatical differences also exist. For example, web sites exist in the present and so content in the present tense is in context as the customer reads it. Printed brochures can be in circulation for months (even years), therefore talking about *now* is not appropriate.

See also **content (2).**

C

Content management

In printed publications the job title of someone who undertakes the duties of content management is the *editor*. The *offline* editor's job is to ensure that the right content is getting to the right reader, at the right time, at the right cost. This is, effectively, the same job that the web site content manager performs.

Content management software (CMS)

A term that is something of a misnomer in that the software doesn't manage content, it only simplifies the process of accessing web sites and changing the content – but that content must still be managed by a human being.

See also **content management.**

Content rich

A search engine term that relates to the fact that **algorithms** give higher ranking to pages which contain the keyword or term for which a user is searching – that is, it is *rich* in content. **Search engine optimizers** should beware, however. To cram a page with keywords simply to attract search engines might make the content unintelligible to human readers, so negating the efforts of getting the web page high in **search engine rankings** in the first place.

Content targeting

See **contextual and behavioural targeting**

Contextual and behavioural targeting

An offline concept that has transferred – and is practised extensively – online. Applications like Google's **AdSense** are built around the concept – which is sometimes called **collaborative filtering**. The *targeting* element refers to the targeting of potential customers with promotions that will (hopefully) be relevant, and so appealing to that segment of the market. Online, that promotion is invariably advertising. Contextually targeted adverts are placed where the adverts are in *context* with the content of the host web site or page. This is an extension of content targeting, though the two are related. With *content* targeting the ads *match* the content – tools being advertised on a gardening-advice web site, for example. Although the tools and gardening mix could still be applied to *contextual* targeting, this model can go further. Ads for creams that alleviate back pain on a gardening web site, perhaps. In both content and contextual advertising the same adverts are presented for all visitors. This is in contrast to *behavioural targeting*, where the presented ads take into account the online behaviour of the user and so are *personalized*. Behavioural segmentation might be based on such things as usage frequency (for example, occasional or frequent), usage status (that is, non-user, user, lapsed user), occasion for purchase (a gift, for example), or benefits sought (for example, convenience or status). Whereas contextual targeting is relatively simple (requiring knowledge only of the web sites' content), successful behavioural targeting demands more information about the user before they can be truly targeted either individually or as part of a segment. The data cannot be collected ad hoc; they must gathered in a formal, structured manner and must then be stored in such a way that they are easily extracted and analysed. This practice is a very close relative of **database marketing** – though that discipline is normally associated with **direct marketing** rather than advertising. The gathering of information required for accurate behavioural targeting can be overt (personal data on a subscription form, for example), covert (for example, using **adware**) or something between the two (**cookies**, for example).

> This definition is based on, or cites, content by the author in R. Gay, A. Charlesworth and R. Esen, *Online Marketing: A Customer-Led Approach*. Oxford: Oxford University Press, 2007.

Conversational media

The offline forerunner of **consumer-generated media** (CGM), conversational media has been around for as long as the printed media – though always as a minor sideline to publishing. Newspapers, for example, have always invited comment in *reader's letters*-type forums. However, due to advances in ICT it is now not only more accessible, but easier than ever to participate in. The popularity of its contemporary manifestation – consumer-generated media – has resulted in it becoming the main event (rather than a sideline) for many web sites.

Conversion

The term used to describe the action when a web site visitor completes whatever the objective of the web site is, that is, they *convert* from being a *potential* customer to being an *actual* customer. For example, a visitor ordering a product or subscribing to a newsletter would be a conversion.

Conversion by acquisition

A **web site analytic**, part of a **conversion path analysis** where the ad campaign or source that a customer used to first visit a web site is recorded so that any subsequent purchase might be credited to that source. For example, a TV ad might feature a specific URL – **landing page** – where the customer can gain more information or place an order. If the customer then visits the site and makes a purchase, the TV ad is identified, and credited, as providing the lead – even if the purchase is made some time after the TV ad aired.

Conversion funnel

An online extension of the **sales funnel** – where many potential customers enter the funnel (at its widest end), but most drop out as they pass through the funnel (to its narrowest point), with only a few making a purchase. The conversion funnel is, by its very nature, linear, with customers having a single path to follow from entering until their exit. As a result, the conversion funnel can be used to help with the performance analysis of the web site. The conversion funnel is made up of a series of stages that together equal the desired result – because the user follows a path down the funnel, the concept is also referred to as *conversion path analysis*. At each stage the prospect chooses to either continue to the next stage, or leave the process – the analogy of losing customers to a pipe losing water has led to the concept sometimes being called *the leaking pipe*. By analysing the actions of users at each stage, the web site publisher can assess user behaviour and address problems where they are identified. As with the sales funnel, a successful segmentation strategy would help to increase the ratio of buyers to prospects by putting only genuine **prospects** in the top of the funnel. Targeted advertising, both offline and online, should drive only those users who have a real interest in the product or service on offer. The conversion funnel is the vendor-side view of the **purchase funnel**. Note, however, that the conversion funnel differs from **persuasion architecture**, which considers the conversion to be a more fluid process, with customers requiring continuous persuasion as they engage in the purchase process.

Conversion path analysis

See conversion funnel.

Conversion Process

See persuasion architecture.

Conversion rate

An element of **web site analytics**, conversion rate calculates the ratio of total numbers of site visitors to the total number of **conversions**.

Cookies

These are electronic calling-cards that are left on the hard drive of the user's computer when they visit a web site. Essentially, a cookie facilitates the recording of data about the user and their visit(s) to the web site that issued that cookie. They have a number of valid reasons for existing. *Login* cookies record details of user's personal login details – facilitating sites such as Amazon to deliver personalized welcome pages when a registered user returns to the site (using the same computer). *Advertising* cookies are left on web sites by downloaded ads. These allow future ads to be served based on the user's previous online behaviour – so improving **clickthrough rates**. *Analytic* cookies help companies understand traffic patterns on web sites. Note that cookie is also used as a verb, for example to *cookie* a site's visitors.

Cooperative web site

See **collaborative web site.**

Copy

See **content (2).**

Copyright

An exclusive grant from the government that gives the owner the right to reproduce a work, in whole or in part, and to distribute, perform or display it to the public in any form or manner – including the Internet. The owner also has the right to control ways in which their material can be used. Copyright is an unregistered right (unlike **trademarks**), coming into effect as soon as something that can be protected is created on paper, on film, via sound recording or as an electronic record on the internet. While it is not legally necessary in the UK, it is advisable to warn others against copying any work by marking it with the copyright symbol – © – followed by the owner's name and the date. Online, copyright covers all web site content, including text and images, as well as the **source code** of the web site.

Co-registration

A tactic used in an **opt-in** email marketing strategy, co-registration is a way of having users opt-in to receiving emails, or subscribing to **e-newsletters**, that are in addition to the one they have originally agreed. The concept is relatively easy to implement. When a visitor arrives at the page in which they are agreeing to receive email or subscribe to a newsletter, they are also offered the option to sign up for other emails or newsletters as well, normally simply having to check the relevant boxes to indicate which they agree to receive.

Corporate cyberstalking

See **cyberstalking.**

Corporate email servers

While most Internet users will send their email through an **Internet service provider** (ISP), larger organizations, corporations and institutions – universities, for example – may have their own email servers. Although they do take resources to maintain, they can be more easily adapted for the specific uses required by the owner organization (**spam filters** can be more specific, for example).

Cost per –

It is worth noting that in many elements of **e-metrics** *cost* per – and *pay* per – (for example cost per order, pay per click) are used almost at random. Effectively the two terms mean the same – that is, how much the advertiser pays per click or how much each click costs the advertiser. Quite why *pay* or *cost* are applied to different terms can only be down to custom and practice. Perhaps the future will see finite definitions for these terms, but in the meantime they are interchangeable.

Cost per acquisition

The total marketing expenses divided by the total number of new customers acquired. In an e-commerce environment, expenses are normally those incurred online only, though they could incorporate offline costs as well.

Cost per order

The total marketing expenses divided by the total value of orders. In an e-commerce environment, expenses are normally those incurred online only, though they could incorporate offline costs as well.

Cost per visit

The total marketing expenses divided by total number of visits to a web site. In an e-commerce environment, expenses are normally those incurred online only, though they could incorporate offline costs as well.

CPA (cost per action)

See **pay per click.**

CPC (cost per click)

See **pay per click.**

CPM (cost per thousand impressions)

A method of charging for **pay per impression** advertising. The 'M' – the abbreviation of the Latin word for one thousand (*mille*) – is used because **ad impressions** are sold in blocks of a thousand.

Crawler

See **spider.**

Creatives

A term that has been used in advertising for some time, this has been adopted for e-commerce when referring to web site development. Creatives are the people who come up with the ideas (they *create*) that make a web site different, normally in an aesthetic context. They will work alongside **techies** who will handle the technical aspects of the site's development. Pushing the grammar envelope still further, any work completed by *creatives* is covered by the noun *creative*, as in 'that image is a creative'.

CRM (customer relationship management)

Customer relationship management is based on the assumption that there is a relationship between the business or the brand and the customer. This is a relationship that needs to be managed both through the individual buying stages and in the longer term. CRM is very much related to fostering customer loyalty and, in the longer term, customer retention.

CRM can be used in call-centre support and direct marketing operations; software systems assist in the support of customer service representatives and give customers alternative means by which they can communicate with the business (such as mail, email, telephone, etc.). Some sophisticated CRM software programs have email response systems which process incoming emails and determine whether they warrant a personal response or an automated response. Recent figures indicate that systems such as this can handle around 50 per cent of the requests from customers (typically requests for additional information, **passwords** and responses to **email marketing**).

Other CRM software systems incorporate the facility for customer representatives to take part in live **chat** rooms or co-browsing, offering the business a less formal environment in which to make contact with customers. CRM software can also queue customers on the basis of their profiles, by requesting that the customer logs in to the web site. It is then possible to pass the customer on to individuals in the customer service team, who may be better suited to dealing with customers who share similar profiles. CRM software also provides the facility to maintain and update a database of information about each customer (in other words, a case history).

CRM is included here because the impact of e-technology on the practice is significant, improving both communications with customers and collection of data.

Sutherland, J. and Canwell, D. *Key Concepts in Marketing*. Basingstoke: Palgrave Macmillan, 2004.

See also **E-CRM**.

Cross-linking

Linking to content on a web site from pages within that site. An example would be to have a link to the site's home page on each page of the site. It should help the user to navigate the site and so increase the chances of the objectives for the site being met.

Cross platform

See **platform**.

Cross-selling

A close relative of **up-selling**, cross-selling has been around offline for as long as sales have been made. Cross-selling involves the sales person offering related or associated products to increase sales. Done properly, the practice is seen by the buyer as being part of good service – it is annoying for the customer to arrive home with their purchase only to find they need a particular **yagahit** to make it work properly. Had the salesperson advised of the necessity for the yagahit the customer would have been grateful. Naturally, loading the customer with useless accessories has the reverse effect. Online, carefully prepared software programs can take the place of the attentive salesperson, with an automated notice of the need for an accessory appearing when a purchase is made. Amazon take the online application further with their 'customers who bought this book also bought this one . . . ' facility.

Crowdsourcing

A play on the business term *outsourcing*, this is the practice of having members of public perform work for an organization, often for little or no financial reward. Although the practice existed previously (some argue that it is a derivative of **open source**), the term *crowdsourcing* – and its subsequent popularity – is credited to a *Wired* magazine article published in June 2006. Often cited as one of the first proponents of crowdsourcing, image provider iStockphoto (www.istockphoto.com) invites contributions from amateur photographers, indexes them, and make those images available to others for a fee. Although each contributor receives a royalty, it is a pittance compared to that which professional photographers and publishers would expect.

CSS

See **cascading style sheets**.

Cue words

Also known as *atomic phrases*, these are words, terms or phrases that alert search engines to the context of a searcher's submission. 'Biography', for example, added to a person's name in a search box prompts the search engine to look for anything **tagged** as being biographical about the person, rather than simply returning every web page that has that person's name in it. For example, searching on 'David Beckham' would return every web page that contains a report of any game he has played in as well as every article published about his personal life. Adding 'biography' will put pages relative to his biography at the top of the millions of returns that his name produces.

Customer evangelists

In a word-of-mouth context, customer evangelists are those individuals who not only spread the message the widest, but are also the ones who can exert most influence on their friends and associates. Although they are targeted at the beginning of **viral marketing** campaigns, evangelists exist outside any endeavours of marketers. When customers act as evangelists, it is because they have received excellent service from the organization (or brand) and are willing to put their own reputations on the line when they recommend that service. Customer evangelists are often early adopters (in the product life cycle) and considered to be influencers of others in their buyer behaviour. Although they can be solicited for **testimonials**, evangelists normally *preach* in their own social circles, though in an e-commerce environment, it is often such individuals who are inclined towards **blogs** and **consumer-generated media**. Businesses should also be aware that while offline the customer evangelist is expected to deliver only a positive endorsement, online they may preach a negative message – see **cyberbashing**.

See also **social proof**.

Customer relationship management

See **CRM**.

Cyber (as a prefix)

Although the word cyber doesn't exist in its own right, the term as a prefix indicates a relationship to computers. More recently, and probably owing much to the use of the term **cyberspace**, prefixing any word with *cyber* gives that word an association with cyberspace, the Internet or being online. For example, a cybercafé is a café that has Internet access available to its customers and *cyber*-law deals with those laws that or specific to the Internet.

See also **online (as a prefix)** and **e (as a prefix)**.

Cyberattack

See **cyberbashing**.

Cyberbashing

Also known as a cyber*attack* or a cyber*smear* campaign, this is the application of Internet technology in expressing a poor opinion of an organi-

C

zation, brand or product. An element of **consumer-generated media**, cyberbashing can range from fairly mild comments of frustration to libellous statements. Cyberbashing is practised by setting up a web site – commonly using a **domain name** that ends in *sucks*, for example, companynamesucks.com, and sometimes called a *gripesite* – and filling it with content that criticizes the target organization. More elaborate cyberbashing sites include forums to allow fellow disappointed customers to add their comments. While legal action can be taken against outright untruths, genuine accounts of actual events are far more difficult to censor. Because of the nature of the cyberbashing sites – pure textual content which feature the company/brand/product name frequently that appeals to their **algorithms** – it is not unusual for cybersmears to appear high in **search engine results pages**. More proactive companies will monitor cyberbashing sites as part of **online reputation management** and move to diffuse potential situations by either contacting the complaining individual, responding in the forums or setting up response sites.

Cybercheck

As the term suggests, this is using the web to find information about individuals, a search engine being an obvious starting point for any kind of *online* check. However, there are numerous other sites that will reveal personal information, from the rather innocent Friends Reunited-type sites (www.friendsreunited.com) to those that offer the online service of tracking personal details of potential dates or business partners.

> *See also* **cyber stalking, MySpace generation** and **vanity search**.

Cybercrime

The generic term for any crime perpetrated using Internet technology. However, it is often more closely related to online credit-card fraud and the theft of card holder's details – which is sometimes referred to as *cyberfraud*.

Cyberfraud

> *See* **cybercrime**.

Cyberjockey (cyber-jockey)

A term from the early days of the web when cyber was commonly used as a prefix to describe any Internet-related activity. A cyberjockey –

jockey being more likely related to *disc*-jockey than a horse rider – is someone who spends long periods of time in **chat** rooms, discussion forums or **newsgroups** and addresses issues raised by other users by answering questions or providing assistance in subjects on which they are knowledgeable or even expert.

Cyberloafing

Also called cyber*slacking*, this is a term used to describe an employee who is on the Internet – surfing the web or sending personal emails – when they should be working.

Cyber Monday

Also known as Black Monday, this is a US nickname for the Monday after Thanksgiving (the last Thursday in November). The term stems from the long tradition in America of the day after Thanksgiving being one of, if not *the*, busiest shopping day of the year – historically the day when high sales pushed money-losing stores into the black. The day has been traditionally dubbed Black Friday. However, research has shown it is the Monday after Thanksgiving that is the peak day for *online* trans-actions – hence Black Monday (piggybacking on the Black Friday theme), and more recently Cyber Monday. Many online retailers gear up for the day by running specific promotions on and around the day. While it is an American tradition, any online store – no matter where it is based – which hopes to do business with customers in the US should look to maximize sales at this time of the year.

Cybersmear campaign

See **cyberbashing**.

Cyberspace

A term coined by author William Gibson in his 1984 novel *Neuromancer*, the word is often used to describe the whole range of information resources available through computer networks in general and the Internet in particular. It was very popular in the early days of the commercial Internet, but its use has declined in recent years.

Cybersquatting

The practice of registering a domain name with the aim of selling it at a profit, normally to the organization that has some stake in the name.

Although domain names can still be *squatted*, the fact that few names remain unregistered means that new examples are limited to new products, brands or companies. This is in contrast to the early days of the web when the early bird really did catch the domain name worm. Before businesses had even become aware of the Internet, let alone domain names, unscrupulous individuals saw the opportunity to extort money from organizations by registering the names of companies, brands and products. Although existing and new laws gave organizations legal recourse to recover the names, many simply paid up to avoid protracted, and expensive, lawsuits. One such law is the US Anti-cybersquatting Consumer Protection Act of 1999, which covers **dotcom** names. In other parts of the word, however, there is no such law and action has to be taken on the *use* of a domain name rather than the actual registering of it. One way that cybersquatters can pick up new names is **drop catching** domain names whose registrations have lapsed. A close relative of the cybersquatter is the **typosquatter**. Although the typosquatter will normally have a different purpose, they may take advantage of the general population's poor typing ability (see **fat-finger typos**) and look to sell to organizations domain names of misspellings of their brand or products.

> See also **domain name parking (2)**, a practice sometimes incorrectly referred to as cybersquatting.

Cyberstalking

Although Google often takes the blame in this concept, a commonly used term being *Google*-stalking, the ubiquitous search engine is far from being the only guilty party in this practice. Cyberstalking takes the **cybercheck** to the next, more sinister, level. An excellent definition of the practice comes from Bocij and McFarlane: 'A group of behaviours in which an individual, group of individuals or organization uses information and communications technology (ICT) to harass one or more individuals. Such behaviours may include, but are not limited to, the transmission of threats and false accusations, identity theft, data theft, damage to data or equipment, computer monitoring, the solicitation of minors for sexual purposes and confrontation. Harassment is defined as a course of action that a reasonable person, in possession of the same information, would think causes another reasonable person to suffer emotional distress.' As this definition intimates, cyberstalking can be against an entity – an organization or corporation, for example – as well as an individual.

> Bocij, P. and McFarlane, L. 'Online Harassment: Towards a Definition of Cyberstalking', *Prison Service Journal*, 139 (February), HM Prison Service, London, 2002.

Database

A collection of data stored in a computerized format.

See also **data warehouse.**

Database marketing

A form of **direct marketing** using **databases** of customers in combination with other databases (products, suppliers, distributors) to generate personalized communications which drive targeted marketing efforts at both strategic and tactical levels. Compared to other forms of marketing (branding, for example), the analysis of outcomes of database marketing efforts is relatively straightforward, and for this reason it can be described as 'marketing with measurable results'. Database marketing involves the gathering, storage and mining of data that can be used to provide information on customers that might be useful in future marketing efforts. Technology has provided the marketer with the means to collect and store masses of data on all their customers. The complexity of any such operation means that only the largest companies can handle **data warehousing** in-house, with the majority outsourcing to specialists. For successful online database marketing (as well as **contextual and behavioural targeting**) the e-marketer might gather data specific to the individual's online habits – such, as: how often does the user access the web? (every day, once a week), how long do they spend online in a single session? (ten minutes, an hour), when do they go online? (weekdays, weekends), at what time(s) of the day do they go online? (morning, evening), what type of access do they have? (dial-up, broadband) and where do they access the web? (home, work, library).

This definition is based on, or cites, content by the author in R. Gay, A. Charlesworth and R. Esen, *Online Marketing: A Customer-Led Approach*. Oxford: Oxford University Press, 2007.

Database of Intentions

A term used by John Battelle in his 2005 book, *The Search*, to describe the phenomenon of how information is now gathered and held. Battelle's definition of the Database of Intentions is: 'the aggregate results of every search ever entered, every result list ever tendered, and every path taken as a result'. Battelle's book is, essentially, about how search technology has, is, and will change both business and our culture.

Battelle, J., *The Search*. London: Nicholas Brealey Publishing, 2005.

Data cleansing

Also known as data *scrubbing*, this is the process of detection and removal (or possibly correction) of data that are no longer accurate and/or useful – that is, they are *dirty*– from a **data warehouse**.

Data mart

A small **data warehouse**.

Data mining

See **data warehouse**.

Data packet

See **packet**.

Data Protection Act 1998 (DPA)

While the legislation underpinning the DPA is complex, with much of it devoted to giving individuals certain rights to access information kept on them, it does have an impact on e-commerce in that it requires that appropriate security measures exist in order to safeguard personal data against unauthorized or unlawful access or processing.

The Data Protection Act is built around eight principles, which state that all data must be:

- processed fairly and lawfully;
- obtained and used only for specified and lawful purposes;
- adequate, relevant and not excessive;
- accurate, and, where necessary, kept up to date;
- kept for no longer than necessary;

D

- processed in accordance with the individual's rights;
- kept secure;
- transferred only to countries that offer adequate data protection.

Although these are *legal* requirements, most not only make common *business* sense, but would also represent good online trading practice. The last point is of particular relevance to the e-commerce trader. Whilst the others are equally relevant to offline businesses, they would be unlikely to transfer data away from their own trading country. Online, however, this might be common practice – particularly if the organization has servers located around the world. It is worth noting that while the UK has the Data Protection Act, and similar laws exist in Europe (there is an EU Data Protection Directive), other countries in the world – including the USA – have nothing comparable.

Data warehouse

A collection of data (a database) designed to support management decision-making. Development of a data warehouse includes development of systems to extract data from operating systems, so-called *data mining*. Data mining goes beyond simply searching for specific data within the database – looking for new and perhaps unknown patterns within the data collection. From such data, information can be developed on (for example) customer behaviour that may allow the organization to predict future actions and so be proactive in its planning.

See also **database marketing**.

Dayparting

Also known as *ad scheduling*, dayparting is a descendant of the **daypart session** and follows the same basic concept – limiting ads to certain times of the day – but does not involve dominance of the medium being used. Google's **Adsense** (from where the term ad scheduling comes) allows advertisers to select times of the day or days of the week in which they want ads to appear. This could be used, for example, by an advertiser who thinks that a certain TV show will prompt users to go online and search for terms relative to that programme – and so they might limit advertising to times or days immediately after its transmission.

D

Daypart session

A form of ad presentation where a single advertiser dominates all the advertising on a publisher's web site at a predetermined time of the day.

Although the innovation is widely attributed to the *New York Times* (*NYT*), several organizations had already dabbled with the concept prior to *NYT*'s adoption of it in the summer of 2002. MarketWatch.com, for example, had sold its Friday afternoon advertising space to Anheuser Busch, allowing the brewer to feature a Friday afternoon *happy hour* on the site. The dayparts are early morning, daytime, evening, late night and weekends. *See also* **dayparting**.

> This definition is based on, or cites, content by the author in R. Gay, A. Charlesworth and R. Esen, *Online Marketing: A Customer-Led Approach*. Oxford: Oxford University Press, 2007.

Decryption

See **encryption**.

Dedicated server

A **server** that hosts a single, or very few, web sites which are normally owned by the **publisher** of the sites. Few web sites will generate sufficient business to make the investment worthwhile, but all the major online brands will have banks of dedicated servers for their web sites. Although the purchase price of servers continues to fall, significant expertise is necessary to keep them running. If a dedicated server is required without the accompanying hassle, they can be hired from **application service providers**. There are a number of advantages to hosting a web site on a dedicated server, namely, that not sharing the facility should result in:

- faster **download** speed for the user;
- less chance of **down-time**;
- more security;
- less chance of appearing on a **search engine blacklist**.

Deep linking

The practice of linking to a web site's interior pages, rather than its **homepage**. The link could come from one of three primary sources:

- **A search engine results page** – if the web site has been optimized for **organic listing**, specific **keyword** searches will take searchers to pages with the relevant content.
- Another web site – the link is to a page with specific content, rather than the homepage, as a benefit to that web site's visitors.

- An ad for the company – rather than taking respondents (to the ad) to the homepage, they are taken to a page that is part of the **persuasive architecture** connected to the ad, normally called a **landing page**.

De facto standard (proprietary standard)

Adopted widely in e-commerce, this term is used to describe a practice or standard that has evolved and been endorsed by industry or government.

Default

In computing this refers to the preselected settings of equipment, electronic devices or software when they are manufactured – that is, *default* settings that operate unless instructed otherwise. The term is used when those settings are optional and can be changed by the owner/operator after purchase.

Defensive domain name registration

The practice of registering **domain names** that are similar to that being registered so as to prevent other individuals or entities registering them – usually for nefarious or mischievous reasons. Defensive registration might include registering the domain name with multiple suffixes (e.g. .co.ok and .com) and similar spellings – and misspellings – of the name.

See also **cybersquatting, typosquatting, cyber-bashing sites** and **fat-finger typo.**

Defensive keyword marketing

The practice of purchasing **keywords** in **paid placement** advertising on search engines to counteract negative publicity. For example, if rumours abound that company A's turbo **yagahits** are faulty, then company A buys the search engine keyword phrase 'faulty turbo **yagahits**', and having achieved high listings in the **search engine results page**, have the link go to a specially prepared web page that refutes – or responds to – the accusation.

Deferred billing service

A method of accepting customer payments that is moving – slowly – online. The model is that the customer orders the product online, and opts to take the deferred billing option. The goods are dispatched from the

D

online store, and the bill is sent to the customer from the deferred billing service. The bill can be paid off within 30 days or over a period of months. The online shop receives payment immediately after the sale, less a service charge which varies depending on the length of repayment. As the retailer decides on the period of repayment being offered (e.g. six months on items over £250), the charges can be built in to any pricing policy.

Deferred conversion

An element of **web site analytics**, this is where a user visits a site and does not buy anything at that time – but returns later and does make a purchase.

De Kare Silver's ES Test

In the early days of the commercial web, many retailers were concerned that they could not operate both physically and electronically without one cannibalizing the other. In attempting to assess the extent of any cannibalization, Michael de Kare Silver (1998) devised a framework to help determine why a product might sell online. The ES Test consists of three elements, each of which must be addressed to determine the product's suitability for online sales.

1 Product characteristics – what is the product's primal appeal to the senses? Does it need to be touched or tried before buying? Products that appeal to the senses of sight and sound make good candidates for ES, while those that appeal to touch, taste and smell are less likely to suit ES.
2 Familiarity and confidence – to what degree does the customer recognize and trust the product, enough to repurchase it?
3 Consumer attributes – what are the customer's underlying motivations and attitudes towards shopping?

De Kare Silver, M., *E-shock*. Basingstoke: Palgrave Macmillan, 1998.

De-listed

In an e-commerce environment this phrase is used to describe web sites that are removed from a search engine's **index**. Normally this is because they have been **banned** – though it is not unheard of to be de-listed through a glitch in the search engine's technology. De-listing should also cleanse the search engines of **broken links** and **ghost sites**.

See also **reinclusion request**.

Denial-of-Service (DoS) attack

The use of specialized software to maliciously disable – close down – a web site or online service. This is achieved by sending to its **server** a flood of erroneous data **packets**, so overloading the system – the same effect as having millions of users try to access the web site at the same time. A *distributed* DoS attack involves the attacker gaining unauthorized access to as many computers on the Internet as possible and using them to flood packets to the target site. E-commerce traders should be aware of, and take steps to combat, such attacks on their web site.

Depth of visit

An element of **web site analytics**, this considers how far – *deep* – a visitor goes into a web site, measured by the number of distinct pages they download during a visit to the site.

Desktop purchasing

A phrase used to describe an offline practice that has proliferated with the advent, and acceptance, of e-commerce. Desktop purchasing is the practice of individuals in an organization being given the authority to make purchases without the express authority of supervisors or the organization's procurement department. Such purchasing can be controlled by software applications that limit or control an individual's purchasing. Despite the title, purchases can be made in the field using remote devices, such practice being the cornerstone of many **e-procurement** systems. Although originally the purchases would be from internal marketplaces, the Internet – and in particular **e-market-places** – have meant that external purchasing can also be conducted.

See also **buy-side e-marketplace**.

Destination site

The web site that is at the end of a **link**. Although the definition for *destination site* is the same as that for **target page**, the latter is normally used by web site designers who are writing the site's programming language – when they include a hypertext link they need a *target* for that link. Destination site is more commonly the term used when considering the link from the user's point of view, as the link takes them to a *destination*. Because it is the destination link from an online ad, another – rarely used – definition is to call a **landing page** a destination site.

D

Development server

A **web server** that is used to host and test web sites while they are under development. The server cannot be accessed by the general public and so the development can be kept private until the site is ready to go 'live'. Such a server is only likely to be used by a major e-commerce site.

See also **dedicated server.**

Dial-up connection

Now largely being replaced by broadband connections where the user has a constant connection, dial-up connections were a once common method of connecting to the web. A user's **modem** dials up to an **Internet service provider**, through which an Internet connection is established – the union with the Internet only lasting as long as the dial-up connection is preserved.

See also **modem.**

Dictionary attack (1)

A method of breaking into **password**-protected security systems using software that systematically tests all possible passwords. Beginning with words that have a higher possibility of being used – such as names and places – the software continues as if all the words in a dictionary were being tried in an attempt to discover the password.

Dictionary attack (2)

Not unlike the software used to perform a dictionary attack on passwords, this software application applies the same logic to finding **email addresses**. The method is used for **spamming** where **domain names** are known but the actual email address is not. The software generates tens of thousands of email addresses based on common combinations of letters in the hope that a percentage will be *actual* e-mail addresses. For example, sending emails to alan, alan2, alan3 (and so on) @hotmail.com will eventually find recipients.

Differentiated traffic

A description given to users who visit a site and become (a) customers for the product offered, (b) supporters of the brand or (c) users of any

D

service provided by that site. Such visitors are often described as *good* traffic.

See also **visitors, intentional traffic** and **undifferentiated traffic.**

Digital

See **analogue.**

Digital (as a prefix)

As with a number of other terms it has become common practice to prefix certain offline concepts or terms with *digital* in order to indicate their association with the Internet. Although this is usually restricted to issues that are directly associated with digital (as opposed to **analogue**) – **digital products**, for example – for others the digital connection is somewhat tenuous – e.g. the **digital economy**.

See also **e (as a prefix), online (as a prefix)** and **cyber (as a prefix).**

Digital brand

See **online branding.**

Digital certificate

Also known as digital ID, this is a method of verifying that an individual on the Internet is who they claim to be.

See also **public key infrastructure.**

Digital divide

The term used to describe the gap between the *haves* and the *have-nots* in the digital world. In essence, it means the gap between those who have access to the Internet and those who do not. In societal terms it means that the quest for knowledge, information and lower prices is easier for those who *have* access to the web. Though finance is a prime determinant in the digital divide, it is not absolute. For example, there are those who cannot gain fast access to the web – they live in areas with no broadband connections, for example – and there are those who have the means to access the web, but have not yet recognized its potential benefits.

D

Digital Economy

Also known as the *New* Economy, this term refers to the influence of information technology (IT) companies on the economy. The concept of the Digital Economy grew during the 1990s, its implication being that information technology (the Internet in particular) was changing the world so dramatically that traditional benchmarks of value were no longer applicable.

Digital footprint

See **clickstream.**

Digital ID

See **digital certificate.**

Digital products

Those products that can be configured into a digital format, so allowing them to be delivered via the Internet. Digital products can come in one of three categories:

1. Products that are digital by composition – e.g. software, computer games, music.
2. Products that can be presented in digital format – e.g. airline tickets and newspapers.
3. The product is information that can be presented in electronic format – e.g. a surveyor's report emailed as a Word document rather than printed and sent by traditional **snail mail**.

Digital Rights Management (DRM)

The term used to describe technologies that can be incorporated into electronic devices to control the use of digital media, DRM is usually considered to be *copy protection* for music, films and video games. However, it has wider applications such as allowing computer software to be rented or providing assurance that only authorized programs are used on a particular computer. DRM permits the creation of new business models where users can buy the right to read a book just once, or pay a very small fee every time they play a piece of music. As a result of this, publishers can exercise greater flexibility in the services they offer, which allows them to increase consumer choice.

Digital signature

A code used to verify the content of messages – including emails – and the identity of the signatory.

Digital subscriber line (DSL)

A data-communications technology that enables faster data transmission over standard copper telephone lines than a conventional **modem**. ADSL (asymmetric digital subscriber line) enables even faster data transmission. Such systems are commonly used in areas where *old* telephone lines are used. Newer housing and business developments normally have broadband-carrying fibre optic lines as standard.

Digital wallet

The term used to describe a consumer account set up to allow online transactions through a particular credit-card processing system. Before the consumer can make a purchase, they must first set up an account with the credit-card processor, who provides an ID and password. These are then used when making a purchase at any web site that supports that transaction system. PayPal (www.paypal.com) is an example of a digital wallet scheme. For the e-commerce site, accepting payments through PayPal (for example) is seen as an advantage in breaking down the barrier of concerns over secure transactions.

Directed information seeker

Something of a misnomer, *self*-directed being a more accurate description. This refers to a web user who knows what they are looking for when they go online, and so strives to go straight to web sites that will meet their needs. A directed information *seeker* is the opposite of a **surfer**.

See also **meanderthal**, **visitor** and **intentional traffic**.

D

Direct keywords

Rather than more generic terms or phrases, these are **keywords** that are directly related to the organization's products or services. Usually descriptive, they can include **trademarks** or brand names specific to the product or service being promoted or the **tag line** being used to promote the product in other media. For example, if a TV ad for a new product features a character who utters the phrase 'it is the bestest ever choco-late', then 'bestest ever chocolate' might be a search query phrase entered by the potential customer because they missed the actual name of the chocolate. This being the case, the online marketer should have purchased the phrase for **paid placement** on search engines. Note, however, that being a tag line to a promotional campaign should mean that the phrase is already part of the web site's **organic listing** opti-mization efforts.

Direct marketing

A form of marketing where customers are contacted personally – *directly* – rather than through an impersonal medium such as advertising. In an e-commerce environment, **email marketing** is a form of direct market-ing, with the most successful proponents of email marketing invariably applying lessons learned offline to their online efforts.

Direct navigation

A term used to describe the practice of typing a web site address directly into a browser window, meaning that the user not only knows the web site they wish to visit, but also has remembered the correct **domain name** (or **URL**) of that site. The practice can have a number of implica-tions for online marketers – see **domain name parking (2)**, **fat-finger typo** and **intuitive domain names**. Note that using a **bookmark** in a browser is not considered to be direct navigation.

Directory

D

A direct descendant of the offline directory, the online directory has human involvement in its development – rather than relying on **spiders** to crawl the web as **search engines** do. In directories, web sites are usually reviewed and placed in a particular category. Although it is now a search engine, Yahoo started as a directory – with the **Open Directory Project** and Business.com currently being perhaps the best known online directories. Most directories, however, are much smaller – normally being geographical, region-, industry- or subject-specific. They are often developed from an offline entity – a local Chamber of Commerce or industry body, for example, listing its members as part of its online presence. Similarly, a Tourist Information Board might have a directory of accommodation listed by type and location. Such directories are often part of a **portal**.

Disability Discrimination Act

Included here as it applies to not only accessibility to buildings and services, but to the Internet as well. As of October 2004, employers and service providers are legally obliged to make their web sites and intranets accessible to disabled people. An estimated 20 per cent of web users have some form of disability, with the majority of disabled people using the keyboard cursor keys rather than a mouse when surfing the web. Blind or partially sited people normally use a special browser that reads the content of a page out loud through a speaker – or access a text-only alternative to the main site if one is available. Despite it being a legal requirement, very few web sites meet the requirements of the Act. A 2005 investigation by the Disability Rights Commission found that 81 per cent of web sites failed to satisfy the most basic web accessibility criteria.

See also **Pas 78**, **Bobby** and **web site accessibility**.

Disaster recovery (1) technical perspective

Although the term is a little extreme – *contingency planning* is perhaps more appropriate – it refers to the organization having a predetermined plan to be put in place in the event of some kind of technical disaster – a web site's main server failing or a **DoS attack**, for example.

Disaster recovery (2) marketing perspective

While the technical issues are being addressed, the organization should also have a public relations response prepared for any and all situations that they think might arise. Any response will differ depending on the size of the organization and how much it relies on the web for its trade and/or marketing. In the contemporary trading environment organizations must be prepared for not only offline problems – e.g. the failure of a product – but also troubles that originate online, comments on a **cyberbashing** site, or in any other form of **consumer-generated media**, for example.

See also **defensive keyword marketing**.

D

Disclaimer

Literally, a repudiation or denial of responsibility or connection – and in law a renunciation of one's right or claim. In e-commerce terms, this is a legal statement – *disclaimer* – that should be included on all web sites to cover the organization in the event of something going wrong during its normal trading operations. Like **terms and conditions** and a **privacy policy**, any disclaimer should be written by someone with legal training and/or qualifications.

Discovery-based search

It can be argued that when we use search engines we perform two kinds of search, (a) *recovery* search – for sites we know exist, and have probably visited, and (b) *discovery* search – where we look for sites we hope exist, but do not know if they do. In an e-commerce environment organizations should develop their **web presence** in such a way that both of these groups find satisfaction when they arrive on the web site.

See also **navigational query**.

Discussion group

See **newsgroup**.

Disintermediation

An economics term first popularized in the early 1980s, disintermediation is the removal of intermediaries in a supply chain – in other words, cutting out the middleman. The ultimate disintermediation is to eliminate every link in the distribution chain, so allowing the manufacturer to sell directly to the end user. Although some touted this concept as being the greatest potential of the Internet, that prophecy has come to fruition in only isolated instances; Dell computers, for example. Although the cost of distribution is reduced significantly, problems of **channel conflict** prevent many manufacturers pursuing direct sales to customers. However, some manufacturers have adopted **multi-channel retailing** and a mix of ownership of those channels. Sony, for example, have independent offline stores – Sony Centres – but trade direct with end users through their own Sony Style online store (www.sonystyle.com).

Distinct visitor

See **unique visitor**.

Distributed denial-of-service attack

See **denial-of-service attack**.

DMZ (Demilitarized Zone)

Based on the offline term that describes a buffer zone between two warring factions, in an e-commerce environment the phrase has been adopted to describe a network area that lies between an organization's internal and external (Internet) networks. The DMZ will contain a **firewall** to prevent unauthorized entry.

DNS (Domain Name System)

A distributed client-server database system that unites **domain names** with their numerical **IP addresses**. The domain name system allows for the registration of domain names within a number of registries known as top level domains (TLDs). TLDs fall into two broad categories: (a) generic top level domains (gTLDs), e.g. those with the **domain name suffix** .com, and (b) country coded top level domains (ccTLDs), such as the suffix .uk for the United Kingdom. Each country has its own naming authority that runs the domain name system for that country and so distributes domain names on that country's suffix. To register a name you must apply to that authority for *permission* to use that name. Effectively, those who register the name are the *owners* of that name and, as such, are the only ones who can use that name. In the USA the authority is **ICANN** (formerly the **Internic**). The UK's ccTLD registry is owned and operated by **Nominet UK**, a not-for-profit, private-sector organization. Other countries have similar arrangements, with ccTLDs often being run by a government department or a university. There are also organizations that act as intermediaries between customers and the naming agencies. It is with these registration agents – or **domain name registrars** – that the vast majority of users register their domain name.

See also **RDNS.**

DNS blocklist

A list used by **spam filters** to block unwanted emails. The list is drawn from **DNS** records of domains that have been identified as being the source of **spam** emails.

See also **spam filter.**

Domain

The term used to identify a group of computers that are on a network and operate under common rules. On the Internet, domains are defined

D

by their **IP address**, with all devices sharing a common element of that IP address considered to be in the same domain.

Domain modelling

A practice which addresses the issue of email deliverability and which is also known as email rendering, *domain modelling* helps email marketers to have emails delivered and read – in their intended state and by the intended recipients – by tracking the different behaviour of the various interfaces used by **Internet service providers** (ISPs) and **email service providers** (ESPs). By modelling the email domains of the various service providers, emails can be developed for specific domains – so increasing the chances of success for any **email marketing** campaign. Potential problems are manifold – including, for example, that with AOL, image blocking is a **default** setting, which is not the case with Yahoo! Similarly, with Outlook and Gmail environments, the image **alt text** tags can give a description of the image in the absence of actual images. AOL, Yahoo! and Hotmail/MSN, on the other hand, do not allow the viewing of alt tags, showing them only as blank or grey areas. The situation is complicated further by the fact that each provider treats emails on their **white list** differently.

Domain name

Commonly described as a web site's address on the web, a domain name is more specifically the unique name that identifies an Internet site, each being unique because each domain name is allocated its own unique **IP address** in the domain name system (**DNS**). Because the *exact* spelling of each domain name is specific to its IP address the spelling of each name must be exact. For example, in domain name terms, amazom.com is a completely different entity to amazon.com. A name is made up of the **domain name suffix** – .com, for example – and the actual *name* (note that in the US the suffix is referred to as the *extension*). As the suffix is considered to be the *primary* domain, combining the name with the suffix creates a *second*-level domain, yagahit.com, for example. When indicating a domain name's use as the **URL** of a web site, it has become accepted protocol to use the prefix www – www.yagahit.com, for example. As the .com suffix now has two distinct *words* before it, technically, this is now a *third*-level domain name. Any subsequent words placed in front of the primary name, but divided by a full stop, make the URL a fourth/fifth-level domain name. Though technically, you can have as many words prior to the domain as you wish, in practice three or four is really the limit – www.sunderland.yagahit.com, for example. The word element of the original US (and many other) domain names can be made up of any combination of the 26 characters of the Latin alphabet, the digits 0 to 9 and the dash (–). More recently, however, names have been made available using other languages (than English) and characters (other than Latin). There can be no spaces in a domain name. Only the registered owner of the name on the primary suffix can add second- and any subsequent-level names. While it is possible to set up the domain name's host so that the name is case-sensitive when used in a browser, in practice this never happens – effectively meaning that domain names are not case-sensitive.

Domain name parking (1)

A service offered, normally by **domain name registrars**, to individuals or organizations who register domain names but do not wish to use them for a web site or email address, the unused names being *parked* on a server, sometimes with a parked page that says something like 'this domain name has been registered but is not in use at this time'. Many organizations practise registration and parking to prevent names falling into the hands of **cyber squatters**. As the name will have been allocated an **IP address** it can be made *live* at short notice, and can be pointed at a web site (see **domain name pointing**). Although a parked page may well include (with its 'has been registered . . . ' message) ads for the services offered by the domain name registrars, some hosts also sell advertising on the parked domains – perhaps to subsidize low **domain name registration** fees. It is this practice of using the parked site to host ads that has seen the term used in another context – *see* **domain name parking (2)**.

Domain name parking (2)

An example of how the meaning of some e-commerce terms have evolved, even changed, over time, domain name parking is now commonly referred to as a business model that is an extension of the practice described in **domain name parking (1)**. Also known as *shell*, *placeholder* sites or *web billboards*, this is where domains are registered and a web page developed that contains nothing more than a list of ads which link to web sites that have some association with the domain name on which the site is hosted. Parked domain owners generate income through **pay per click** agreements with the likes of Google and Yahoo. Visitors find their way to the parked sites by either:

D

- Typing the domain name directly into their browser – a practice dubbed **direct navigation**. This is popular in the USA where .com is overwhelmingly the most common suffix. For example, to find information on 'shows', type in www.shows.com.
- Mistyping a popular domain name into their browser.
- Finding the sites listed in a **search engine results page** (SERP), where it is not obvious that they are not sites that contain information. Parked names can often appear high in search engine rankings because their content appeals to the **search engine algorithms**. For example, the parked domain web site flashgames.com contains lots of content about games that use **Flash** technology, and so any search on the **keywords** 'flash games' will return flashgames.com high on the SERP.

Because of the reasons described above, domain names used in this practice normally fall into one of two categories. They are (a) based on generic words – shows.com, for example – or (b) they are misspellings of popular domain names – see **typosquatting**. A negative aspect of this practice is that many users are frustrated by pages that appear at the top of SERPs for a specific term, only to find the link goes to an ad site and not a site that has more specific content on the sought-after subject. The practice has gained an element of legitimacy through schemes such as **DomainSense**, a Google application that allows advertisers to puts ads on parked domains. It is worth noting that although some refer to parking as **cybersquatting** this is not the case, as a cybersquatter registers the *squatted* name with the purpose of selling it on to the rightful owner. The confusion comes about because a cybersquatter might park the name in an interim period prior to them selling the name – or losing it as the result of legal action.

Domain name pointing

This is when a domain name is registered, but its new owner does not want to host a web site on it, so they have it *point* at another site. This means that if a user types the domain name into a browser that request will be re-routed to the other, specified, web site. It's most common use is where duplicate names have been registered – e.g. the company name with both .com and .co.uk suffixes – yet only one web site maintained. It is normal for the delivered web site to appear under its own hosting domain name. It is possible, however, for the web site to appear under the domain that is being *pointed*, and this is known as *masked web direction*. Note, however, when a domain name has been withdrawn or made redundant (for example, if a company moves its web site from one domain name to another) this is known as *domain name redirection* – though for the user, pointing and redirection result in the same thing.

Domain name redirection

See **domain name pointing.**

Domain name registrar

A business that makes a profit by handling the registration of domain names for its customers, effectively acting as a third party between the end user and the naming authority. Note that for an individual or organization to register names directly with the naming authority it must operate two *name* servers on which the domain names are hosted. Normally, only domain name registrars will have this facility – with most also offering hosting services or acting as **application service providers**.

See also **DNS, domain name** and **domain name registration.**

Domain name registration

In order to have use of a domain name, the prospective owner must register it with the relevant naming authority through a **domain name registrar**. Although legally recognized as the *owner* of a domain name, the person or entity that *registers* the name actually does little more than buy the permission to use it. This is because ownership of a name is useless without its presence on the **DNS**, something over which the owner does not have complete control.

See also **domain name** and **domain name registrar.**

Domain name suffix (in the USA, domain name extension)

All domain names have a suffix denoting the top level domain (TLD) on which it has been registered. The most common is .com, the suffix for the TLD of the USA. Other countries use country-specific suffixes (ccTLDs), with additional codes to indicate the use of the name. In the UK, for example, .co.uk denotes a *commercial* entity, .ac.uk an *academic* institution and .gov.uk a *government*-sponsored web site. There are over 250 countries with a country-specific domain, for example: .de for Germany, .jp for Japan .fr for France and .gr for Greece. One of the latest suffixes is not country-specific, but *union*-specific – that being .eu for the European Union. Like .com (and other US suffixes such as .info and

.net), registration of .eu names is open to individuals and entities wherever they are in the world – though this is not the case for every ccTLD, with some limiting domain name registration to businesses or organizations from that country.

See also **DNS**.

Domain Name System

See **DNS**.

Domain name warehousing

The practice of **domain name registrars** registering multiple domain names and keeping – *warehousing* – them for future sale or use. While it is permissible for any individual or entity to register as many names as they wish, this is not the case for registrars who should facilitate registrations, not hive off the best names for themselves. The spring 2006 launch of the .eu top level domain was blighted by problems attributed to domain name warehousing, and as a result many popular names were suspended until the problems were sorted out.

DomainSense

See **domain name parking**.

Do not use words

A phrase that comes from **spam filters**. One way in which the filters work is that they reject emails with certain words in their **subject line**. Email marketers are aware, therefore, that there are certain words that they do not use in subject lines. *Do not use words* include such words as *free* and *cash* – the sort of thing that spammers would use to encourage or fool recipients into opening an email.

D

Doorway page

Also known as gateway, bridge or jump page, this is a web page created purely to feature highly in a **search engine's ranking**. A doorway page offers little, if anything, of value to users. Normally consisting of no more than a link to the organization's main or promotional site, the user may even be redirected automatically. Although the concept is sometimes used by legitimate marketers, it is more often the practice of less scrupulous operators – sometimes using **cloaking** to forward users to sites with no association to the search terms used on the doorway page. Because of this, search engines take a dim view of the practice.

See also **hosted doorway pages.**

DoS attack

See **denial of service attack.**

Dotcom

Based on the US **domain name suffix** of .com, dotcom became the description given to **pure online businesses** financed by massive injections of investors' cash in the late 1990s – the so-called dotcom *boom*. As stock markets discovered that most dotcoms offered little in the way of profits, this turned into the dotcom *bust*, and the companies becoming dot*bombs*. The term dotcom lives on in the popular press to describe almost any company associated with the Internet.

Dot pitch

The space between **pixels**. The smaller the space, the sharper the image will appear on a computer screen. For example, a dot pitch of 0.28mm gives a sharper image than .32mm.

Download

The transfer a file or files from a remote computer to the user's computer. In an e-commerce environment the term is used to describe the transfer of files from a **web server** to a user's computer – in other words, the files that make up a web page being *downloaded* to the user's **browser**.

D

Download time

Although the term refers to how long any document takes to download on a computer, in e-commerce terms the only download time that really counts is how long it takes for a web page to download on to the user's browser. People using the web are seldom patient; if a web page does not appear straight away they move on. The maxim that, online, your competitor is only a click of the mouse away is as valid now as when it was first penned. In the early days of the web it was said that users would wait around 8 seconds for a page to download, after which they moved on. In the day of the **broadband** connection, this is now much less. There are a number of factors that can affect a web page's download time:

1 Some are beyond the control of both user and web site designer – **bandwidth** and how busy the network is, for example.
2 Those beyond the control of the site's developer include the configuration and specification of the user's PC.
3 The design of the site is beyond the control of the user.

It is the latter that is of most interest to the e-marketer, for it is the one over which they have most control. As it is the **home page** at which visitors normally arrive on a site, that page's download time is paramount. In an attempt to guarantee fast download, the best practitioners of web site design aim to keep their home page size below 40,000 bytes. At the time of writing (April 2006), the size of the home pages of the following web sites were: Google 1,500, MSN 8,763, Amazon 13,501, Yahoo 16,160, AOL 21,595, The Times Online 23859, the BBC 30,002.

See also **view page info.**

Down-time

In an e-commerce context, down-time refers to any period when a web site is not available to users – the site being *down*. Down-time can be caused by a number of things, either planned (server repair or maintenance, for example), or unplanned (some kind of technical fault). While the former can be prepared for and its effects minimized, the latter should also be prepared for so that any potential damage can be restricted.

See also **disaster recovery.**

Drop catching

A close associate of **cybersquatting** (the same person or entity will probably practise both), drop catching is a way of making a profit by taking advantage of the domain name registration system. Key to this practice is that domain name registrations must be renewed on an annual basis (though it is possible to pay annual fees for years in advance). If the owner of a domain name does not renew its registration the registration lapses and, eventually, the name is made available on the free market. As the original owner may be using the name for a business its loss can be significant. The drop catcher uses software to check on names that come back on to the market (an estimated 20,000 a day) and registers any that they feel might be valuable. Having taken ownership of the name the drop catcher can:

- offer to sell it to the previous owner;
- auction it, perhaps to competitors of the original owner; or
- as the domain might have a high ranking on search engine rankings, use it to host a web site loaded with ads, so earning significant income.

Note that the practice of drop catching breaks no laws, though the owner of a domain name that might be copyrighted or trademarked can seek to recover the name by appealing to an arbitration panel under **ICANN**'s dispute-resolution policy. The downside to this is that the process takes time, and any site previously hosted on the name will be unavailable for the period of the dispute.

Drop-down menu

Also known as a *pull*-down menu, this is a method of displaying extensive navigation menus without taking up too much space on a web page. The idea is that a single word or phrase can be clicked on so that it opens up – *drops down* – into more links on the same subject.

Drop shipping

A concept that has existed offline for many years but has risen to prominence in the e-commerce era. Some online sales companies carry no inventory of the goods they are selling online. Instead they take the order and pass it on to distributors or manufacturers who then pack and dispatch (ship) the goods directly to the customer – this is drop shipping. Drop shipping performs a similar function to **fulfilment houses** and is an essential element in the concept of the **virtual business**.

DSL

See **digital subscriber line.**

Dynamic content

Also known as dynamic **HTML**, this is web page content that changes each time it is viewed. For example, the parameters of the page could be set up to react to such things as the time of day, or the geographic location of the visitor – with content pertinent to each being delivered.

D

Dynamic pricing

The offline concept is that prices charged for a product may vary over time and across customers, usually based on supply and demand. Online, technology is employed to automatically change prices as and when demand changes. An example would be budget airlines, where pre-programmed software will change the online prices of remaining seats depending on availability – for example, (a) if the majority of seats are sold, the price of available seats increases, or (b) if seat sales are poor, the price will be dropped to increase demand.

Dynamic rotation

See **ad rotation.**

Dynamic URL

A **URL** that results from the search of a database-driven web site generated from specific queries to the site's database. Any pages that reside on such a URL are deemed to be **dynamic web pages**.

Dynamic web pages/sites

Pages that are developed from database content, the page only being produced in response to a user's request – selecting a particular product from an on-site search, for example. Dynamic pages are also known as being developed *on the fly* and are identifiable by their long and nonsensical URLs. Although they serve a valuable purpose in web development their main drawback is that search engines have difficulty in indexing such pages, causing product pages held in databases to be excluded from a search engine's **index**.

D

E (as a prefix)

In many of the following concepts and terms 'e' is a prefix used as short-hand for 'electronic' – which normally denotes the word, and its meaning or application has been adapted for use in an online environment. In all of the terms listed below, the 'e' could be replaced by the full word, 'electronic', but it is common practice to simply use the 'e' and a dash as a prefix – as in e-commerce. Note that when the prefix 'e' is used it is normally followed by a dash, as in e-commerce. However, this is not absolute, as is exemplified by *email* being most commonly presented without a dash.

See also **cyber (as a prefix)** and **online (as a prefix)**.

Easter egg

In a computing environment an Easter egg is a message hidden in an application by its developers. The message normally consists of credits for the development team, though often it is light-hearted or humorous. To access the message users must know the secret sequence of keystrokes.

E-auction

See **online auction**.

E-banking

The use of Internet technology in providing online banking services. While this has caused a revolution in the way banks conduct business with retail customers, and so generated most publicity, the use of the Internet to transfer funds in a B2B environment is also a significant element of e-banking.

See also **electronic funds transfer**.

E-book

The description, e-book, covers two primary models of electronic book. Those that are distributed in digital format over the Internet for (1) printing out before being read, and (2) those to be read in digital format.

1 To be printed. The advantage to this format for authors is twofold: (a) a publisher need not be found, and (b) there are no printing costs. The book is normally presented as a **PDF** file and, when printed, resembles a published book. The concept is particularly useful for minority-interest books that would never sell enough copies to warrant being published traditionally. E-books can be used as a promotional vehicle for organizations or individuals. A number of online businesses offer print-on-demand facilities for books that would not warrant the expense of a print run.

2 To be read in digital format. This concept has been *coming* for a number years, but has always been defeated by the lack of suitable hardware and software. The key problem is that humans find it difficult to read from a screen for long periods, and so prefer to read print on paper. Recent innovations claim to have addressed this issue (the Sony Reader in March 2006, for example) by replicating the look of the printed word on a paperback book-sized screen. If this technology works, and is accepted, the future might see users simply downloading any text they wish and reading it on a handheld 'reader'. Readers sceptical of this concept are reminded that a not too dissimilar scenario revolutionized music distribution in the recent past.

E-business

For many, the terms e-business and e-commerce are interchangeable, both having the same meaning. If there is a difference it is that e-business represents a broader definition than e-commerce – addressing the impact of Internet technology on *all* elements of business, with e-commerce concentrating on the practice of the online buying, selling or exchange of goods or services. That e-commerce is the most prevalent term is perhaps due to it being in common use for longer. Although no one has staked a claim to inventing the term – though the domain name e-commerce.com was registered in April 1994 – Kalakota and Whinston certainly helped promote it in the public eye in their 1996 book, *Frontiers of Electronic Commerce*. IBM are credited with the first definition of e-business in 1997, saying that it is 'a secure, flexible and integrated approach to delivering differentiated business value by combining the

E

systems and processes that run core business operations with the simplicity and reach made possible by internet technology'. This IBM definition purports that e-business pertains to any element of business where Internet technology is employed – so can e-commerce be considered to mean the same? The *Collins Concise Dictionary* defines *commerce* as 'The activity embracing all forms of the purchase and sale of goods and services.' This, more limited, application within a business environment would support the IBM-based argument that e-commerce is actually a subsidiary, rather than equivalent, of e-business.

Kalakota, R. and Whinston, A. B., *Frontiers of Electronic Commerce*. Harlow: Addison-Wesley, 1996.

E-checkout

See **shopping cart.**

E-commerce

See **e-business.**

E-commerce service providers (esp)

The online manifestation of **fulfilment houses**.

E-contracts

Contracts formed, taken out or completed online. Note, however, that rules governing contract formation apply just as much in *cyberspace* as they do offline.

E-CRM (e-customer relationship management)

Those elements of **CRM** that are practised using Internet technology. Arguably, it is Internet technology that prompted the rise in CRM applications in the latter part of the 1990s, and so intrinsic is the Internet to contemporary CRM that the term e-CRM is almost redundant. However, the term can be applied to how much (or little) a web site contributes to an organization's CRM strategy. For example, prominent contact details, a **frequently asked questions** page and the facility for the web site to be personalized by the user might all add to the organization's relationship management efforts.

E

Edge networks

Companies that provide the service of handling an **Internet service provider's** (ISP) email connection and filtering incoming traffic for **spam**, **viruses**, **phishing** and other malicious attacks. The term comes from the idea that the software sits on the *edge* of the ISP's network.

EDI (electronic data interchange)

A forerunner to and an older form of electronic commerce, EDI allows the transfer of data between companies using proprietary networks. Although it is still used, it has been largely replaced by Internet technology. The high cost of the hardware and software required for EDI systems means that only large corporations could, and still can, afford them.

Effective frequency

A term given to the number of **ad impressions** that are required for a particular ad, or ad campaign, to become effective in meeting its objectives. Those objectives might include such things as a sales quota, brand or product awareness or visitors driven to a web site.

EFT

See **electronic funds transfer.**

E-fulfilment

See **fulfilment.**

Ego search

See **vanity search.**

E

E-government

The provision of goods, services and information from a government entity using Internet technology. This can include G2B (government-to-business) and G2C (government-to-citizens). There has been a commitment from the EU itself as well as individual governments in the EU to implement e-government. In the business environment this e-transformation has been relatively straightforward, with businesses being *obliged* to use the Internet as the medium by which government business is conducted – 'if you want to tender for this work you must do it electronically'. In the G2C environment governments have used the Internet as a medium to disseminate information and services. Not only is information being made available online, but services that once required the citizen's physical presence in a specific place and at a certain time now being made available online (in the UK, car tax, for example). The use of e-technology as a medium for communication between a government and its citizens might raise issues with regard to the **digital divide**.

E-jurisdiction

Online jurisdiction. By its very nature, the Internet is global, therefore e-commerce traders and e-marketers should be aware of each country's jurisdiction under which their web site might fall. What is legal and acceptable in one country might not be so in another.

E-learning

The online delivery of education or training. The term is something of a misnomer in that it is invariably used to describe the delivery of education, in which case it should be e-teaching – it is the student who does the learning, or e-learning.

Electronic Commerce (EC Directive) regulations 2002 (ECRs)

One of the EU regulations that cover e-commerce practices, including requiring online traders to provide certain information about the operation of online transactions and to acknowledge receipt of orders without undue delay by electronic means. Also to make available to the customer appropriate and accessible technical means to allow them to identify and correct input errors before they place the order. ECRs are relevant to businesses that sell products online or by email, including both B2B and B2C trading.

See also **Consumer Protection (Distance Selling) Regulations 2000 (DSRs)**.

Electronic Data Interchange

See **EDI**.

E

Electronic dropouts

Those people who were once users of the Internet, but no longer go online. Research suggests that lack of access to a computer is the main reason for this, followed by 'no interest', 'too expensive' and 'it consumes too much time'. Interestingly, privacy or security concerns are no longer cited as significant reasons for abandoning the Internet.

Surveying the Digital Future, September 2004, www.digitalcenter.org.

Electronic Funds Transfer (EFT)

The technology that facilitates the electronic transfer of funds from the bank account of one person or entity to that of another. It is one of the group of technologies without which e-commerce would not exist.

Electronic press room

The early days of public relations (PR) on the web saw organizations do little more than include a 'press releases' page on their web site. This developed into a more comprehensive section with an archive of past releases for both press and researchers to access. Contemporary online PR has evolved still further, with best practice now including *virtual press kits*. As well as the press releases, the online kit includes such content as individual press contacts within the organization, downloadable company logos, full details of the company, biographies of senior staff, descriptions of products or services and a photo library of staff, products, head office, manufacturing centres, distribution centres and so on.

Electronic Product Code (EPC)

A successor to the ubiquitous bar code, the EPC is an electronically coded tag that identifies each individual product to which it has been assigned. This is a significant advance on bar codes which can identify only groups of products – for example, every copy of a book carries the same bar code; with EPC individual books are tagged with a different code. The system not only aids electronic point of sale (EPOS) but also inventory, storage and logistics of goods. Products with EPC allocation are identified using a **RFID** system.

Electronic shopping (ES)

A term popular in the early days of e-commerce, meaning shopping conducted online. As online shopping has increased, so the term has fallen out of favour.

Electronic Shopping Test

See **De Kare Silver's ES Test.**

E-logistics

In an e-commerce context e-logistics refers to the delivery of ordered goods, also known as **fulfilment**. In **B2C** trading this will involve many – normally small – parcels being delivered to many customers. In a **B2B** environment the situation normally involves fewer deliveries to fewer buyers, but those deliveries will be much larger in size. In a wider context, the term can be applied to any element of a business's logistical strategy that involves the use of e-technology.

E-loyalty

A web user's loyalty to an online entity. This may be a brand, web site, trader, **portal** or **virtual community**.

Email/e-mail (electronic mail)

Messages, usually in plain text but which may include images, sent from one person to another via computer. Email can also be sent automatically to a large number of addresses at the same time. The use of email as a vehicle for sending messages is perhaps the greatest contribution of the Internet to business – providing, as it does, a comparatively cost-free method of communication.

Email accreditation

In order to help legitimate emails pass through **spam filters**, **Internet service providers** use a number of methods to reject those emails they consider to be **spam**. One such method is to give senders *reputation scores* depending on how well that organization's email complies with legal and ethical practices. Things taken into consideration include the number of **email bounces** the organization has, the number of customer complaints about irrelevant emails from **IP addresses** owned by the organization, and the number of **honeypot emails** sent from that organization.

See also **email delivery protocol standards.**

E

Email address

An Internet user's electronic mailbox name and address. An email address is made up of two parts that are divided by an @ sign, effectively making the address *someone* or *something* at (@) a **domain name**. As with domain names there can be no spaces in an email address. The last part of the email address, the domain name, must follow the regulations for all domain names, that is, a suffix and a second-level name made up of any combination of the 26 characters of the Latin alphabet, the digits 0 to 9 and the dash (note, however, that the www prefix is normally omitted). Before the @ sign, mail servers can be set up to accept any characters, though it is most unusual for anything outside the Latin alphabet and digits 0 to 9 to be used. The use of the full stop has also become common practice in defining a person's first and family name (for example, Alan.Charlesworth). It is also worth noting that, like domain names, email addresses are not **case sensitive**.

Email address appending

The practice of merging a database of email addresses with an existing database of customers, users or potential customers. The **email list** is usually obtained from a third party. This means that as those people listed have not given explicit permission to the marketer whose data-base to which their email addresses are appended, any emails sent to them may be conceived as **spam**. Once common, the exercise is less so now as it is the norm for contemporary databases to be developed with email addresses included.

Email advertising

The use of emails as vehicles for carrying ads. The practice is most commonly carried out by organizations who provide email services that are free to the user – Google's gmail, for example – with costs of the service being recouped (or profits made) by selling space on the free emails.

Email aliasing

A close relative of the **email redirect** (though that practice refers to the forwarding of emails from multiple domain names), email aliasing is where multiple email addresses are formed on the same domain name, but they are all redirected to one address – normally one employee. For example, a small business might set up sales@yagahit.com and service@yagahit.com, accounts@yagahit.com, enquiries@yagahit.com – but have all of them delivered to employeesname@yagahit.com. The practice would save the employee having to check all four email accounts for messages sent to those addresses.

Email analysis tools

In this context the emails under analysis are those of competitors. Email analysis software allows the e-marketer to view individual emails being sent from organizations to customers (normally by covertly registering on an **email list**). Early applications were limited to monitoring networks for email list-management purposes. For example, if company A rents out an email list to company B, then company A will check on the emails being sent out by company B to ensure the list is not being used for **spam** purposes. However, the use is now more commonly being expanded to include analysis of the frequency, type, tone or offer of emails being sent. For example, if an organization knows that a competitor sends out weekly email special offers, they can adjust their marketing efforts to address this. As with other online applications, this is not a new phenomenon. It is the technology-enabled equivalent of a retailer visiting a competitor's shop to check on prices or a marketer for a bank having an account with another bank in order to receive that organization's promotional mailings.

Email analytics

As with web sites, email has a number of **metrics** that can be used to assess the success, or otherwise, of an email marketing campaign. Metrics for email analysis might include:

- the total number of emails sent – as a benchmark against which to gauge success;
- the **email delivery rate**;
- the total number of emails that were rejected and not delivered – there are a number of reasons for this (*see* **email bounce**);
- the **email open rate**;
- the **email response rate**;
- **viral marketing** referrals.

Although these calculations can be used to determine a number of process-oriented metrics, such as revenue per email, ultimately the organization is interested in the return on any investment made in that campaign. It is also the case that for the vast majority of direct marketing emails the recipient will demonstrate interest by following a link to a web site – this being the case, any **web site analytics** should be synthesized with those of the email campaign.

Email black hole

The term used to describe email that is sent, but never arrives in the intended receiver's in-box. That is, it disappears – as if into a black hole. Although the reasons for email *vanishing* are manifold, most are described in **email bounce**.

Email bounce

A bounced email is one that does not reach the intended recipient's **in-box** and is returned – *bounced* – to the sender with an message saying that the email was not successfully transmitted. The transmission of an email involves the sender's system looking first for the **domain name** of the intended recipient, and then the **email server** of that domain. If the domain is not identified – the element of the address after the @ sign is misspelled, for example – the email is immediately bounced. Then, if contact is made with the domain, the recipient's mail server checks the message to determine whether or not it will allow the message to pass through the server. It is possible that the message will be rejected by the recipient's mail server simply because it is busy. It is more likely, however, that the mail servers include **spam filters**, designed to prevent unwanted emails getting to the user's in-box. Both being rejected by a spam filter and a busy server will result in the email being bounced back to the sender. As the email was not accepted by the recipient's mail server, this is known as a *hard* bounce.

Being accepted by the mail server is not the end of the journey for the email – other obstacles exist. The mail server has to determine if the recipient actually exists within its system and if that recipient is allowed to accept emails. Potential reasons for rejection include:

- The recipient's address not existing on the mail server – for example, if I left my current employer, my email account with them would be closed.
- The sender has misspelled the recipient's address – in which case the system will recognize this as a nonexistent address.
- The recipient exists but does not have enough disk space to accept the message – their email application is filled to storage capacity.
- The message is too large – some mail systems predetermine the maximum message size that they will accept. Note that this would include any **attachment** to the email.

When an email is returned to the sender after it has been accepted by the recipient's mail server – as described above – this is called a *soft* bounce.

It should be noted that email delivery is not an exact science, with a lack of consistency in classification across **Internet service providers** (ISPs). Also, it is common that when an ISP is blocking or filtering emails, no bounce-back is provided. This is problematic for the email marketer in that they then assume that the message has been delivered to its intended recipient, when in fact it has disappeared into the **email black hole**.

Email client

Also known as a mail user agent (MUA), this is a software application that runs on a PC which enables the user to send, receive and organize email. Email messages are passed from the *client* to a mail transfer agent.

Email deliverability

See **domain modelling**.

Email deliverability reputation tool

Something of a misnomer in that the *reputation* element is better described as *score*, this is a software tool used in **email analytics** that allows email marketers to assess how their **email delivery rate** compares with others in a market sector or industry. Essentially, it gives the email marketer a benchmark. For example, knowing that 50 per cent of emails were delivered during a specific campaign means little, if the only comparison is with previous, similar campaigns. However, if the email marketer knows that their biggest competitor achieves a 75 per cent delivery rate, then the figures are put into context and they know they are underperforming in that market sector.

Email delivery protocol standards

Although a number of bodies are moving towards the development of such, there is no single set of standards that an email must meet in order for it not to be considered as **spam**. A universal set of email delivery protocol standards would be a massive boost to legitimate email marketers because it would help eradicate spam, and so make legitimate email marketing more acceptable to users. Most non-standardized protocols work on the principle of giving each email a credit score based on certain predetermined criteria. Depending on the way the criteria are

E

counted, the email must either exceed a certain score or not pass a threshold before it will be forwarded to its destination. Criteria considered include such things as **authentication tagging, email accreditation** and **honeypot email address**.

See also **SpamAssassin.**

Email delivery rate

The total number of emails delivered to the intended recipients in an **email marketing** campaign – calculated by subtracting the number of **email bounces** from the total number sent.

See also **email deliverability reputation tool.**

Email dictionary attack

See **dictionary attack (2)**

Email discussion group

A group of people who communicate with each other by email, with the messages being managed by a software application (for example, a **mailing list**). Such groups – who would normally share a common interest – were popular in the early days of the Internet, but have been largely replaced by online discussion groups.

Email forwarding

The facility to forward an email to another person without re-typing it. For the e-marketer, it is an essential technology in encouraging **viral marketing**. The term is sometimes used as an alternative to **email redirect**.

Email guaranteed delivery

See **sender certification.**

Email harvester

A type of **spider** that visits web sites and records any email addresses found on those sites. Harvested email addresses are used for spam mailings; see **email list (2)**. Email harvesters are one reason for using contact forms rather than listing email addresses.

E

Email list (1) *permission*-based

An element of **permission marketing**, this is a database of email addresses of people who have confirmed that they are willing to receive emails from a specific source, often on a specific subject. They have made the decision to **opt in** to that email list by giving the sending organization permission to use their email address. It is sometimes known as a *subscription* list as people can be described as *subscribing* to the email list – though that term is more commonly used with reference to newsletters or the like, where people feel they have actually taken out a subscription in that they may well have competed an *application form* to do so. Lists developed within the organization are called *house* lists. List owners maintain, and monitor basic data such as:

- the list total – the number of people, currently on an email list, who have agreed to receive mailings;
- **email bounces** – which subscribers are not receiving emails;
- new subscribers – the number of people who have opted in to the list since the last mailing;
- unsubscribers – the number of people who have requested they be removed from the list since the last mailing.

Although all of these points are important, it is the latter that may give cause for concern. Large numbers of people leaving the list could be a result of (a) poor targeting – the wrong segment being made the wrong offers, (b) significant changes to the email messages – for example style, content, or (c) list burn-out – people have tired of the content.

Permission based lists are developed and maintained in-house or by a trusted outsourced partner – normally a specialist email marketing service provider. They are extremely valuable to the organization and so should be protected from outside interference or influence and never sold or passed on to any third party.

Email list (2) *non-permission*-based

As the name suggests, these are lists of email addresses that have been developed without the knowledge of the addressees, and so do not carry the marketing value of those lists where people have opted to receive mailings. They are, effectively, **spam** lists. Such lists are sometimes developed in-house, but more often they are produced by **email list brokers** who specialize in the trade of selling on lists to organizations that do not have their own in-house list. While some of the list-developers are reputable, many are not. The less reputable will simply gather email addresses from any source they can, usually using some kind of

E

email harvester. Reputable companies will take more care over their gathering of addresses, sometimes asking people to opt in to a number of lists and completing a questionnaire of personal details (an inducement may be offered for subscription). Those reputable companies will then offer their customer organizations targeted lists, the email addresses of 10,000 dentists, for example, or perhaps 20,000 people who have said they watch a certain TV programme on a regular basis. Organizations will buy the lists for specific campaigns and/or as the foundations for their own in-house lists.

Email list broker

An individual or entity that, as a business model, acts as a third party to compile or source **email lists**, either permission- or non-permission-based, and then sells them on to interested organizations.

Email marketing

Although often defined as '**direct marketing** using the Internet as the medium of communication', that definition – though correct – is only part of how email can be used in a marketing context. Email offers potential for targeted and personalized communication and so is a suitable medium of communication for a number of purposes over and above the *direct sales* message. These include such things as new product announcements, promotional discount offers, press/publicity releases, order confirmations, reminders for event purchases, shipping status, newsletters, reminders to frequent purchasers, customer surveys and thank-you messages. Note that the same email – if correctly composed – can address more than one of the issues listed above.

Email metrics

See email analytics.

Email open rate

An element of **email analytics**, the open rate is calculated by taking the total number of emails delivered (note: not *sent*) divided by the total number of emails opened. The open rate is the first action required of the recipient, without which no other objective will be met, making it perhaps the most important element of email analytics. While the subject of how to ensure recipients open their email is a specialized discipline, marketers will recognize that the action constitutes a first test

E

for the successful implementation of the **AIDA** model. Note, however, that the fact that a recipient has opened an email does not necessarily mean they have read it.

Email redirect

A term that has one *technical* meaning, and another that has become more commonly used outside that. Technically, an email redirect is an email sent from person A to person B which is redirected to person C. A redirected email is identified by the inclusion of 'by way of' in the sender information. The more common *redirect* is processed by domain name hosts who will redirect emails sent to a registered domain name. This is particularly useful for owners of multiple domain names, who can have emails set up for each name, but by having them all redirected to a single account does not have to check a number of accounts for messages. This is sometimes also referred to as **email forwarding**, though that term can be confused with the *forward* facility on email systems. Email redirect is also a close relative of **email aliasing**, though that practice refers to multiple addresses on one domain name.

Email rendering

See **domain modelling**.

Email response rate

That part of email analytics that calculates how many of the total emails sent in a campaign generate a response from recipients. Response rates vary across industries, but low single figures are the norm.

Email server

Although its technical name is a mail transfer agent (MTA) – and it is also known as an (e)mail server or (e)mail exchange server – an email server is the computer program that transfers email messages from one computer to another. Emails are passed to the server from an **email client**.

Email service provider (ESP)

Although many users have email access through their **Internet service provider** (and so are both *Internet* and *email* service providers), others

E

use email services from providers who do not offer Internet access as part of their product portfolio. The major Internet brands dominate the market, with AOL, Hotmail and Yahoo making up nearly 60 per cent of all B2C email addresses. It should be noted that many, if not most, users have more than one email address.

Email signature

See **signature file.**

Email specification

Emails can be sent in one of two configurations – text only or **HTML**, the latter making it possible to include images in the email. Text and HTML are email specifications. Although HTML is most commonly used, there is still some debate in **email marketing** circles as to the advantages and disadvantages of each. That images are more aesthetically pleasing and can be used to give emails the same appearance as web sites is the prime argument in favour of HTML. That not all **email clients** download images in the same format – or not at all, is a significant problem with HTML. Text-only emails, on the other hand, present in the same way on all email systems, and are also small (in **byte** size) and therefore download quickly and easily. Good practice in email marketing maintains that emails should be tested for all service providers, the main players using **visual rendering tools**.

Email spoofing

The practice of making an email appear to have come from someone other than the actual sender – for example, you get an email that has my email address in the *sender* box, but I know nothing of the message. A tactic used in spamming, it is illegal in some parts of the world. It can be extremely harmful to businesses and brands whose name has been spoofed (as senders) because recipients of those emails assume the **spam** has come from that company.

Email subscription list

See **email list.**

Email trackability

A significant benefit of email as a medium for **direct marketing** is that each communication (email) can be tracked and its effectiveness assessed. The practice of assessing that effectiveness is addressed in **email analytics**.

Email white list

See **white list**.

E-marketing

See **online marketing**.

E-marketplace (or virtual marketplace)

Although sometimes used as a generic description for any kind of marketplace that exists online, e-marketplaces are more normally associated with B2B trading in specific markets. An e-marketplace brings together multiple purchasers and multiple sellers in a virtual environment facilitating such things as **reverse auctions** and **online tendering**. The e-marketplace is run – normally as a business model – by a third party (or parties) who facilitate trade between the various buyers and sellers, taking a percentage of transactions or a fixed fee for the service. The e-marketplace will normally be industry-centric and can be horizontal (a wide range of products and services in many industries) or vertical (more specific products and services in limited industries). Note that although e-marketplaces are business models and so should generate income for their publishers, it is common for **portals** offering similar services to be operated by industry or trade bodies on a no-profit basis. When considering the overall economic value of e-commerce, if transactions made or arranged through B2B e-marketplaces were identified in the equation they would dwarf all other online business (that is B2C) simply because of the size of some of those transactions.

See also **butterfly model**.

E-metric

The online version of a **metric** – used in **web site analytics**.

Emoticon

A series of keyboard characters grouped together so as to depict a small image that represents a human facial expression that conveys an emotion. For example **:-)** is a smile, **:-(** a frown. Emoticons are used extensively in emails, **bulletin boards** and **chat** rooms.

Encryption (and decryption)

Derivatives of the Greek word for secret or concealed – *crypto* – both encryption and decryption have come to be associated primarily with electronic technology. Encryption is the encoding of data to prevent unauthorized access, and decryption the act of decoding that data. It is not unusual, however, for 'encoding' to be used to describe the *process* of both the encoding and decoding – the assumption being that anything *encoded* has to be *decoded* to be of any value.

See also **public key infrastructure.**

Engagement

Although the term exists offline, normally referring a customer accepting – *engaging* with – a marketing message. Online, the term is used to describe how a web site takes the interest and attention of users, in other words, how the site *engages* with the visitor. The theory is that if a site – or more specifically, its content – can develop *engagement* with the visitor then the web site is more likely to achieve its objectives.

E-newsletter

Simplistically put, this is a newsletter delivered electronically. A newsletter is, however, a tried and trusted method of disseminating information that is significantly enhanced by Internet technology. As well as the obvious advantage (over offline) of cost of production and distribution, the e-newsletter can be more concise – and so appealing – and use hypertext links to take the user to extended content on web sites. Potential subscribers should be aware, however, that some emailed newsletters carry little content and are thinly disguised vehicles for **direct marketing**.

Enterprise invoice presentation and payment (EIPP)

Used mainly in a B2B environment, this is a software application that facilitates the presentation and payment of invoices online.

Enterprise Resource Planning (ERP)

A business management model that uses an integrated software system to merge all facets of the business, including planning, manufacturing, sales, and marketing. It is included here as Internet technology was frequently cited as providing the communications medium through which ERP could be implemented.

Entry page

The page at which a visitor enters a web site, which is not necessarily the **homepage** – a **search engine results page**, for example, might list a page deep in the web site. The entry page would be identified in a **log file** analysis. Note also that the last page downloaded before the user leaves the site is the **exit page**.

E-procurement

The use of Internet technology to source and purchase products and services in a B2B environment, either directly or through an **e-marketplace**. Advocates of e-procurement argue that the Internet can transform procurement's role from administrative to strategic. By automating paper-intensive purchasing processes, procurement professionals are able to focus on value-added tasks, including the development of procurement strategy and improving supplier performance.

> *See also* **buy-side e-marketplace, catalogue services, forward auctions, reverse auction** and **desktop purchasing.**

ERDRP (the Eligibility Requirements Dispute Resolution Policy)

A body set up to oversee the arbitration system for resolving disputes on .me.uk domain names. As the web has evolved and the number of domain names available has increased, so the task of resolving disputes over who is the rightful owner of a particular domain name has increasingly been devolved down to smaller organizations that deal only with a specific **ccTLD**s. This is an example of such a domain name disputes body.

E-recruitment

The use of Internet technology in the recruitment of staff. Essentially this is the use of a web site to promote job vacancies and display details and specifications of both the jobs and the organization. CVs could be forwarded by email or application forms be available to download or complete online. The processing of forms completed online might also be carried out electronically before any human involvement. Note that

E

potential recruits could be driven to the e-recruitment pages by ads on other web sites. This practice would, however, be as much an element of **online advertising** as it is e-recruitment.

ERP

See **enterprise resource planning.**

Error code

A series of code numbers, each of which represents an HTML error when a web site is requested but cannot be downloaded – of which **404 file not found** is by far the most commonly recognizable to web surfers. Others that users may come across include:

- 202 Accepted – the request has been accepted for processing, but the processing has not been completed;
- 301 Moved Permanently – the requested resource has been assigned a new permanent **URI**;
- 307 Temporary Redirect – the requested resource resides temporarily under a different URI;
- 400 Bad Request – the request could not be understood by the server due to malformed syntax;
- 401 Unauthorized – the request requires user authentication;
- 403 Forbidden – the server understood the request, but is refusing to fulfil it;
- 408 Request Timeout – the client did not produce a request within the time that the server was prepared to wait;
- 410 Gone – the requested resource is no longer available at the server and no forwarding address is known;
- 503 Service Unavailable – the server is currently unable to handle the request due to a temporary overloading or maintenance of the server.

ES (electronic shopping) test

See **De Kare Silver's ES Test.**

Escrow service

A means of transferring confidential material through a third party. Sometimes used to transfer **source code**, but its most common use in an e-commerce environment is for the purchase and transfer of domain names.

E

E-service

Although it might be described (like many other 'e' terms) as the delivery of an offline service using Internet technology, Hewlett Packard (HP) have taken this a stage further by developing a concept based on the term. HP argue that e-service is actually a continuation of e-commerce, with e-commerce ending when a sale is completed and e-service providing *after-sales* service.

E-shopping basket/cart

See shopping cart.

ESP

See e-commerce service providers.

E-supply chain

A supply chain that uses Internet technology in its management and operation, so improving its operation. Administration of such a chain is deemed e-supply chain management.

E-tail

A rarely used term for electronic – or *online* – retail. It is practised by e-tailers.

E-telephony

Also known as IP telephony, this is the use of Internet technology to make voice calls or send video sequences. It can be a great cost saver for businesses when making global phone calls as – if broadband is used – there is no charge for individual calls.

E

E-ticketing

A ticket that is processed and delivered online, normally in response to an online order and payment. Although seen as little more than a convenient add-on to online purchasing in some market sectors (that is, printing, handling and postage are not required), for other industries the e-ticket has revolutionized their business practices. A prominent example is the airline industry, where customers not only make their flight selection and purchase online (so reducing human resources), but then also facilitate their travel arrangements by:

- using the ticket number to check in for their flight online prior to arriving at the airport; and
- by either printing out the ticket or simply quoting its reference number, bypass the physical check-in desk and proceed directly to the security check and departure lounge.

EU Directive on Privacy and Electronic Communications

Although this directive is wide-ranging, its main impact on e-commerce is in the areas of commercial email and the collection of data online. It lists requirements for each of these, with some being mandatory and others being advised as 'best practice'. Points raised include:

- Email – a link to unsubscribe, clear evidence of who the email is from and a link to the organization's Privacy Policy are all mandatory. A link to the organization's Legal Notices and a statement of purpose and origin are best practice.
- Collection of data online – at the point of personal data collection, visitors should be provided with a clear and conspicuous notice as to the purposes for which the personal data are collected and they should be offered an **opt-in/opt-out** facility.

EUR*id*

The .eu domain name registry. As their web site (www.eurid.eu) says: 'EUR*id* is the not-for-profit organisation, established in Belgium, and has been selected by the European Commission to operate the new .eu top level domain. EUR*id* was established in a partnership between DNS BE, IIT CNR and NIC SE, operators of the country-code top level domain registries for Belgium (.be), Italy (.it) and Sweden (.se). EUR*id* is in the process of setting up offices in those countries as well as in the Czech Republic to support 4 geographical regions. EUR*id* headquarters are located in Brussels.'

E-voting

The use of Internet technology in a voting process including registration, voting and counting of votes polled. Allowing constituents to vote online is seen by many governments as a means of increasing votes cast (voter turnout), though misuse of the system is a concern. E-voting might also raise issues with regard to the **digital divide**.

Exchange portal

See portal.

Exit page

The last page downloaded before a user leaves the site as identified in a **log file** analysis. Note that the first page downloaded is the **entry page**.

Expandable banner ad

See banner.

Extension

See file extension and domain name.

External link

See link.

Extranet

An **intranet** that is partially accessible to authorized outsiders who can only access it with a valid username and password.

Eye candy web site

Although the term *eye candy* has a number of interpretations offline, online it is used to describe web sites that are aesthetically pleasing, but do not meet the objectives of the site's owner or publisher. Packed with **whistles and bells**, an eye candy site might, for example, have a **flash front page** but lack the content and **persuasive architecture** required to promote sales of the products on offer. In many ways they are the antitheses of the **white van web site**, which might not look good, but gets the job done.

E

Eye tracking

A research technique with a number of offline applications but in an e-commerce context most significantly, web site **usability** and advertising. The idea is to track the pattern of a user's eye movements and so determine which elements of a web site or advertisement they take most notice of. The practice has helped web designers to place the most important content, or **PPC** ads, in those parts of a web page that users look at most. Eye-tracking *studies* show that when people are viewing web pages, their eyes start in the upper-left corner and follow along the top navigation, until they hit the end of the browser, at which point they travel diagonally through the centre of the screen until they stabilize at the left navigation. The sight path then proceeds back and forth across the centre area, between left navigation and right column, then back and forth, back and forth, engaging within the central area, hence the term active window.

Eye-tracking studies content from Joshua Hay, *GrokDotCom Newsletter*, 6 December 2005.

Eye-tracking studies

See **eye tracking**.

E

Faceted navigation

Also known as *guided* navigation, this is a kind of in-site search facility where users refine the search by being allowed to either:

(a) Exclude products in which they have no interest. For example, if the user takes a size 9 shoe, they can exclude all other sizes, and the search then presents them with only those styles of shoe that are available in size 9.
(b) The user selects a feature, and is then shown only products with that feature. For example, the user selects to see red shirts, and so is then presented with all styles of shirt that are available in all variants of red.

Exclusion or inclusion can be more complex, and only sites with a comprehensive database of the products on offer can successfully offer faceted navigation. Note that this is another example of technology being adopted to replicate common offline sales practice. Good sales staff will always ask pertinent questions to determine the products that will best meet the needs of the potential customer. The answers to those questions either *exclude* or *include* products within the organization's inventory.

False logic

A **copy**-writing term (attributed to Michael Masterson) that refers to copy that does not tell untruths but that manipulates the reader through skilful representation of facts. For example, a clothing vendor might say on a web site or email that 'only one person in ten thousand has such a shirt'. The reader might perceive this as meaning that the shirt is exclusive, the truth being that not many of the shirts have been sold.

False positive

In an e-commerce environment this term is used to describe the result of a **spam filter** which incorrectly identifies a legitimate email as **spam**.

Fascinations

A term used in direct marketing, fascinations are elements of sales **copy** – often bullet points – that are very specific and tease the reader into continuing to read and, eventually, buying the product (or whatever the objective of the communication is). Online, fascinations would be used on web pages (particularly the first page of the site) and email **subject lines** and introductions. Fascinations are an integral element of **persuasion architecture**.

Fat-finger typo

The light-hearted term used to describe typing errors where the typist hits the key next to the one which they meant to press – as if they had fat fingers. The typing error has a significant role to play in e-commerce in two ways:

1 It can change a domain name typed into a browser. Instead of going to the intended Amazon.com, for example, the fat-finger typist could be taken to Amazom.com – a very different site to what they were expecting.
2 A searcher might mistype a keyword in a search engine, and so be served not only with a results page which lists sites that do not meet their needs, but also displays irrelevant **paid placement ads**.

The e-marketer should therefore consider registering misspelt versions of their domain name (to prevent **cybersquatters** getting them), and it might also be worth buying misspelt keywords in paid placement ads to accommodate fat-finger searchers.

FAQ

See **frequently asked questions**.

F

FFA (free for all) link pages

Web pages that are set up with the sole purpose of allowing users to submit a link to their site. Despite what they may say in their self-promotion, they are of no practical use in **search engine optimization** as the search engines recognize them for what they are.

Field

In an e-commerce environment, a field is a space (for example, on a web site) that has been allocated to a particular piece of information that is being gathered in a database. For example, a simple online form might have *fields* for surname, first name and email address. It is common for extensive forms to have fields that are *required* or *optional* – with submitted forms being rejected if a required field has not been completed. Good practice in developing online forms has the developers set the fields to accept only specific data. For example, in a field designated for an email address any collection of characters without an @ sign would be rejected.

File extension

The two-, three- or four-letter extension on the end of a file name designating the file type. The extension is separated from the file name by a full stop. For example, alan.gif would identify that file as a **gif** image, and alan.doc a Microsoft Word file.

File Transfer Protocol

See **FTP**.

Filtering database

A database of domain names, organizations or individuals who have been identified as perpetrators of **spam**. The list is used by **spam filters** to block unsolicited emails from reaching their addressees.

See also **DNS blocklist**.

Filter words

See **stop words**.

Firewall (fire wall)

A system of hard and/or software that is designed to prevent unauthorized access to or from a private network. In an e-commerce environment a firewall would be used to prevent unauthorized users from accessing private networks that are connected to the Internet. Although firewalls can prevent both web and email access, they are most commonly associated with blocking **spam**.

Fixed placement

A term used in search engine **paid placement**, fixed placement is a program where a specific **ad listing** position can be purchased for a keyword for a fixed fee.

F

Flame

A personal attack on other Internet users via **email**, **USENET** or **mailing lists** – normally with multiple, automatically generated messages. Flame wars occur when a series of flames are sent back and forth between two or more people. At their most extreme, flames can develop into **denial of service attacks**.

Flaming logo

See **spinning logo**.

Flash

A generic term that relates to web pages that have **Flash**–type graphics – though not necessarily graphics generated by Macromedia's Flash™. Used in this sense the meaning is derogatory, as in the term 'flash Harry', meaning someone who is all front but actually has little substance. Some use the term **splash page** in the same context, although that description is a little more specific.

Flash™

The trade-marked name of a vector-based moving graphics format created by Macromedia for the publication of animations on the world wide web. In layperson's terms, it's what makes most web sites active rather than static.

See also **Flash front page**.

Flash front page

A web site that uses **Flash** (in either form of the definitions above) on its front page. Often it will have a 'Flash intro' – a series of moving graphics that go together to produce an introduction to the web site. Such pages can normally be identified by a message that says 'skip intro', clicking on which bypasses the activity and takes the user to the navigation page. Flash intros are normally the domain of web designers who wish to show off their abilities with the format. In marketing terms they are rarely a good idea. Usability guru Jacob Neilsen has declared flash technology '99 per cent bad', and numerous surveys have revealed that Flash intros are high on users' lists of the most annoying aspects of the Internet. Note that flash front pages which do not use Flash™ technology are sometimes called **splash pages**, in practical terms, and

F

certainly from the point of view of the end user, there is no discernible difference between flash and splash pages.

Flash intro

See **Flash front page.**

Floating ads

The floating ad, also referred to as a *voken* (a virtual token), is a close relative of the **pop-up ad**, but more sophisticated. This is an image that *floats* over the top of a web page's content rather than appearing in a small **browser** box. Most are static images, but some move around the page – an aeroplane flying around or a car driving across the page, for example. Unlike the standard pop-up, which appears and stays put, the floating ad moves around the page, often following the user's cursor. Although aesthetically more pleasing that standard pop-ups, floating ads come with all the negative aspects of their pop-up cousins plus the added irritant that the 'close' button is often difficult to locate. Many are programmed to stay on the page for a specific length of time, so disappearing only when that period (for example ten seconds) has elapsed. As with standard pop-ups, however, they can be effective if used judiciously.

Flog (flogging)

A type of **blog** that is developed by marketers as a covert promotion for a product, brand or organization. Such is the nature of blogging, however, that it is difficult, if not impossible, to keep the true nature of such a blog from users – at which point it will be derided by the blogging community. This is not to say that marketers cannot develop successful blogs promoting a product or brand, but they should be overt in their intentions.

See also **commercial blog and boss blog.**

Folksonomy

A combination of the words folks and taxonomy, the term folksonomy refers to the simplistic, rather than centralized, way in which information is categorized on the web. Users are encouraged to assign keywords – **tags** – to pieces of information or data. Part of search engine **organic listing** is based on what the search engines sees in various tags on a web site, **alt tags**, for example. Although tagging has been around for longer, the features that would become known as *folksonomy* appeared on the web site del.icio.us in late 2003. Web services that use tagging include those designed to allow users to publish and share photographs and most blog software, which permits authors to assign tags to each entry.

There are also more vague applications of the term *tagging* used in e-commerce vocabulary. For example, an e-marketer might refer to visitors to a specific web site or ad being *tagged* so that their future actions might be tracked. Although in this example the term is used almost as slang, it is still based on the basic concept of a piece of data – the site visitor's identity – being recorded for future use.

Forward auction

Normally a B2B practice, this is where sellers put surplus or obsolete stock or equipment up for sale and invite bids on it. In an e-commerce context the auction is held online, so expanding the marketplace in which the goods can be seen. The auction is often part of the services offered by a B2B portal. This is common practice, particularly in specialized industries.

Frames

An **HTML** web site design which allows two web pages to be viewed as one page divided into distinct areas – or *frames*. Usually one frame will remain static while the other changes. For example, one frame is used to list navigational aids while the site's content is featured in the second frame. The use of frames has diminished to the point that they are now rare. This is for two main reasons: (a) that newer design technologies replaced them, and (b) pages in frames are not read by search engine **spiders**.

F

Freeware

Software that is made available free of charge – usually online – for personal use.

See also **open source**.

Frequently Asked Questions (FAQs)

A document that lists and answers the most common questions raised on a particular subject. Popular amongst the technical community, the concept was readily accepted online, with its ability to disseminate information to those who sought it easily and cheaply appealing to both users and organizations. Where each question can be answered in a sentence or short paragraph it is the norm to have both questions and answers presented as a list. More complex questions, however, are often answered by the user clicking on a **link**, taking them to a new page (or **pop-up window**). This method allows software to be used that tracks the most popular questions (that is, those clicked on most) and presents them in descending order of popularity.

Front end/office (operations)

See **back office.**

Front page

See **home page (3).**

FrontPage

A registered trademark of the Microsoft Corporation for a program that creates web pages using a **WYSIWYG** format. It is included here to differentiate it from the generic use of the term *front page* when used in an e-commerce environment

See **home page (3).**

FTP (File Transfer Protocol)

An Internet tool/software utility which allows users to transfer files between two computers that are connected to the Internet. Its most commonly recognized function is the uploading of files to the web. Web site designers develop pages as files on their own computers, and then transfer those files to a web server by means of FTP transfer. Anonymous FTP allows connection to remote computers and the transfer of publicly available computer files or programs.

F

Fulfilment

When used in terms of Internet trading, fulfilment is normally seen as the after-order processing and delivery of goods. In the main, fulfilment is an element of e-commerce that has not succumbed to having an 'e' prefix (that is, e-fulfilment). This is perhaps because when dealing with tangible products (a CD, for example) the fulfilment has to have a physical element, that is, it cannot be purely *electronic*.

See also **fulfilment house** and **back office**.

Fulfilment house

An organization that, as a business model, handles the *fulfilment* element of another company's trading activities. Benefiting from the economies of scale it can generate, the fulfilment house will store, process orders, pick, pack and distribute goods on behalf of the business that has sold those goods to the consumer. It might also handle directing orders to suppliers and keep customers updated on order progress, as well as handling order cancellations and returns. Fulfilment houses offer services that are an extension of those provided by **drop shippers**, and are sometimes referred to as third-party logistics (3PL) suppliers. The service is particularly useful to **virtual businesses** that operate online stores but do not want to commit resources to stock holding and logistics.

Full-scale landscape banner

See **banner**.

Full-scale takeover banner

See **banner**.

Functionality

In an e-commerce environment this term is sometimes used to describe how quick and easy a software application is to use. While the term can be applied to a web site, it is more usual to refer to the site's **usability**, though **navigation** also has a part to play in a site's functionality.

Fusion retailing

See **multi-channel retailing**.

Fuzzy logic/search

See **Boolean search**.

G2B (government-to-business)

See **e-government.**

G2C (government-to-citizens)

See **e-government.**

Gateway

That part of a **network** that acts as an entrance to another network. For example, for accessing the Internet from home, the **Internet service provider** acts as the gateway between user and Internet.

Gateway page

See **doorway page.**

Geek

A term that has been around a long time, and historically has been taken to mean a number of things – from 'a boring and unattractive social misfit' (*Collins English Dictionary*) to 'a person who is fascinated, perhaps obsessively, by obscure or very specific areas of knowledge and imagination' (www.wikipedia.org). In an e-commerce context, however, geek has become the description of a person who is particularly interested in technology, especially computing. It has become common practice, therefore, to refer to computer-programming **techies** as geeks. Once considered a derogatory term, its meaning has softened to the point that people apply the description to themselves as a kind of badge of honour.

General Packet Radio Service

See **GPRS.**

Generation My

See MySpace Generation.

Generic domain names

See intuitive domain names.

Geo-destination targeting

An **online advertising** model that combines **IP-based targeting** and **keywords** used in searches on search engines to deliver geographic and destination relative ads. For example, if a user in London is searching on the term 'hotels in Berlin', published ads might promote cheap air fares between the two cities.

Geographic portals

See portals.

Ghost site

A web site that remains live on the web, but is no longer updated or maintained. Most are on hosted-free servers (of **Internet service providers**, for example), those on their own **domain name** being withdrawn when the domain name's registration expires. The browser's **view page info** facility will give details of when the page was last updated.

GIF (Graphic Interchange Format)

A common format for **image** files, GIF files are particularly suitable for images containing large areas of the same colour. GIF-format files of simple images are usually smaller than the same file would be if stored in **JPEG** format. However, the GIF format does not store photographic images as well as JPEG. It is common for web site designers and developers to refer to images simply as a GIF or JPEG (depending on their format), as in 'a GIF of a church will go in that space'.

Gigabyte

See byte.

G

Global sites

This is something of a misnomer as, theoretically, all web sites are available – that is, they can be viewed anywhere in the world – state intervention notwithstanding (for example, see **Great Firewall of China**). However, the term is commonly used to describe a web site that is designed for global viewing, but makes no changes to facilitate local visitors. An example would be an international entity or brand that publishes only one web site for all of its global customers. This is, however, uncommon, as most global corporations tailor their online presence to suit local tastes and markets.

See also **localization, IP recognition** and **localized domains.**

Global village

A concept popularized by media culture guru Marshall McLuhan in his 1964 book *Understanding Media: The Extensions of Man* some thirty years before the Internet was developed. The global village describes the way that communications technology has made the world a smaller place. That the Internet improved that communication in a way that McLuhan could only imagine has meant the phrase is still popular in describing the effects of the Internet on society.

Golden Shield

See **Great Firewall of China.**

Good traffic

See **differentiated traffic.**

Google (verb) to *google*

To look for something or someone using a search engine. Perhaps the brand manager's greatest dream is that one day the function that their product serves will become known by that product's brand name – Hoover is the classic example, and Google is its contemporary. The legal department at Google are not keen on the term as a verb, however, and came out and said so in public in August 2006. They argue that there are some serious trademark issues if the distinction is not made between using the word 'Google' to describe using *Google* to search the Internet and using the word *google* to generally describe searching the Internet. Those *trademark issues* are *perhaps* based on the effect on trademarks of

G

those marks becoming a *generic trade mark* – that is, that those marks can be commercially exploited by others.

GoogleBombing

So named because Google was an obvious target for the practice that is actually **link bombing**.

Google bowling

Working on the assumption that **link popularity** is a good thing, Google's **algorithm** rewards sites that have links going into them with a higher ranking. Realizing that this was the case, **black-hat SEOs** would attempt to trick the search engine by purchasing site-wide text link ads (on legitimate web sites) and so get lots of incoming links in a hurry. For example, if the legitimate site had 500 pages and an ad was placed on each, the result would be an instant 500 incoming links to the promoted site. Naturally, it didn't take Google long to realize this, and soon began filtering sites that indulged in this kind of link-scam and either penalized or removed guilty sites from its database. Bad news for the business employing the black hats; good news for their competitors. Black hats being black hats, however, they looked to turn this to their advantage, which they did by buying site-wide text link ads for their competitor's site. The result is that the competitor's site gets penalized by Google, and the black hat-promoted site gains more customers. That particular trick is Google bowling.

Google dance (or **Google dance** *syndrome*)

From time to time Google, like all search engines, changes the algorithms by which each web site's ranking are determined. These changes are always unannounced and, like the algorithms themselves, secret. The changes only come to light when, suddenly, the results on key word searches change dramatically – leaving search engine optimizers doing a *dance* to address the changes and so restore their sites to the top of **search engine results pages**. Rather like hurricanes, it has become the norm for each new *dance* to named – Florida, Jagger, and Big Daddy being the most recent at time of writing.

Google stalking

See **cyber-check**.

G

GoogleWhack

Originating in 2001, a Googlewhack is a query consisting of two words (with no quotation marks) entered into Google's search page that returns a single, solitary result. Googlewhacking is the activity of seeking such a result. Anyone successful in discovering a googlewhack can add it to the 'Whack Stack' at googlewhack.com.

Gopher

A software tool predating, and mainly superseded by, the world wide web. It is used in search applications, allowing information to be presented in a hierarchical menu system – such as a table of contents.

GoTo

See **paid search.**

GPRS (General Packet Radio Service)

A data service used to send Internet information to mobile telephones. It is sometimes described as falling between second and third generations of mobile **e-telephony**.

See also **1G/2G/2.5G/3G/4G.**

Graphic design

See **graphics.**

Graphical Search Inventory

A somewhat confusing title given to online adverts – **banners, pop-ups, rich media** and so on – which can be synchronized to search engine **keywords**. For example, this means that if a user searches on the term 'New York hotels' any ads on subsequent pages will be related to that subject. The term *graphical search inventory* has a rather convoluted composition. In the phrase, *graphical* refers to *graphics* – the ads. *Search* refers to the association with search engines, and offline it is common practice to refer to blocks of ads that have been allocated space on media as *inventory*.

Graphical user interface (GUI)

See **usability.**

G

Graphics

Visual presentations that can be functional or artistic, these are those elements that determine the physical appearance and aesthetics of a web page – as opposed to textual **content**. Someone who performs the function of graphic design is a graphic designer.

Great Firewall of China

A term used originally by academics – and picked up by the press – to describe the technical infrastructure used by the Chinese authorities to censor the Internet. Although inside China the project is known as Golden Shield, to the rest of the world it is known by the play on the description of the centuries-old Chinese fortification. As part of an Internet censorship law in the People's Republic of China, a censorship system is implemented by state-owned **ISP**s, businesses and organizations. Although the block on content is not absolute, users in China are unable to access sites containing certain content – those of political opposition groups in Taiwan, for example. Controversially, the main search engines have contributed to the censorship by blocking searches on the banned keywords and phrases – such as 'democracy'.

Gripesite

See **cyberbashing**.

Grok

A term taken from Robert A. Heinlein's 1961 novel *Stranger in a Strange Land*, in which Grok is part of the Martian language meaning 'to understand completely'. Originally adopted by hippies and then Star Trek fans, the term has been taken up by computer **geeks** – hence its presence in e-commerce terminology with the same definition as that in the book's Martian language, a grok being someone who understands something completely. In other words, they are an expert in that subject.

GUI (graphical user interface)

See **usability**.

Guided navigation

See **faceted navigation**.

G

Hacker

Although when used in a technical context the term refers to a person who creates and modifies **hardware** and **software**, in both the e-commerce environment and to the general public *hacker* has a more sinister connotation. For most people, a hacker is someone who gains unauthorized access to 'secure' computer systems. Based on the old cowboy axiom, such hackers can be 'black-hat' (malicious or criminal), or 'white-hat' (ethical or doing it for fun).

HAN (home area network)

A **network** contained within a user's home, connecting digital devices – computers, telephones, VCRs, televisions, etc.

Hard bounce

See **email bounce**.

Hard-to-find product

In marketing terminology this is commonly known as the *niche* product, but to the consumer it is the *hard-to-find product*. It also has a close relative – the *didn't-know-it-existed* product. Before the advent of the Internet there were many products that were difficult, if not impossible, for the person in the street to find. Some argue that it is this kind of product that makes the most successful online business.

See also **long tail**.

Hardware

Intrinsically linked with **software**, *computer* hardware describes the tangible aspects of computing, that is, anything that can be physically touched. The term is used generically. For example, if a computer fails with a mechanical, electrical or technical fault it would be described as 'a hardware problem'.

Heading tag

An **HTML** tag that designates a heading in a piece of text on a web site. Because a headline to a piece of text is deemed to be a good indicator of what the body of the text is about, heading tags are given extra credit by search engines. For that reason all heading tags should be **keywords** for the page on which they are featured.

Helping the buyer to buy

Arguably one of the most significant developments the Internet has brought to marketing is to give impetus to marketers' objectives shifting from *helping the seller to sell* to *helping the buyer to buy*. Consumers now expect to be aided in their research on the product or service that best meets their wants and needs. The web is significant in that, unlike others, it is a **pull media**. An integral element of the concept of helping the buyer to buy is the development of **consumer-generated media**.

Hexadecimal code

The six-digit code used to specify what colour text will be displayed on the web. For example, black is 000000, white FFFFFF.

Hidden text

Also known as *invisible* text, this is content on a web site that cannot be read by humans. This is usually achieved by having the text in the same colour as the background (for example, white on white). The idea is that although humans cannot see the text, search engine **spiders** can – so **search engine optimizers** put **keywords** in hidden in the hope of increasing their **search engine ranking**. Although this might have worked in the mid-1990s, all search engines now recognize the practice as **spam**.

Hit

Used in reference to the Internet, a *hit* means a request from a web **browser** for a single file from a web **server**. Therefore, a browser displaying a web page made up of three graphic images and a paragraph of text would generate five hits on the server – one for the HTML page itself, one for the file of text and one for each of the three graphics. In the early days of the web (and occasionally still today), hits were the way of expressing how popular a web site was. In contemporary e-commerce, however, a hit is a next-to-useless term of reference. Saying a web site has a thousand hits a day, for example, is an almost pointless statement. It could mean ten visitors went to a web site that has a hundred files, one visitor who downloaded a thousand files, or anything in between. The chances are, however, that the first is most accurate. The use of hits (in a press release, for example) to indicate the success of a web site would suggest that the organization is (a) using hits as a metric in order to inflate numbers as the visitor count is relatively low, or (b) out of touch with contemporary practice.

Hit bolding

The practice used by most search engines of emboldening the actual search query where it appears in the web site description on a **search engine results page** (SERP). Although this may appear to be altruistic on the part of the search engines, it is a deliberate tactic. The idea is that if the search query repeatedly appears in bold on the SERP then the user's eye is drawn to it – the more hit emboldening there is, the stronger the subliminal confirmation that this search has produced the required results. The practice works on the concept of **trigger words**.

Homepage (1)

The web page that a browser opens each time it starts up. This can be set as a preference by the computer user, though software developers will set the **default** to their advantage. For example, new PCs with Microsoft software will open on MSN.com.

Homepage (2)

The main web page, or even entire web presence, of a business or organization. This definition in a business context is rare, though it is not unusual for an individual to use the term *homepage* when referring not only to one page, but to their personal web site. For example, members of a family with the surname Johnson might refer to their web presence as the 'Johnsons' homepage'.

Homepage (3)

In this definition the homepage is commonly referred to as the 'front page', in the same way as the first page of a newspaper is called the front page. It is the first, or opening page of a web site, that is, the one

H

that introduces the site to the **visitor** and carries the primary navigation aids. It would be the page that opens if the domain name is entered into a browser that is without any directory or file names. For this reason it is also known as the web site's *index page* because of its file name within the **URL** of the page – it carries the extension .index.

Honeymonkey

Used in an IT environment, the prefix *honey* is used to describe anything that attracts wrongdoers to some kind of security device so that they can be identified and their actions detected and stopped (see also **honeypot email address**). A honeymonkey is a software application that has a computer imitate the actions of a human user while surfing the web on a **browser**. Programmed to search out web sites that target specific user vulnerabilities (e.g. **phishing** sites), the honeymonkey is able to track down such sites. Once identified, the effect of such sites can be analysed and action taken to prevent any potential damage.

Honeypot email address

In an IT environment, a honeypot is a security measure that sets a trap to detect or deflect attempts at unauthorized use of systems (the prefix *honey* being used to describe anything that attracts wrongdoers to some kind of security device). More specifically to e-commerce, the term is used in email marketing. The email honeypot address (also known as a *trap* address) is a fake email address that **ESPs** put into a mailing to see if **spammers** pick them up and try to send emails to them. As there would be no legitimate reason for anyone to use the honeypot email address, sending an email to that address identifies the sender as a spammer.

See also **email accreditation**.

Hops

See **traceroutes**.

Horizontal e-marketplace

See **e-marketplace**.

Horizontal hub

See **hub**.

H

Host server

A **server** that hosts a web site or sites.

Hosted doorway pages

A practice that has similarities to **paid links** in that it can only be successfully offered by web sites that have a good reputation with not only users, but – more importantly – with search engines. While **doorway pages** are generally frowned on by the search engines, if they are hosted – *hidden* – on reputable sites the search engines may not identify them as being *doorway* pages. Like paid links, the strategy is risky as the selling host is risking its own search engine reputation by participating in the practice, and for that reason it is rare.

Hot spot

A term used to describe a zone in a public space, a hotel or airport, for example, where wireless (**Wi-Fi**) access to the Internet is available.

Hotwired

Included here as it was *one* of the first commercial content web sites – the Global Network Navigator (GNN) was another. First published in 1994, Hotwired (www.hotwired.com) was the online incarnation of *Wired* magazine, and is also reputed to have carried the first online ad **banner** – for AT&T – in October of that year. For many, this date represents the birth of the commercial web.

House ads

A practice that has transferred online from traditional advertising, house ads are those ads that promote the publication in or on which they are presented, a magazine that carries ads for the next edition of that magazine, for example. Online, the model would be for a web page to carry ads for another part of the same web site. While cross-promoting internal products and services can work for multi-product organizations, the use of house ads is a sign that the ad space could not be sold to external advertisers. Although they have the same premise, house ads differ from **nested ads** in that the house ad is reactive (to unsold ad space), whereas nested ads are part of a deliberate promotional strategy.

H

House list

See email list (1).

HTML (HyperText Markup Language)

The coding language used to create documents for use on the world wide web. Directions, or *instructions*, are used to instruct the browser in the way it presents the text. The example below shows some of the basic commands.

The short paragraph as seen by the user would be:

It was the **best** of times, it was the *worst* of <u>times</u>.

The HTML version of this paragraph is:

<p>It was the <b>best</b> of times, it was the <i>worst</i> of <u>times</u>.</p>

In this example, <p> means open new paragraph, <b> means 'bold', <i> 'italic' and <u> is 'underline'. The same command preceded by a / (slash) ends that command, for example, </b> means 'stop bold'.

HTML (only) email

See email specification.

HTTP (HyperText Transfer Protocol)

The protocol for moving hypertext files across the Internet – hence the full **URL** of any site will start with http. Note; if the site is hosted on a **secure browser**, the suffix becomes https, the 's' standing for 'secure'.

Hub

A term sometimes used to describe a B2B **portal**, the definition coming from the offline context where *hub* is used to represent the radiating point of spokes in a wheel – that is, the centre of elements of a subject. A *vertical* hub is one that has a narrow but deep focus, as opposed to *horizontal* hubs that have a very wide focus covering more aspects, but each element is not covered in great depth.

Human computer interface (HCI)

See usability.

Hyperlink

See link.

Hypertext

The text on a web page that can be clicked on by a web user because it acts as a **link** to another document – usually another web page. For this reason it is also known as *link* text. Unless the designer stipulates otherwise, the **default** setting for web browsers is for hypertext to be a different colour (to the standard text) and underlined. This is to make links easier to identify on a web page. The actual words used in hypertext links are considered in search algorithms, so using intuitive words as links not only helps the user in their navigation of the site, it can help with **search engine ranking** as well. For example: if on a page about gardening there was a link to a page that included advice on growing tomatoes, then the hypertext should be the words <u>advice on growing tomatoes</u>. As such it is obvious to the human reader what the linked-to page contains, but also the search engine will assume that a page with an inbound link from the phrase 'advice on growing tomatoes' should contain something relevant to a search on that, or a similar, phrase.

HyperText Transfer Protocol

See **HTTP**.

H

ICANN (Internet Corporation for Assigned Names and Numbers)

The successor to the **InterNIC** as the body responsible for a number of Internet-related tasks, primarily the assignment of **domain names** and **IP addresses**. A non-profit organization contracted by the US Department of Commerce, ICANN also oversees an independent panel of arbitration to settle domain name ownership disputes.

Icon

An image, usually small, used on computer screens which, when clicked on, performs an action. Icons can be used on web sites to represent **links** to other pages or sites, or on a computer's **toolbar** to represent actions. A small image of a printer is the icon used to represent the command 'print', for example.

ICT (information and communication technology)

See **IT**.

Ideavirus

A concept put forward by Seth Godin in his 2001 book, *Unleashing the Ideavirus*. Godin gave his own definition in the *Harvard Business Review* as 'managing digitally-augmented word of mouth'. Godin argues that **viral marketing** is an ideavirus (though not all ideaviruses are viral marketing), and many see the book as a seminal work on the subject of what we now recognize as viral marketing. Interestingly, although the book can be purchased in paperback form, it is available free on www.sethgodin.com (if you accept his concept, Godin is actually practising his *ideavirus* by doing this). It is said to be the number one most downloaded e-book in history.

Image

In web site terms, an image is anything created as a **graphic**, rather than text. An image could be a picture (for example, a photograph presented in digital format), or text represented as an graphic – company names and logos, for example.

See also **alt text**.

Image map

A graphic **image** on a web page that is divided into parts, each of which acts as a **link** to different pages or sites. The parts might be clearly visible to the user – as on a map of Europe divided into countries, for example – or invisible, so that the user must move their mouse pointer across the image to detect the different links.

iMP (interactive media player)

A multimedia application which downloads videos on to computers, so allowing them to be played without **streaming**.

Impression

The downloading of a specific file onto a browser. In an e-commerce environment the most common application of the term is in **page impression** and **ad impression**. Note that a file being downloaded does not necessarily mean the ad or page has been viewed by the user – a phenomenon common in offline advertising. For example, a TV ad being aired does not mean anyone has seen it, or an ad might be included in a magazine, but readers may not take any notice of it.

Impression ratio

The percentage of **impressions** that an advertising banner receives against the number of visitors the web page that hosts the banner has. For example, if a banner is hosted only on the **home page** of a web site when a visitor arrives on that page, the impression ratio is 1/1 – that is, one impression, one visitor. If the same visitor goes to another page on the site and then returns to the home page, the ratio is 2/1 – two impressions, one visitor.

I

Inbound link

See **link**.

In-box

That part of a user's email system that acts as a recipient of, and storage facility for, incoming mail.

Incidental offline advertising

The description given to offline advertising where the primary objective is not to drive traffic to a web site, but does so *incidentally*. This could be because the domain name of the product, brand or organization is included in the ad. More recently, however, search engines have started to record **search spikes** in searches for products, brands or organizations that coincide with the broadcast of TV ads, suggesting that offline ads trigger searches for the product or organization being advertised. This phenomenon was noticed particularly in the Superbowl ads of 2006. The synchronization of ads being broadcast and searches made online also suggests that people watch TV and surf the web at the same time.

Incubator

A term used to describe premises provided for a new business to develop and grow – as an incubator does for plant seeds. The business incubator is normally provided by a company, university or not-for-profit organization, and will include not only space and facilities, but expertise and advice as well. Although the concept is used in *general* business scenarios, it became popular in the **dotcom** boom era, and so has become associated with business start-ups in IT in general and the Internet in particular.

Index

The searchable catalogue of documents created by **search engine** software that those searching can query against. With **spider**-based search engines, the index consists of data from all the web pages they have found on the web. With **directories**, the index contains the summaries of all web sites that have been categorized by the human developers.

Index page

See homepage (3).

Information architecture

As with many terms in e-commerce, information architecture is virtually self-descriptive, it being the way in which a web site's content is constructed and presented to the user. For example, a university web site might be broken down into undergraduate and postgraduate programmes, full-time and part-time courses, UK, EU and international students, and so on. Successful information architecture means that the site's **navigation** is intuitive and easy.

Information portal

See portal.

Information retrieval (IR)

A science that predates search engines by a nearly 50 years, it is at the heart of **search engine algorithms**.

Information superhighway

A term made popular by (then) US Vice-President Al Gore to describe the Internet. While Gore's speech resulted in most people equating the information superhighway to the Internet, the term was previously used to describe an electronic communications network that would connect every government agency, business and citizen not only nationwide, but globally. To date, the Internet is the closest we have come to such a network. Although now somewhat redundant, in the early days of the commercial Internet using a *highway* analogy was common when describing what the Internet was and how it worked – with **broadband** being a six-lane motorway and a **dial-up connection** a country track.

Infomediary

An electronic *intermediary* who controls the flow of information online, often aggregating and selling it to others. Rappa (1998) puts forward the infomediary concept as a business model whereby data about consumers and their online buying habits is deemed valuable enough to be gathered and sold on to interested parties.

See **Rappa's online trading business models.**

Infomercials

See **advertorials.**

Informed purchase

The term used to describe the practice of retail shoppers who use the Internet as part of search for information in making their purchase decision. Research suggests that this is becoming more common.

See also **online purchase behaviour matrix** and **helping the buyer to buy.**

Instant messaging (IM)

A software application that facilitates real-time communications between individuals in a private **chat** room – effectively, a keyboard-generated online conversation.

In-store kiosk

In e-commerce terms this is where a retailer brings together its offline and online offerings by allowing customers to use an in-store connection to the Internet (or store **intranet**) to search for products without physically walking around the whole shop. In-store kiosks would normally be an integral part of a **multi-channel retail** strategy.

Integrated marketing

The synthesized use of all available media in strategic marketing efforts. In an e-commerce context this means the integration of offline and online marketing. Also known as *connected* marketing and *multi-channel* marketing, this is still far from standard practice, with many traditional **bricks-and-mortar** organizations treating the Internet as a marketing tool that operates in isolation from other marketing efforts. There are a number of ways in which the marketer can combine use of the Internet with other elements of the marketing mix. These include – but are not limited to:

- online ads and **paid placement** on search engines to complement offline promotion

- use of a web presence to enhance marketing messages made in other media
- sponsorship of offline events to publicize web sites
- using referral to web sites from ads in other media to reinforce the marketing message
- the web site as a point of purchase for offline promotions
- the use of a web site as a point of contact for applying for promotional offers
- the use a web presence to develop a relationship with customers that has been initiated offline.

Integrated retailing

See **multi-channel retailing**.

Integrity

In an e-commerce environment this term is used in relation to security. For example, the integrity of data, or a network, is judged by how secure it is from unauthorized access.

Intellectual property

A generic title given to the various forms of protection against unlawful copying, reproduction or other forms of unauthorized acquisition or use of intangible aspects of a product, service or business. In e-commerce, the main concern would be for web site content – text, images, etc. – and the program used in its design, both of which would be covered by **copyright** and/or a **trademark**.

Intelligent search

Many predict that this concept will become the norm in the not-too-distant future – it has been an optional feature for a while with most search engines. The concept is that the search engine tracks the individual user's search behaviour and adapts its **algorithm** to their habits. For example, the author is a supporter of Nottingham Forest Football Club, and so has searched on that term a number of times. Therefore, a search on the word 'forest' would return pages associated with that football club and anything to do with collections of trees would be much further down the **search engine results page (**SERP). While the search engine is striving to give the searcher a better service, intelligent search is not wholly altruistic on the part of the search engines – they can better target the advertising on the SERPs as well.

Intentional traffic

The **traffic** to a web site (or page) that arrives with an intention to act on the objectives of that web site – make a purchase or subscribe to a newsletter, for example. Naturally, intentional traffic is much more desirable – an obvious assertion exploited by Bill Gross at GoTo.com (see **paid search**). The visitor might well arrive at a page as the result of a **call to action** on an ad, another site, email or combination of the two (for example a **landing page**).

> See also **differentiated traffic, undifferentiated traffic, directed visitors** and **qualified traffic**.

Intermediary

A third party who operates between buyers and sellers providing a service to both, and making a profit for providing that service. Contemporary intermediaries utilize e-technology to facilitate the transactions – though the term *e-intermediary* has not gained popularity.

Internal link

> See **link**.

Internesia

A term formed by combining Internet and amnesia, which refers to the inability of users to remember where on the Internet they came across specific information.

Internet (lower-case i)

When two or more networks are connected together they form an *internet*.

Internet (upper-case I)

According to the *Collins English Dictionary*, when used as a prefix 'inter' means between or among (as in international) or together, mutually or reciprocally (as in interdependent and interchange). When two or more networks of computers were connected it became the practice to not simply add the prefix *inter*, but also to shorten the resulting word, making it *internet* (always fond of acronyms and jargon, computer engineers perhaps considered *internetworks* a bit cumbersome?). When the vast collection of interconnected networks that evolved from the **ARPANet** of the late 1960s and early 1970s came along it was more than just *an* internet, it was dubbed *the* Internet. Effectively, it became a proper noun that was the name of that internetwork, so we have the Internet, with a capital 'I'. All other internets are spelt with a lower case 'i'.

Internet advertising

See **online advertising.**

Internet Protocol (IP)

The most important **protocol** on which the Internet is based. It defines how **packets** of data get from source to destination.

Internet service provider (ISP)

An organization that, as a business model, provides access to the Internet for individuals and businesses. Originally this was through **dial-up connection**, but this has progressed through to **broadband**. Most, but not all, ISPs are telephone or telecoms companies.

InterNIC (Internet Network Information Center)

The InterNIC, an integrated network information centre developed by several companies in conjunction with the US government, was the governing body of the Internet until 1998 when its authority was assumed by **ICANN**. Although it is not the whole of their responsibility, both the InterNIC and ICANN are best recognized for their control of domain name and **IP address** allocation.

Interstitial

See **pop-up ad.**

Intranet

A private network inside a company or organization that uses the same concepts, technologies and **protocols** as the Internet, but which is for internal use only – hence their being commonly known as 'private web sites'. An intranet is normally exclusive to the employees of the organization that publishes it. An extranet follows the same principles (as an intranet) but allows access to users outside the organization. Those users would be associates of the organization – suppliers or affiliates, for example. The whole concept is designed to aid the dissemination of information. Both intranets and extranets have a **login** and are normally **password**-protected, with each login having access to all or some of the content.

Intrusion detection systems (IDSs)

Software designed to monitor all the activity on a network or host computer and identify suspicious patterns that may indicate a potential problem involving an attack on that system – a **hacker**, for example – and take automated action to prevent that attack.

Intuitive domain names

Closely associated with **direct navigation**, these are domain names based on generic words – that is, not the name of an organization, brand, person or entity – which are registered because users might type them into a browser with the hope that they will host a web site whose content matches the domain name. For example: house.com, carhire.com or careerinfo.com. The two domain names that have sold for the highest sums – loans.com (($3m) and business.com ($7.5m) – host web sites whose content reflect the meaning of the domain name. However, many multi-word phrases are registered and used to host faux-**shopping comparison sites**.

See also **domain name parking**.

Invisible text

See **hidden text**.

Invisible web

The concept that many web sites are not found by users because those sites do not feature in the **index** of **search engines** because they are *invisible* to their **spiders**. Protagonists of the invisible web normally lay the blame at the door of web site developers who either (a) do not optimize those sites for search engine ranking, or (b) use design features which rebuff search engine spiders.

IP

See **Internet Protocol.**

IP address (Internet Protocol address)

A unique number (IP number) consisting of 4 digits, 0 to 255, separated by dots, e.g. 165.113.245.2, that are allocated to devices (computers or **routers**, for example) for them to identify and communicate with each other on the Internet. While technical staff will be versed in using IP addresses for many purposes, for the e-commerce practitioner the term is normally associated with IP numbers that are designated to **domain names**. When applied to a web site an IP address is commonly referred to as a business's 'Internet address'. While not technically correct, the term is accurate in that the IP address (particularly in its guise as a domain name) is a web site's – and so the organization's – address on the Internet.

IP-based targeting

An **online advertising** model that uses **IP recognition** to target ads based on the location of a user. This means that visitors to **global sites**, no matter where in the world they are, can see ads that are relevant to them.

IP delivery

A **black-hat search engine optimization** practice that is a form of **search engine cloaking**. The concept is to present one set of content for a web site to a search engine and another set for a human user. This is accomplished by presenting the two sets of content based on the **IP address** of the user. The idea is this. For nefarious reasons, a web site publisher might like its web site to feature high on a **search engine ranking**, but not for its *actual* content. Although some legitimate businesses use this illegitimate method of SEO (usually following ill-judged advice to do so), the practice is most common for **adult web sites**. The idea is that 'legitimate' content is shown to search engines, so hiding the real 'adult' content. In its worse form the search engine sees a web site with content aimed at children – for example, with the key phrase 'Barbie doll' – but the *actual* web site is full of pornographic images. The search engine is fooled because the web site runs software that recognizes the IP address of any search engine **spider** and so delivers to it the 'Barbie doll' content. Search engines constantly look for the practice and ban any sites that they identify. The practice is a close accomplice of **IP spoofing.**

IP number

See IP address.

iPod

Included here as the brand name, for this product has become the generic term for all similar **MP3**-playing devices (rather like Hoover and the vacuum cleaner) and so should be considered a marketing success for its manufacturers, Apple. Apart from its brand name, the iPod does differ from other MP3 players in that it does have the capacity to download and play iTunes – music files available only at the iTunes Music Store, an online shop run by Apple.

IP recognition

A software application that identifies, by their **IP address**, where in the world the user is. There are a number of applications for this, the two most common being (a) its use to serve a local language web site depending on the geographic location of the web site's visitors, and (b) the targeting of online ads based on the location of a user; see **IP-based targeting**. **Geo-destination targeting** uses IP recognition as a basis for its application.

IP spoofing

Like **IP delivery** this is a form of **search engine cloaking** and, as such, is an unethical, and potentially illegal, practice that serves the same purpose. This method of **black-hat search engine optimization** (SEO) involves connecting to the web but not using the **IP address** that you have been assigned. The result is as with that in IP delivery, where one set of content is presented to search engines and another to web users. As with all black-hat methods of SEO, legitimate organizations are ill-advised if they get involved in practices like this one.

IP telephony

See e-telephony.

IPTV (Internet Protocol television)

An umbrella term for video delivered using Internet technology through a broadband connection to a television which is connected to a device that decodes the **IP** video and converts it into standard television signals. Applications for IPTV can be as fundamental as streaming video on the internet or as complex as being a complete substitute – and so competitor – to digital television.

ISDN (Integrated Services Digital Network)

A method of transferring digital data over existing standard phone lines. Providing speeds of around 128,000 bits per second, ISDN was a considerable step up from **dial-up connections** before **broadband** became more commonly available.

ISM (industry-sponsored marketplace)

An online **e-marketplace** developed by a number of players in a specific industry.

ISP

See Internet service provider.

ISP reputation system

A software application that allows **Internet service providers** to run 'reputation checks' on the **IP addresses** of email senders. These checks monitor each IP address for the number of user complaints and how much invalid email originates from it.

IT (Information Technology)

Loosely speaking, the 'I' stands for the management and processing of information and the 'T' for technology. The ubiquitous term has, however, become synonymous with virtually anything to do with, or related to, computers. Originally simply IT, it has become common for a 'C' – for communication – to be included (i.e. Information and Communication Technology), an addition that makes the term more applicable to e-commerce. For the e-commerce practitioner, it is worth noting the quote: 'We have spent the last fifty years focusing on the "T" in information technology (IT). We should spend the next fifty years focusing on the "I"' (attributed to Peter Drucker).

iVideots

See citizen cinema.

Jagger

See **Google dance.**

JANET

Funded by the Higher Education Funding Councils (HEFC) for England, Scotland and Wales, JANET is a dedicated Internet network for education and research in the UK. According to its web site (www.ja.net) over 18 million end-users are currently served by the JANET network. Any student in a UK college or university will benefit (or have benefited) from the JANET system. Early UK Internet use relied heavily on JANET.

Java

A programing language invented by Sun Microsystems that is specifically designed for writing programs that can be safely downloaded to a computer and immediately run without fear of viruses or other harm to the computer or its files. Using small programs called **applets**, Java makes it possible for web pages to include functions such as animations and calculators.

See also **ActiveX.**

JavaScript

A programming language used in the design of web pages, usually to add interactive features. When JavaScript is included in an **HTML** file it relies upon the browser to interpret the JavaScript. Developed by Netscape, JavaScript was so named to benefit from the popularity of **Java**. It is worth noting, therefore, that JavaScript and Java are two different programming languages from two different companies – Microsoft's application that competes with Java is **ActiveX.**

JPEG (Joint Photographic Experts Group)

JPEG is most commonly mentioned as a format for **image** files when used on the web. The JPEG format is preferred to the **GIF** format for photographic images as opposed to line or simple logo art. It is common for web site designers and developers to refer to images simply as a jpeg or GIF – depending on its format – as in 'a JPEG of a church will go in that space'.

Jump link

See **within-page link**.

Jump page

See **doorway page**.

J

Keylogging (keystroke logging)

Although originally a diagnostic used in software development, keylogging is more commonly known for its nefarious application in obtaining users' data. The keylogger program, normally transmitted by a **Trojan horse,** infects computers, captures login names and passwords for online bank accounts and the like, and then sends them to the attackers.

Key performance indicators (KPI)

A concept that has existed offline for many years, but has become a popular term in an e-commerce environment, the KPI is a close relative to **web site analytics**. However, KPIs consider the performance of a web site from more of an underlying business perspective, rather than simply the performance of the web site itself. Loosely defined as a quantifiable measurement that can be tracked and evaluated, a KPI must be associated with what the organization wants to achieve from its web presence. For example, while a simple visitor count might be a valuable element of a web site's analytics, it would not be a KPI. Common KPIs for an e-commerce trader might include any or all of the following:

- product conversion rates;
- percentage of new and returning visitors;
- sales per visitor;
- average order value;
- average number of items purchased;
- repeat order rate;
- repeat order rate value;
- cost per visit;
- profit per website visit.

Keyphrase

See **keyword(s)**.

Keystroke logging

See **keylogging.**

Keyword(s)

Also known as a search term or query term, most web users recognize a 'keyword' simply as being the word, words, phrase or term that they enter into a search engine's **search box** with a view to finding web sites that include content pertinent to that keyword. It is worth noting that, as it is rare for users to search on a single word, the term *keyphrase* is becoming popular, and the future may see it replacing *keyword*. The reverse of this definition is that that keywords are an essential element of how **search engine algorithms** attempt to match the sites they deliver on their results pages to what the searcher was looking for in the first place.

Since the early days of the commercial web, however, *keyword* has taken on a different, though associated, meaning for those who use the web as part of their business operations. In an e-marketing environment, 'keyword' has taken on the following mantles:

- The word, words, phrase or term for which a web page should be optimized in order for it to feature highly on the **organic listings** of a **search engine results page**.
- The word, words, phrase or term on which bids can be made as part of **paid placement**.

See also **search engine optimization, search engine marketing, direct keyword** and **negative keyword.**

Keyword advertising

See **paid placement.**

Keyword density

A search term that refers to the number of times a keyword appears in the text of a web page. The more it appears, the greater the density. Density that is too high causes problems, however, as text with little more than a repeated keyword makes no sense.

See also **keyword stuffing** and **content rich.**

Keyword domain name

A **domain name** that is chosen because it contains the main **keyword** for which the site is being optimized.

K

Keyword Effectiveness Index (KEI)

A calculation that attempts to place a value on the **keywords** used by web surfers when using search engines to find information on a specific subject. Typically the KEI is calculated by considering the ratio of searches for a keyword (normally per day, but it could be a shorter or longer period) divided by the number of websites that are listed for that keyword. For example, if a specific keyword (A) has a hundred searches that returns only one website, it will have a much higher ratio than a keyword (B) that has a hundred searches but returns four web sites – so keyword (A) has a higher ratio (100 rather than 25). Note: some applications of the KEI are more complex than this example, but follow the same principle. The KEI can be used in selecting key words for optimizing web sites in **organic listing** or the purchase of keywords in **paid placement** or **paid search**.

Keyword stuffing

The practice of excessively repeating – stuffing – keywords in the text and **meta tags** of a web site. The idea is that this will appeal to the search engines and give a high listing in their index. While this may have been true in the web's early days, the tactic is now recognized and penalized by the search engines.

See also **keyword density**.

Killer application

A slang term given to the application that will be the panacea to all problems in the field to which it will be applied. Suffice to say, many seek to develop a killer application, but very few are successful.

Killer content

The **web content** that 'does the business' for a web site, so helping the site achieve its objectives. The killer content could be *content* – information that meets the needs of the visitor – or *copy* – the textual content that prompts the visitor to take the action desired by the site's publishers/owners.

See also **call to action**.

Kilobyte

See **byte**.

Knowledge worker

Although the term was first coined by management guru Peter Drucker in 1959 – and has been used in management studies since – it has seen a recent revival in e-commerce circles to describe the type of worker who can develop and use knowledge in the workplace. The resurgence is (probably) down to it becoming a buzz-phrase in Silicon Valley and Eric Schmidt, CEO of Google (in December 2005), using it to describe the type of worker Google want to recruit.

KPI

See **key performance indicator.**

K

LAN (Local Area Network)

A computer network that is limited to a relatively small area, usually the same building or floor of a building. Businesses would use a LAN to connect all computers to each other and the Internet and/or an **Intranet**.

Landing page

A web page specifically developed as the place to where the user is directed when they respond to a promotion. That promotion might be presented offline or online. Offline, a TV advert might refer to a specific URL for the user to access in order to follow up on the promotion. Online, an ad will **link** directly to the landing page rather than the front page of the promoting organization's web site. If the user is referred to the site's home page the momentum of the potential sale is lost, as the prospective customer has to find the relevant product page. By referring users to a specific landing page the vendor has a greater chance of converting a lead to a customer. The landing page can pick up where the **call to action** on the ad leaves off, so taking the user on a seamless journey to the objective of the promotion – be that a purchase, a newsletter sign-up, a white paper download, etc. The landing page would be close to the top of the **conversion funnel**.

Latent semantic indexing (LSI)

Also known as latent semantic *analysis* (LSA), this technique was developed around 1990 and aims to tackle problems with **information retrieval** that originate with vocabulary diversity in human–computer interaction. More specifically, in real life people use words in context, and so we interpret their meanings accordingly. For example, we have:

- Different words to describe the same object (for example, car boot and trunk).

- Different words to describe the same concept (e-commerce and e-business, perhaps).
- Words that are spelled the same but have more than one meaning depending on how they are pronounced (for example, bow could be an archer's weapon or the front of a ship).
- Words that have multiple meanings that actually contradict the others (for example fast can mean moving quickly or stuck in place).
- Different words that have the same meaning (for example, Jupiter, Zeus, Odin).
- Words that have the same sound but a completely different meaning (for example, to, too, two).

While there are obvious implications of LSI for large search engines, there are also repercussions on the e-commerce practitioner. These are most significant in choosing **keywords** for **paid placement** and also for on-site search facilities. In the latter, it is important to have search fields address LSI; for example, the online clothes shop might list 'burgundy pullovers', but the customer might search for 'red sweaters'.

It is also the case that our existing knowledge and experience influences what we might expect from a search facility – so-called *semantic mapping*. For example, two searchers who use the keywords 'digital camera' in a search engine might be (a) a grandmother who knows nothing about cameras, but wants to buy her grandson one for his birthday, or (b) a professional photographer who is looking to update her equipment. The **search engine results page** would be the same for both users. Semantic search allows the searcher to further quantify their search by having them select other criteria for the search – a service already offered by some search engines under the guise of *advanced* search (or similar such title).

Law of convenience

A phrase coined by Jerry Michalski, his definition being that 'every additional step that stands between people's desires and the fulfilment of those desires greatly decreases the likelihood that they will undertake the activity'. In an e-commerce environment, this means that every click on a web site a user has to make to meet their needs reduces the chances of them actually meeting those needs. Amazon's one-click facility is an example of the law of convenience being applied.

See also **usability**.

Lead generation

A marketing term that refers to the development of associations between vendors and well-matched consumers. **B2B** marketing in particular is dependent on companies seeking out *genuine* potential customers – sales leads – for the products or services they have on offer. It is important to note that a *lead* is not a *sale*, only the opportunity to deliver a pitch that might lead to a sale. The better the lead, the greater the chance of converting prospect to sale. In e-commerce both email and web sites can be used in lead generation. An email must create enough interest in an offering to encourage the target to give contact details to the advertiser, or visit a web site. The majority of B2B web sites have an objective of lead generation rather than online sales. The web site must generate enough interest in whatever the organization has to offer for the user to either contact the company directly – normally by email or telephone – or by completing an online form giving name, contact details and any other pertinent information. Once the initial contact is made the 'generation' element of the process is over and representatives of the organization must use their sales skills to convert the lead – as has always been the case in any form of lead generation in any industry.

Legacy system

A computer program in which an organization has invested considerable resources, usually running on **mainframe computer**s. Advances in information technology (IT) – in all its guises – have greatly reduced the use of legacy systems.

Link

Originally known by its full name of *hyperlink*, but now more commonly referred to in its abbreviated form, it is the (hyper) link that makes the web the communications medium that it is. Clicking on a link (an image or text) takes the user to another document. Normally this will be another web page or site, but it can be virtually any other form of file, a word document or PDF file, for example. Links come with a number of functions, including:

- External links (also known as outbound links) – though more specifically referring to a link that takes the user to another web *page* (possibly in the same web site), it is common practice for it to mean another web *site*, that is, *external* to the one being visited.

- Internal links – that take the user to another page within the same web site, or even to a different place on the same page.
- Inbound links (also known as *back links*) – those links that come from another site.

Links also play a role in **search engine optimization**; *see* **link popularity**.

Link baiting

A tactic in a **linking strategy**, link baiting is the practice of encouraging people to link to a site by producing quality content that attracts – *hooks* – those links. Baits could include:

- *News* hooks, normally in a specific environment, industry, etc.
- *Contrary* hooks, where the writer takes up a contrary stance to expert, or public, opinion on a given subject.
- *Resource* hooks, where the web site gains a reputation as the place to go for information.
- *Humour* hooks, attracting those looking to pass on some light relief to others.

With all of these hooks the subject should be relevant to the product or service on offer, so ensuring that **link popularity** scores are high by having the links come from sites (and blogs) that address the same subject areas.

Link bombing

Although this concept is all about achieving high ranking in a search engine's **index**, it is normally associated with light-hearted rather than purely commercial or even malicious intent. The notion is that a page will be ranked higher if the sites that link to that page all use consistent **anchor tags** – a link bomb being created if a large number of sites link to a specific page using the same text in an anchor tag. Such are search engine's algorithms that the **target page** need not have any content on the subject of the text used in the tag. Although it might have been discovered by accident in 1999 (a search on the phrase 'more evil than Satan' returned the Microsoft home page), the first deliberate *bomb* was instigated by Adam Mathes who, in 2001, succeeded in making a search on the phrase 'talentless hack' return the web site of his friend and journalist Andy Pressman. More recently, and to demonstrate that link bombing is not confined to one search engine, the summer of 2005 saw

L

a search on the phrase 'miserable failure' return the official George W. Bush biography web site as number one on Google, Yahoo and MSN.

Link equity

See **link popularity**.

Link farming

The process of exchanging numerous **reciprocal links** with web sites in order to increase search engine optimization. However, the practice is pretty much a waste of time as search engines consider link farming as a form of **spam** and may banish sites that participate in the practice.

See also **FFA link pages**.

Linking campaign

A limited application of a **linking strategy**.

Linking strategy

Web site owners and publishers are well aware that to attract visitors to their site they need to feature highly in **search engine ranking**. One element that **search engine algorithms** favour is the site having quality links coming into the web site – so-called **link popularity**. It is, therefore, common practice to have a deliberate strategy of actively seeking out web sites that might add a link to their site, and such practice is deemed to be a linking strategy. Note however, that a linking strategy employs legitimate methods of gaining links into a site, and not **link spamming**.

Link popularity

Also known as link equity, this is a **metric** of how popular a page is based on the number of **inbound links** it has. Search engines might use this metric to help determine the page's **ranking**. However, the search engines set greater store by the context and quality of the links. A link from a web site that is considered to be an authority on the subject in question will carry greater ranking value than one from a **link farm**. For example, a link to a page on growing tomatoes might be deemed more valuable if it comes from the BBC's gardening pages (www.bbc.co.uk/gardening).

See also **PageRank** and **TrustRank**.

Link rot

A collective term used to describe a problem that plagues the web, that of **broken links**.

Link spamming

In an effort to take advantage of **link popularity**, less scrupulous search engine optimizers (so called black hats) look to create links into their site by nefarious means. They do this by visiting web sites where users are able to leave comments (for example, **chat rooms**, **bulletin boards**, in fact, any source of **consumer-generated media**, including **blogs**), and leave a message that includes a **link** to their web site. Although this can be done manually, it is more likely that a software program would be employed on the task. Like other such activities, the search engines are aware of, look for, and penalize the practice.

Link text

See **hypertext**.

Listing

See **search engine listings**.

List poisoning

See **opt-in/opt-out**.

Listserver

A software application that handles the sending of emails to a large number of individuals simultaneously. Email marketers might use a list-server to draw from their database those addresses to which emails are to be sent.

L

Localization

Whether to sell the same product in all countries or to adapt (localize) it to the local market is always an essential decision for international marketers. Similarly, for the organization that trades globally the deci-sion has to be made as to whether there should be one *global* web site or localized versions for each country being traded in. There are three basic options:

1 The single web site. Normally it would be in the host language of the organization, though verbatim translation of some or all pages into other languages may be included.
2 Different web sites for local countries. The content is predominantly translations of the *home* site, though the presentation and content may be adapted to address local issues.
3 Local web sites are developed for each country in which it has a physical presence. In this case each web presence would have a standardized corporate design and structure but content would be localized.

Localized domains

The term used when domain names have been registered for specific countries in which the organization has a presence – normally to host local web sites (see **localization**). For example, Google uses google.de, google.fr, google.es, google.it and google.co.uk for its European sites.

> See also **DNS**, **localization** and **global sites**.

Local search

Many argue this is one of the ways forward for search engines, with the major engines already practising the concept. The idea is that the user's search can be geographically *localized*, making the resulting listings more appropriate – and so useful – to the searcher. While the practice is of no use if the search has no geographical context, it will make it easier to find, for example, a vegetarian restaurant in midtown Manhattan – if that is the kind of food the searcher wants to eat in the location they want to eat it.

Log file

Also known as a *web log* (note that this is not to be confused with the origin of the term **blog**), this is the software application that records all activity on a web site. The web site's log file is the source of all data used in **web site analytics**. To the uninitiated a log file is a mass of confusing, coded data. Once familiar with them, however, the e-marketer can draw data such as:

- Where the request for pages comes from.
- The nature of the link used to arrive at the site (the referral link). For example, was it a textual link on another web site or a banner ad?

- The type of browser being used by the visitor, for example, Internet Explorer, Netscape, Firefox.
- If the visitor found the site on a search engine, which search engine was used and the keyword entered.
- On what page the visitor entered the site, their path through it (clickstream) and at what point they left.

Note the more the in-depth the log file analysis, the more comprehensive the data gleaned.

Login/log-in/log in (noun)

Also known as a username, this is the account name used to gain access to a computer system or **network**. For example, all staff at an organization could be allocated user1, user2 and so on, or their initials and a department code, e. g. AC002 and so on. Usernames are not normally confidential, unlike a **password**.

Login/log-in/log in (verb)

The act of entering a computer system. Note, being a verb, a user can have *logged in*.

Long neck

A distillation of the **long tail**, this concept, introduced by Gerry McGovern (www.gerrymcgovern.com), emphasizes the importance of popular content on web sites. McGovern's research suggests that where web site content is concerned, there is a 25:5 rule – with five percent of content being read by 25 percent of people. Viewed in graphical form this creates a *long neck*. While niche operators might concentrate on the long tail, the long neck concept reminds web site managers that in order to best satisfy the majority of visitors they should include the content that is most commonly sought. McGovern's original research respondents were asked to vote on their favourite tourism-related words/phrases from 147 put forward. The top seven words (McGovern refers to them as *carewords*), representing 5 per cent of the total words, received 35 per cent of votes, with the top seven actually getting more votes than the bottom 120.

L

Long tail

A phenomenon introduced by Jakob Nielsen in 1997, but given greater prominence by Chris Anderson in his *Wired* magazine article 'The Long

Tail' (2004) and later in his 2006 book, *The Long Tail*. The concept takes the 80/20 rule (also known as 'Pareto's principle' after Vilfredo Pareto, an Italian economist who devised the concept in 1906), which says that 20 per cent of products are responsible for 80 per cent of sales, a stage further. Anderson suggests that the 80 per cent of sales volume comes from high-maintenance, low-profit products and that the remaining 20 per cent of sales come from products that make high profits for niche operators. Because the 20 per cent comes from sales as they 'tail off' (on a sales graph, for example), perhaps over a long period, they are the long tail of sales. The notion relies heavily on the concept of **niche marketing**.

Anderson, C., 'The Long Tail', *Wired*, October 2004.

Anderson, C., *The Long Tail: How Endless Choice Is Creating Unlimited Demand*. London: Random House, 2006.

L

M (as a prefix)

As with the prefix 'e' (for electronic), 'm' is used to represent the 'mobile' incarnation of whatever word or term it precedes. In this instance mobile refers to the use of wireless devices – they are portable in their use, making the user and their activity *mobile*. For example, m-commerce is business conducted on the move. Other common applications include m- shopping, marketing and banking. Although the term originally referred to any portable (mobile) device, including laptops, technology has moved along and now 'mobile' is normally restricted to **PDA**s and web-enabled mobile (cell) phones. Given that the same basic technology is used to download web sites and ads on a mobile device as on a PC, it is worth noting that m-commerce could be legitimately regarded as a sub-division of e-commerce rather than a separate element of business.

Mailbot

See **autoresponder**.

Mail filter

See **spam filter**.

Mailing list

Also known as a mail list, this is software that permits users to send an email to one address, whereupon the message is copied and sent to all of the other subscribers to that mail list. Note that a mailing list is not an **email list**.

Mail server

See **email server**.

Mail transfer agent (MTA)

See email server.

Mail user agent (MUA)

See email client.

Mainframe computer

A large (and normally expensive) computer that can be used by hundreds, even thousands, of users at the same time. With the exception of a small number of specialized industrial applications, mainframes have been replaced by personal computers.

Malware

A generic term for malicious software that is secretly downloaded on to a user's computer to cause damage or steal data – **viruses**, **worms**, **Trojans**, **spyware** and the like.

Margin landscape banner

See banner.

Marketing blog

See commercial blog.

Marketing engine

If their advertising is to be believed, this is what Yahoo! considers itself to be. It has a certain logic to it, as the organization offers marketers (and the general public) much more than a search engine. Only time will tell if the term catches on – or if Google et al. come up with their own version.

Marketing funnel

The marketing funnel is used to demonstrate how all marketing efforts rank in capturing a share of the market, taking potential customers (represented by the wide end of the funnel) through to being paying customers (the narrow end). Like the **sales funnel** and its online compatriot, the **conversion funnel**, the marketing funnel's value is as a diagnostic tool, with marketers analysing at what stage potential customer leave the process. Key to developing a successful funnel is segmentation of the market. This is because only those potential customers who are in the target market for a product or service should be enticed into the funnel in the first place. Though generally used as part of a strategic marketing initiative, the marketing funnel is relevant to e-commerce in two ways:

- For the **pure online business** most, if not all, elements of marketing are online. Therefore, the marketing funnel will refer to all marketing efforts.
- For the business that either trades online as part of its distribution strategy (that is, **bricks-and-clicks** trader) or the offline business (**bricks-and-mortar trader**) that uses the Internet for promotional purposes, the Internet could well be an important aspect of some elements of the marketing funnel.

Marketing-led SEO (search engine optimization)

The notion, championed by search engine guru Mike Grehan, that **search engine marketing** is no longer a matter of code and technology, but is more about quality marketing. The argument is that **search engine optimization (SEO)** is just one element of the contemporary marketing mix, not a stand-alone discipline practised by outsiders. To be successful, therefore, SEO must be performed as part of the organization's marketing mix.

Market research

See **online market research**.

Marketspace

M

A term used to distinguish between electronic and conventional markets, a marketspace is a virtual *marketplace* that exists intangibly – in *space* – rather than as a tangible entity which can be physically visited by a customer.

Mash-up

Although its origins are in the hip-hop music practice of mixing two or more songs, in e-commerce the term mash-up refers to a kind of web-based application that mixes services from different web sites. Originally associated with **hackers**, a mash-up is often created against the wishes, and normally to the detriment of, the web site and its legitimate developers. In the past it was something that e-commerce practitioners were a victim of, but never exercised. More recently, however, it has gained more legitimate use. Google maps, for example, can be overlaid with data from an estate agent's database of houses for sale to give a visual representation of where those properties are located.

Masked web direction

See **domain name pointing**.

M-commerce

See **M as a prefix**.

Meanderthal

A rather unkind term for people who **surf** the web mindlessly, that is, with no great purpose – the online equivalent of the couch potato who flicks around TV channels in search of entertainment. They are significant to the e-marketer for two main reasons: (a) they can be converted into customers, and (b) the effect they have on web site **metrics**.

See also **screensucking**.

Megabyte

See **byte**.

Memory

M

Computer memory is the term given to the elements of a digital computer which retain data over a limited period of time, that is, until the computer is turned off. Long-term memory is referred to as *storage* or hard disk space (or *hard disk* memory). Storage retains any data it holds even after the power is turned off. In a home computer, memory often takes the form of random access memory (RAM), which is used to temporarily store things as programs and data while the computer is using them. Unlike memory, which can be slow to access, RAM can be accessed at very high speeds, making it ideally suited to personal computing. Memory storage is measured in **bytes**.

Meta

In computing circles meta is a prefix that means *about*. For example, web site **meta tags** are tags that give data about the web site on which they are located.

Metadata

Data about data – metadata describe how and when and by whom a particular set of data was collected, and how the data are formatted. Metadata are essential for understanding information stored in data warehouses.

Meta refresh

A close relative of the **web site redirect**, a meta refresh is where a user arrives at a page and, in a predetermined period of time (usually a few seconds), is taken to another site. The practice is used when a site or page has moved from one **URL** or **domain name** to another. Unlike web site redirects, however, the meta refresh presents the user with a page on which a message is normally presented – 'please wait a few seconds while we take you to our new web site', for example – before the new page is downloaded.

Meta search engine

A search engine that extracts listings from other search engines, rather than compiling its own **index** by having **spiders** crawl the web.

Meta tag(s)

In web site design, the meta **tag** is used to describe the contents of a web page. Some meta tags are used for static information; the author's name, for example. Others are more important as they can be used by search engines to determine **search engine rankings** of pages. Web site meta tags include:

M

- meta description tag, which allows page developers to say how they would like their pages described when listed by search engines;
- meta **keyword** tag, which allows page developers to add text to a page to help with the search engine ranking process;
- meta robots tag, which allows page developers to keep their web pages from being indexed by search engines.

It should be noted that while early search engine indexing relied heavily on meta tags, their significance on **search engine optimization** has diminished in recent years.

Metaverse

A term taken from Neal Stephenson's 1992 book *Snow Crash*, a metaverse – as in universe – is a virtual world accessed through the Internet. Although a number exist, the most popular metaverse at the time of writing is Second Life (www.secondlife.com). This role-playing alternate-world game was created by San Francisco-based Linden Lab and features personalized **avatars** representing each player which interact to find and create experiences using 'linden dollars', which players buy with real dollars and can cash in at any time. Second Life's audience – reported to comprise mainly stay-at-home moms and young professionals – can use their skills to conduct business within the game, with some making significant profits from their *virtual* dealings. Not only does a metaverse present opportunities to marketers by way of advertising and promotion within the virtual universe, but more proactive companies are seeking other models for profits – US retailer American Apparel has already opened a virtual store in Second Life (so that participants can dress their avatar).

Metric

Used in **web site analytics**, a metric is a specific measurable standard against which actual performance is compared. When used in an online, e-commerce or e-marketing context, metrics are known as e-metrics.

Microbrowser

A web browser, normally wireless, that is designed to operate on a small screen and with limited bandwidth. It is used in **m-commerce**.

Microbusiness

A very small business, often a one-person operation run from home, sometimes on a part-time basis. While such activities have always existed, they have flourished with the advent of the Internet (eBay-type auction sites in particular), it being a perfect medium for conducting a small, often **niche marketing**, enterprise. It is not unusual for these businesses to be run as a part-time undertaking.

See also **mom and pop operation** and **SME**.

M

Microcontent (1)

A notion popularized by Amy Gahran (www.contentious.com) in 2000, microcontent is the content on a web site that addresses the reality that users tend to scan pages – rather than read them – and so each page should be presented in such a way that it facilitates this *at-a-glance* mentality. Microcontent includes such things as page titles, headlines and subheadings, navigation bar links, bold text and captions.

Microcontent (2)

A second, more recent (2002) interpretation of microcontent comes from Anil Dash (www.dashes.com), who says that 'microcontent is being used as a more general term indicating content that conveys one primary idea or concept ... a day's weather forecast or the arrival and departure times for an airline flight are examples of microcontent'.

Micro-gains

A term used in **web site analytics** to represent the value of the compounding effect of small gains in a number of elements of an online promotional campaign. For example, small performance increases in **pay-per-click** response rates, **landing page** conversions and completed **shopping cart** transactions can combine to deliver significant improvements in overall revenue. Micro gains would be an integral part of the **conversion funnel** and **persuasion architecture**.

See also **micro-improvements**.

Micro-improvements

Although micro-improvements could be seen as being the same as **micro-gains**, in reality the *gains* should come from the *improvements*.

Micropayments

Electronic payments for small-value purchases. Although systems to facilitate such payments are fairly common offline (public transportation systems, for example), the **killer application** online has yet to be determined. The main problem for an online merchant is that they have to pay a fee (to the credit-card company) for any credit-card payment they accept. The fees are normally a percentage of the sale, but with a minimum amount stipulated. So if, for example, a merchant pays a minimum of 50p for every transaction, making sales of less than £5 is (realistically) unlikely to make them sufficient profit. Accepting a micro-payment of less than 50p will actually cost them money. The answer is likely to come in some kind of **digital wallet**-type arrangement. The argument in favour of such a system is that it would make it easier for web sites to charge for content. For example, a user might want to look at one article from a magazine which they rarely read and so would not pay a £50 yearly subscription, but would be willing to pay 20p for that single article.

Microsite

A small web site, usually one page. The term is generally used to describe one of two types of web presence:

1 where the organization's objectives can be met by the contents of one web page;
or
2 a web page that is on a different domain to the organization's primary site because it serves a different purpose to the rest of the web presence, for example, a **landing page**.

MIDI (Musical Instrument Digital Interface)

A **protocol** used to exchange musical information between computers, synthesizers, and instruments.

MIME (Multipurpose Internet Mail Extensions)

A specification for attaching non-text files to standard Internet mail messages. Non-text files include graphics, spreadsheets, formatted word-processor documents and sound/video files. An email program is said to be MIME-compliant if it can both send and receive files using the MIME standard. MIME is important (especially) to email marketers who might wish to send MIME-compliant messages – the concern being that the receiver might not use a MIME-compliant email system, and so not receive those messages. Multipart MIME allows senders to mail both text and HTML versions of a message to each recipient.

Mirror site

A web site that has exact copies hosted on duplicate **servers**, where those servers act as a kind of **cache** for the site. The advantage of such

M

a strategy is that the mirror site can be in different geographical locations in order to provide more widespread access to the site at greater speed. For example, a site might be located in Europe and mirrored in the USA, meaning that users on each side of the Atlantic would access the appropriate site without their request travelling thousands of miles. Note that mirror sites use the same **IP addresses**, and so are recognized as being the same site by search engines. This is important, as duplicates of web sites hosted on different IP addresses, with the intention of gaining greater recognition from search engines, are normally penalized by search engines.

M-marketing

While the comments made in **M (as a prefix)** are certainly relevant to marketers, they should also be aware that that mobile devices can be used for more that a medium for advertising. Provision of a service, both pre- and post-sales, can be delivered to a customer while they are on the move – the use of mobile search facilities helping a tourist find a specific type of restaurant in the area of a city they are visiting, for example. The technology can, however, be utilized to greater effect. During the Cellular Telecommunications and Internet Association Wireless trade show in Las Vegas (in April 2006), the Luxor Hotel demonstrated a new methods of connecting with customers. On landing at Las Vegas Airport, delegates staying at the Luxor could turn on their mobile (cell) phone and the Luxor could check them in before they even exited the aircraft. No queuing at the hotel check-in, just straight to their room. Even the delivery of ads can use the technology available. Using the phone's **GPS** capabilities, the Luxor also knew if a guest had left the hotel premises and so sent tailored mobile promotions to lure the delegates back to the hotel.

Mobile commerce

See **m as a prefix.**

Modem (MOdulator, DEModulator)

A device that allows digital data to be transmitted over an **analogue** system. Although modems are used widely in other fields, in the e-commerce environment they are associated with connection to the Internet. An Internet user's computer is connected to a telephone line by a modem that *translates* the digital content at each end of its journey

M

over the (analogue) telephone lines. Essentially, the modem allows a computer to *dial up* other computers through the telephone system – hence the common term, dial-up connection. In the early days of the Internet, modems were separate devices to the user's PC, though now most are integral to the machine.

Although it operates on the same basic principles as traditional telephone modems (analogue/digital conversion), the computer–Internet connection using **broadband** is better described as a *broadband adapter* (rather than modem). However, users' familiarity with a device that connects them to the Internet being called a *modem* prompted vendors to market broadband adapters as modems to ease their acceptance. Broadband modems are far more advanced appliances, often including the functions of a **router**.

Mom and pop operation

An American expression meaning a very small business (**microbusiness**) that is normally operated from the family home. Such businesses may also be run at home by the female parent of the family, known as 'stay-at-home moms' (SAHM).

Monitor

Though mainly used to describe the display screen of a computer, *monitor* also includes the box in which it is housed.

Mosaic

Developed by the National Center for Supercomputing Applications at the University of Illinois, Mosaic was the first web **browser** that was available for Macintosh, Windows and UNIX all with the same interface. It was also the first browser to facilitate images, and it became the basis for many subsequent browsers. It is generally recognized that the introduction of Mosaic signalled the birth of the popular commercial Internet as we know it. Its actual date of birth is not too clear, however. Although the official release was in November 1993, the timeline of Mosaic's browser capacity on different platforms (for example, Unix, Macintosh) differed. January 1994 saw the first version 2 release, October 1995, the last version 2 release, and a number of upgrades between those dates are frequently proffered as *the birthday of the web*, as is March 1993, when the pre-release version of Mosaic was first announced.

Mouseover

An online application (which uses **javascript**) where moving the on-screen pointer of a mouse over an element of the web page (e.g. an image) triggers a change in whatever the mouse is hovering over – usually signifying that the item is part of the site's **navigation**.

Mousetrapping

The use on a web site of software that disables a browser's back button. This means that the visitor is *trapped* on the site as they cannot go back to previously visited sites. Not considered to be good practice as it defies **usability** conventions, mousetrapping is most common on **adult web sites**.

Moved to Atlanta

A slang term for a web page that has disappeared, leaving a **404 file not found** error message in its place; see also **broken link**. The phrase comes from the US telephone area code for Atlanta, Georgia – 404.

MP3

Technically, the acronym for the specification of the MPEG-1 Audio Layer-3 – to the lay person it is a common format for compressing sound into very small files. MP3 files can be played on a computer or any MP3 player. Widespread adoption of the MP3 files led to the popularity of music downloads and **podcasting** (see also **iPod**). Although the technical definition is more convoluted, MP4s are commonly recognized as being MP3 players that also show video clips.

MP4

See **MP3**.

MPEG (Motion Picture Experts Group)

A format for compressed video files.

M-shopping

See **m as a prefix**.

M

MSN adCenter

MSN's **pay-per-click** advertising system.

See also **AdWords**.

MTA

See **mail transfer agent**.

Multi-channel retailing

Where a company uses more than one retail distribution channel to sell goods to its customers. The practice is not new. Sears, Roebuck & Co., the US retail giant, has sold its goods through mail-order catalogues *and* retail outlets since 1893. The same company has brought the concept up to date with its *fusion retailing* – where customers can not only shop in-store or online, but combine – *fuse* – the channels, with online purchasers having the option of home delivery or collection from a local store. An additional fusion is that when the online shopper visits the store to collect their purchase, they are encouraged to make additional purchases while they are at the store collecting those goods.

See also **disintermediation, channel conflict** and **online purchase behaviour matrix**.

Multipart MIME

See **MIME**.

MySpace Generation

A term that originated in a *Business Week* article (December 2005) and owing much to the users of MySpace.com, the MySpace generation is one that has grown up with the Internet – and online networks in partic- ular (note that a play on the generation X/Y descriptions of certain age groups has spawned the term *Generation My*). Where most adults see the Internet as an add-on to their daily lives, MySpacers make no distinction between online and offline interactions. At the same time as watching TV and playing video games, they are using the web for as social networking as well as interacting through email, telephone and face-to- face contact. There is even a MySpace economy, with web sites that offer MySpace users free tools to upgrade the aesthetics of their profiles, personal page redesigns for a fee, and software designed to automate tasks within the MySpace network. The challenge to the e-marketer is to

M

develop, or take advantage of, online networks. The challenge to marketers in general is to work out how to reach this new generation of consumers who eschew traditional marketing methods. Note that this is an example of how the name of the first organization to be associated with a new trend or model can become the generic term by which that concept is known. In the UK, for example, August 2006 saw Bebo (bebo.com) overtake Myspace in visitor numbers, yet those users are not known as the Bebo generation.

Mystery surfer

The online manifestation of the offline 'mystery shopper'. The mystery surfer will visit e-commerce sites and, depending on the objectives of the visit, seek information, contact the organization or make a purchase. A report on aspects of **navigation**, **usability**, product pricing, product descriptions (see web **content**) and even **fulfilment** is then provided for the publisher of the site. For the practice to be objective – and so of any value – the mystery surfer should have no affiliations to either the publisher, vendor or any person or organization involved in the development of the site. The practice is particularly useful for smaller traders who outsource web design and maintenance as it provides a third-party check on the skills and output of the design company. E-commerce vendors can also employ mystery surfers to visit competitors' sites to compare the 'customer experience' against that of visitors to their own site. Any positive lessons learned can then be adopted for the vendor's site.

M

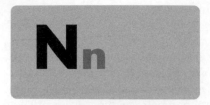

Naming authority

See **DNS (domain name system)**.

Napster

A search engine for music that put the power of seeking, finding and acquiring music into the hands of the consumer and raised public awareness of the concept of peer-to-peer (P2P) trading. Napster is included here for its significant impact as a business paradigm, in particular its impact on the pre-existing model of the music industry.

Natural listing

See **organic listing**.

Navigation

In an e-commerce context, navigation refers to *web site* navigation. That is, how easy or difficult it is for a **visitor** to find their way around a site. More specifically, and in marketing terms, how easy or difficult it is for a visitor to find whatever it is on the site that meets the need that prompted them to arrive at the site in the first place. Navigation is an integral element of **usability** and **web site accessibility** and it is the practical side of **information architecture**.

Navigational query

The practice of typing a word into a search engine that the user knows will return the specific web site that they want to visit. The practice is born out of the fact that a **domain name** must be typed in *exactly* in order to reach the required web site. With a few notable exceptions, specific spellings of domain names can be tricky to remember – including which suffix is used. If the surfer wants to return to a web site they have been on before, what they do is type into the **search box** a word or phrase they know is part of the domain name. For those who may doubt that navigational queries take place, consider that in November 2005 the **keywords** that were the first and second most searched term (on Google, Yahoo and MSN) were 'eBay' and 'Google'.

Negative keywords

Words that are used as a filter to exclude certain phrases or terms from the results of a search engine's search. Essentially they are used to make search results more specific to the intended subject. For example, if a user wished to find out about the city of Manchester and they entered 'Manchester' in a search engine, the returns would include sites that feature Manchester United Football Club. If the searcher wanted to exclude pages about the football team they would add 'united' as a negative keyword. Note that search engines differ, but the most common way of adding a negative keyword is to put a minus sign and the negative word after the main search term. In the example cited, 'Manchester –united'. As with search **keywords**, the practice has an application for the e-commerce practitioner. When bidding on keywords for **paid placement** on a search engine, the e-marketer can use negative keywords to more closely match the listings with the products or services offered.

Nested ad content

Normally, when a user clicks on an ad banner they are taken to another web site – that of the product or brand being advertised. With nested ad content anyone who clicks on an ad is taken to a web page within the same site as the page on which the ad is displayed. The concept might be used for an online retail outlet where (for example) a special offer within the store is being promoted. Nested ads differ from house ads in that they are part of a deliberate promotional strategy, whereas **house ads** are normally used to fill unsold ad space.

Netiquette

The unwritten *rules* of etiquette used on the Internet. Perhaps the most commonly recognized is the (mis)use of upper-case characters. On the Internet, particularly in emails, to capitalize words is to shout – and so be perceived as being rude.

See also **Netizen.**

N

Netizen

Deriving from citizen, a netizen is a citizen of the Internet. The term connotes civic responsibility and participation. Like **netiquette**, the term was popular in the early days of the Internet when most users were idealistic about what the Internet would bring. The rise in commercialization of the web saw a corresponding decline in utopian hopes for the new technology, and the use of terms that reflected those hopes.

Net (network) neutrality

A subject being discussed and debated – in the USA up to Congressional level – the outcome of which may have an impact on the fundamental use of the Internet. The question is whether or not web sites should be served in the same way to all users – that is, in a *neutral* way. Opposing neutrality are the telecoms and network providers who would like to see a two-tier system which creates fast lanes and slow lanes for web access – the fast access going to web sites that are willing to pay for it. Note that when presented from the non-net neutrality standpoint the concept is often referred to as *tiered web delivery*.

Netroots

The name given to political activists who use **blogs** or web sites to get their views across to a wider public. The term is a play on 'grassroots' when used to describe politics at a community level.

Netscape

A web **browser** and the name of a company. The Netscape browser was originally based on the **Mosaic** program. Distributed as **freeware**, Netscape was the browser that introduced many to the web. The distributive power of Microsoft saw Internet Explorer replace Netscape as the number one browser, a situation that exists today.

Network

When two or more computers are connected together so that they can share resources they are a network. Connecting two more networks together creates an internet.

N

Networks (commercial and social)

In the network of relationships that affect our lives, the *commercial network* is our relationship with products, services and brands. The *social network* is our relationships with other people. Prior to the Internet, the majority of our commercial network was short-lived, with us developing relationships with very few businesses – as a customer in a B2C context, perhaps only our local bar or newsagent. Networks in a **B2B** context would vary depending on career or employment, but perhaps half a dozen customers or suppliers. However, the Internet introduced a medium of communication that made it easier to maintain commercial relationships, both as customer and vendor. Instead of (expensive) direct personal contact (in person or by telephone, for example) an organization's web site is available 24/7, with a wealth of information that can help maintain and enhance the customer–supplier relationship at comparatively little cost. Consumer product manufacturers and retailers can also reach thousands – if not millions – of customers on a one-to-one basis by email at a negligible cost per person.

A more significant impact of the Internet on our personal relationships comes in social networking. Also known as *social computing*, our online social network exists predominantly by way of **virtual community**-type web sites, popular with the **MySpace generation**. In social networking the Internet – both the web and email – has opened up our potential for developing relationships with not only more people, but with individuals and groups from all around the world. The concept extends also to **consumer-generated media**, where although the communication is generally one-way, the opportunity to get a message across to a wider social network far exceeds anything that has gone before it.

For some commentators, it is the use of the Internet in developing and maintaining relationships in both commercial and social networks that is the main contribution the new medium brings to the world. Both commercial and social networks should now play a significant part in any organization's strategic business and marketing planning.

See also **portals**.

Neural Net (NN)

A ranking technology added to the ranking algorithms of search engines from the beginning of January 2006. Technically speaking, NN is an adaptive system that not only changes its structure based on external or internal information flowing through the network, but it is able to learn from its previous operations. In search terms this means that search results are improved because, based on users' searches, the neural net model produces results that get better over time. For the SEO, NN will emphasize the value of relevant content and quality inbound links.

Neutral web

See **net (network) neutrality.**

Newbie

Someone who is new to the Internet (or to computers in general). No matter how close to saturation use of the Internet might become, there will always be people who are visiting a web site for the first time, therefore best practice in design takes such users into account. Newbies might be an element of the **rule of one**.

News aggregator

See **content aggregator.**

Newsgroup

A **USENET** discussion group related to one topic. Internet users can subscribe to many different newsgroups. Major newsgroup categories include:

- alt: alternative discussions on a wide variety of topics;
- comp: computer-related information and discussion;
- misc: miscellaneous categories;
- news: issues concerning USENET and newsgroups;
- rec: recreational activities, such as movies, books, sports, etc.;
- sci: science news and information;
- soc: topics related to sociology and psychology.

Actual subjects covered within these groups know no bounds, with some topics seeming bizarre to the majority of the population.

NIC (Networked Information Center)

Generally, the term used to describe any office that handles information for a network. The most famous of these on the Internet is the **InterNIC**.

Niche marketing

The practice of finding and serving small, but potentially profitable, market segments. Niche marketing is normally the domain of small businesses (SMEs) who are better equipped to deal with fewer customers who have specific buying needs. Because they concentrate on a limited range of products or services, the SME can offer greater and deeper expertise in those products, so presenting a better service to customers. With the notable exceptions of the likes of Amazon and some of the major bricks-and-mortar retailers who have an online presence, it is with niche markets that most web sites have found success – the ability of the Internet to reach a wide market, with relatively little expense being the key. It is the concept of niche marketing to which the **long tail** theory applies.

See also **niche product.**

Niche product

A product that is sought by only a small number of customers. Although sales volume for sellers of niche products is small, potential profit is high. Niche sellers normally offer a high level of expertise in the product or service they offer, something that allows the seller to demand premium prices. Large manufacturers normally eschew niche products, as the opportunity for economies of scale are limited.

See also **niche marketing.**

Node

Any single computer connected to a **network**.

Nofollow

A **tag** used on web pages, often mistakenly as a command to prevent a web site being indexed by a search engine (the correct method for that being a **robots.txt** file). The nofollow tag is actually a message to the search engine robots (or **spiders**) telling them that the link in question was not necessarily a **trusted link** put there by the owner of the site. The main reason for the inception of the nofollow tag was to thwart **blog spam**.

N

Nominet

The licensing authority for the UK's ccTLD domain name registry. The Oxford-based organization also runs an arbitration procedure for disputed .uk domain names.

See also **DNS**.

Non-standard link

Good **usability** practice dictates that all **links** should be obvious to the users; for example, textual links should be in coloured, underlined text. Non-standard links are those which are not obvious to the user – that is, they do not follow accepted practice and common expectation.

N

Offline

See **online** (1) and **online** (2).

OLGA (the Online Lead Generation Association)

A not-for-profit company, set up at the end of 2005, to promote best practices and standards among web sites, marketers and **lead generation** providers.

One-click purchasing

Although the patent for the technology involved was challenged in court, Amazon are generally recognized as the first practitioners of the one-click online shopping experience. The concept is that when a customer has registered with the vendor and made an initial purchase, the vendor has all the information necessary (credit-card number, delivery address, etc.) for that customer to make subsequent purchases. For any future purchases, the buyer identifies the product(s) they want to buy and simply clicks on one 'buy now' command button. The system then completes the purchase and **fulfilment** using the data already held on record. The one-click purchase is an integral element of **pursuasive architecture**.

Online (on-line) (1)

The term used to describe the state of a computer being connected to something, including the Internet. **Hardware** can be offline or online – a printer and a PC, for example, can be connected (online), or not connected (offline). When a connection is broken or disconnected it becomes offline.

Online (on-line) (2)

In e-commerce terms, and in this book, online and offline are used to describe something that is either on the Internet (online), or not on the

Internet (offline). For example, offline shopping is the practice of shopping without the use of the Internet (also sometimes referred to as *traditional* shopping) – as opposed to online shopping, where retail purchases are made using the Internet. It has become common practice to use **online (as a prefix)** generically to describe any Internet-related function, online marketing, for example.

See also **online (1)**.

Online (as a prefix)

In an e-commerce environment it is common practice to prefix a word, term or phrase with *online* to denote its practice or application in an Internet environment – *online* branding, for example. Much the same can be said of 'cyber', 'e' – and to a lesser extent 'digital' – as prefixes. Why some terms gained the prefix 'online', 'cyber' or 'e' is based on chance and/or personal preference (and thereafter, custom and practice) rather than any kind of logical explanation. For some terms, the prefixes used are frequently interchanged – online marketing and e-marketing, for example. In this text the selection of prefix is based on either most-common practice, or in the case of equal use, the author's own preference.

See also **cyber (as a prefix)**, **e (as a prefix)** and **digital (as a prefix)**.

Online advertising

The term used to describe the use of the Internet as a medium for hosting ads (as in *TV* advertising, *radio* advertising, etc.). This includes all types of advertising on all types of web sites as well as emails and **blogs**. Though not universally accepted, it is also argued that a web site that does not offer any kind of transactional facilities is simply promoting the organization, product or service and is, therefore, an advertisement. A further complication of the concept of advertising *on* the Internet is where Internet technology is used to transport an ad, yet the viewer would not identify the ad as being seen on the Internet – that is, on a computer. For example, if a user sees an ad on their **PDA**, is that *online* advertising, *Internet* advertising or *mobile* advertising? Furthermore, Internet technology can be responsible for the delivery of dynamic messaging seen on the street, in lifts (elevators), and in public washrooms –are these *Internet* ads? Further complication is added by crossovers of technology. For example, if a user watches a TV programme on their computer, are any ads shown *TV* ads or *online* ads? They are in a TV show, but transmitted by Internet technology. Further technical developments in this area may serve to clarify or only confuse the issue further.

Online advertising network

A network of brokers, or aggregators, of **online advertising** inventory. While some **web publishers** handle the sale of all of their advertising space themselves – if they choose to do so – it is rare for them to sell 100 per cent of what they have available. Other publishers, particularly small ones, find it easier to not even try to sell their ad space themselves. This is where the ad network specialist comes in, acting as the conduit between those who have advertising space and those who wish to advertise. The advertiser can stipulate the types of web site on which they wish their ads to run, or they can use a *blind network* where they do not know the exact places where their ads are being run. The first is more expensive, but the advertising is better targeted, and so should be more productive. The online ad network would normally use its own **ad server** to deliver the ads.

Online auction

An auction conducted online using Internet technology. Though popularized by the media as a **B2C** and **C2C** phenomenon (eBay, for example), it is a common practice in the **B2B** environment.

See also **forward auction** and **reverse auction**.

Online banking

See **e-banking**.

Online branding

Branding and the Internet are associated in three significant ways:

- Branding online – as a medium of communication the Internet can be included in any branding efforts the organization might undertake. Although a web site should always be considered as an important aspect of the organization's brand, it is becoming more common for the web or email to be integral to branding strategies.
- The online brand – also known as the digital brand, where a company uses a different brand for its Internet marketing than that used in its offline environment. This is common among banks and credit cards, the Co-op Bank and smile.co.uk and the Prudential and egg.com, for example.
- The pure online brand – where an organization trades as an online

O

entity only, those businesses will be a brand in their own right; Yahoo and Amazon, for example.

Online buyer behaviour

Traditional, offline, buyer behaviour considers: who buys, how do they buy, when do they buy, where do they buy and why do they buy? The answers to these questions might depend on:

- psychological factors, such as the customer's perceptions of the product or business, their motives for the purchase, the benefits sought from the purchase, their personality and their learning;
- social factors, such as the customer's social class, culture and family role.

If the marketer can appreciate these issues better than the competition it is a potentially significant source of competitive advantage. When considering the ways in which consumers behave on the Internet there are two key aspects of online behaviour that can be monitored to help assess that customer's behaviour:

- explicit behaviour – based on data provided by the user. This would include such things as a user profile if membership or registration details are required to access the site or make a purchase. Also included would be any recorded actions on the site, like signing up for an e-newsletter or placing an order;
- implied behaviour – based on data derived from the observation of a user's actions as they interact with the site.

The collection and analysis of buyer-behaviour data provides the under-pinning for the concept of **contextual and behavioural targeting**.

This definition is based on, or cites, content by the author in Gay, R., Charlesworth, A. and Esen, R., *Online Marketing: A Customer Led-Approach*. Oxford: Oxford University Press, 2007.

O

Online buying cycle

Offline, the buying cycle follows the purchaser's path from recognizing that they want or need a product through to its purchase. The *online* buying cycle suggests that, although rare, it is possible that a *purely* online buying cycle can exist. Facilitated by interactive advertising, a person *could* go online, recognize that a problem exists, seek information on solutions to that problem, evaluate the alternatives identified in the search and take action to solve that problem. If this is the case, then the online marketer should not only be aware of the concept, but be prepared to take advantage of it. The marketer should also be aware that in contemporary marketing, online activities are part of the (overall) buying cycle, with purchasers having the potential to use the web at all stages of the buying cycle. To help marketers ensure that a customer's path along the buying cycle is unhindered they can use the **AIDA** model. **Persuasion architecture** owes at least some of its origins to the online buying cycle. The *pure* online buying cycle is one element of the **online purchase behaviour matrix**.

Online community

See **virtual community.**

Online credibility

Offline, customers are reluctant to do business with a vendor who has no credibility – online, the same applies. The difference is that online, any judgement on credibility can only be made based on the content of the web site. While measurement of credibility can be apportioned to specific elements of a site (no contact details, for example, does nothing to inspire confidence), visitors actually form an impression of the organization based on the whole of the experience they have whilst navigating the site. Stanford University has a 'Persuasive Technology Lab' which applies scientific research to the web by accessing the credibility of web sites in the Stanford Web Credibility Research Centre (http://credibility.stanford.edu). In 2002 the Centre published ten credibility guidelines based on three years of research:

1 Make it easy to verify the accuracy of the information on your site.
2 Show that there's a real organization behind your site.
3 Highlight the expertise in your organization and in the content and services you provide.
4 Show that honest and trustworthy people stand behind your site.
5 Make it easy to contact you.
6 Design your site so it looks professional (or is appropriate for your purpose).
7 Make your site easy to use – and useful.
8 Update your site's content often.
9 Use restraint with any promotional content (for example, ads, offers).
10 Avoid errors of all types, no matter how small they seem.

O

While a number of these could be viewed as subjective (for example in 6, what is *professional*?), they do represent the primary concerns with regard to online credibility. That the same points are likely to appear in a 'good practice' guide for any e-commerce web site emphasizes the intrinsic importance of credibility to online trading.

See also **online reputation management.**

Online customizing

See **online personalization.**

Online event

See **reverse auction.**

Online focus group

The criteria for the online focus group is the same as that for its offline contemporary – to gather qualitative research data on consumers' attitudes and perceptions about a product or brand. Rather than attending a group discussion in a physical facility, online focus groups log in to a virtual environment and use chat-room-type facilities to express opinions on subjects raised by a moderator. The obvious advantage over offline groups is that of reduced cost, though it is possible that greater geographical representation and participants being more inclined to give honest opinions while in their own environment (home) are also positives.

Online incentive marketing (OIM)

A practice that sits, sometimes uncomfortably, between referral schemes, **viral marketing** and pyramid sales schemes – online incentive marketing is a legitimate and lucrative method of customer acquisition. Often recognized for its association with 'free iPods', the first successful campaign attributed to the concept, OIM is popular with 18- to 24-year-olds who use the Internet as an integral part of their **social network**. The concept is simple: take individuals and offer them a gift (where the iPod comes in) if they can introduce x amount of customers, or **prospects**, to the organization. The *online* element stems from the fact that the *lead generators* use chat rooms and emails to pass on the marketing message and so earn themselves a gift.

Online individualization of products

A close affiliate of **online personalization** – so much so that they might easily be interchanged – online individualization of products applies more to products individually manufactured for the end user. For example, Timberland's 'Bootstudio' (www.timberland.com) allows buyers to 'build a boot as original as you are', which includes adding the buyer's own monogram. It should be noted, however, that individualized products are made up from a set pattern rather than being bespoke.

Online marketing

As with the use of both 'e' and 'online' as a prefix to other words and terms, in the case of marketing both terms – e-marketing and online marketing – are normally accepted as being the same thing, and so are interchangeable. Essentially, the terms refer to any aspect of the discipline of marketing that is performed or practised in an Internet environment. However, like their offline equivalents, most aspects are known by their function, with e-marketing being the parent of the family which includes, but is not necessarily limited to **advergaming, affiliate marketing, database marketing, e-CRM, email marketing, etailing, online branding, online market research, online advertising, permission marketing, search engine marketing**.

Online marketplace

See **e-marketplace**.

Online market research

As students the world over have discovered, the Internet is an excellent medium for conducting research, and it is the same for market research. The Internet can be used for both primary and secondary research:

- Primary: Questionnaires being distributed by email as well as being included on web pages. Mini surveys ensconced in other content within a web page. Easy-to-use feedback facilities to encourage customer replies.
- Secondary sources include: competitors' web sites, industry **portals** and **consumer-generated media** sites. Published information is also available online, including both government (for example the DTI) and commercial (for example Mintel reports).

Marketing managers can also use the web to seek out new customers, new markets and ideas for new products and services.

Online personalization of products

The advent of the Internet has allowed businesses to offer customers personalized products that do not require the personal contact normally associated with mass customization. Using the web, consumers can personalize their product remotely – not only from the comfort of their own home or workplace, but without any pressure or influence from a salesperson. In addition, because online selection and ordering are relatively inexpensive for the vendor to offer, the price of personalized products can be reduced. The concept of using the web as a medium for mass personalization has, however, limited application. Not least is the issue that manufacturers are so used to dealing with customers through intermediaries – wholesalers/retailers/agents – that they are ill-equipped to deal directly with end-users. Also, manufacturers soon learned that selling direct to customers online could alienate offline distribution channel members, so compromising offline sales – see **channel conflict**. In essence, there are only two types of business that can benefit from using the web in a mass customization strategy:

1 The manufacturer that has no bricks-and-mortar distribution channel: Dell Computers, for example.
2 The intermediary that takes component parts of a product from various suppliers and offers the buyer a choice of multiple combinations: the travel/holiday industry, for example.

See also **online individualization of products.**

Online purchase behaviour matrix

A consideration of how the contemporary shopper might go about researching, purchasing and taking possession of goods in the modern shopping environment. Note that this matrix includes only those activities that are completed purely online. If offline elements are included – a customer going to a bricks-and-mortar store for any of the three activities, for example – the matrix increases to around thirty possibilities, and that does not include such things as the use of the telephone to make product enquiries. Similarly, the matrix makes no consideration in the 'research' element to how many web sites a user might visit in doing that research, including the use of **shopping search engines.** The matrix is important in that it not only makes vendors aware of the options open to web-enabled shoppers, but guides them on how they should manage their marketing in order to make these options available to their customers. Failure to do so could result in customers using the organization to gain information (research) but not make the purchase from them. It would be used in tandem with the **conversion funnel**.

The online purchase behaviour matrix.

Research	Purchase	Fulfilment	Purchased from
online	online	home delivery	same vendor that provided the original information
online	online	home delivery	different vendor to that which provided the original information
online	online	online	same vendor that provided the original information
online	online	online	different vendor to that which provided the original information

Adapted from R. Gay, A. Charlesworth and R. Esen, *Online Marketing: A Customer-Led Approach*. Oxford: Oxford University Press, 2007.

Online reputation management

Where **online credibility** considers the web site from in a static context (that is, information provided within the site's content), reputation management considers credibility from an ongoing standpoint. The practice of online reputation management involves the monitoring of all web sites that feature **consumer-generated media** in order to track – and, if appropriate, respond to – any adverse comments about the organization, brand or product that might be made on those sites. In a wider context, online reputation management might be seen as an aspect of brand management.

See also **cyberbashing** and **RSS tracker**.

Online social shopping

An element of **consumer-generated media**, this is where users visit a dedicated web site to give their opinions of all kinds of goods. Unlike the more formal review-type sites, the online social shopping sites are less formal – to the degree that detractors refer to the content as gossip. In essence, however, the concept is designed to promote discussion between like-minded individuals about shopping for and buying a wide variety of goods in much the same way as they might do while social shopping in an offline environment.

Online tender

Although the online business community often favour the term **reverse auction** for this practice, the use of Internet technology to open tendering to a wider audience is one of the business successes of the medium. Tendering (offline) has been a staple of business practice for as long as business has been carried out. Associated more with major contracts and both local and national governments, the concept is that the buyer makes available the specifications and criteria of the product or service they wish to purchase. Potential suppliers then put forward their proposal – tender – for the contract as a sealed bid, so that its details are not known to other bidders. After a submission date is reached the buyer reviews each tender and awards the work to the most suitable. The significant benefits that the Internet brought to the practice are that:

- When posted on a web site the jobs are more widely available, not only nationally, but internationally.
- The medium makes it easier for joint tenders, with different organizations using the web and email to contact and liase with other companies who can provide complementary expertise. Many B2B or industry **portals** facilitate contact between organizations that might work together in putting forward tenders.
- Online applications mean that the paperwork involved is reduced. The EU's tendering system, for example, allows frequent bidders to store information and reproduce it for multiple bids rather than completing a full application for every proposal.

Online trading business models

See **Rappa's Online Trading Business Models.**

Open Directory Project

According to its web site, this is 'the largest, most comprehensive human-edited directory of the Web'. Developed and maintained by a global community of volunteer editors, it aims to follow in the footsteps of the *Oxford English Dictionary* to become 'the definitive catalog of the Web'. It can be found on www.dmoz.org.

Open rate

See **email open rate.**

Open source

Although some might argue that open source is more of a philosophy or way of working, it is more commonly known for its reference to software that is freely available and that the creators are not only happy for others to use it, but modify the source code for their own purposes. It is not unusual for groups of enthusiasts to work on a project remotely in order to develop or perfect products to be made available in open source.

See also **crowdsourcing.**

Open source content

Web site content whose author is happy for other people to use uncredited. Effectively, the author has relinquished **copyright** on the work. This is extremely rare – even online – though many authors give permission for their content to be used providing a reference and link to the originating web site are given. This is a common practice (a) as a marketing tactic to promote the author and/or their business, and (b) to create **inbound links** that may improve **search engine ranking** for the author's web site.

Opt-in/opt-out

Generally, opt-in/opt-out is an agreement that requires users to take specific steps to *allow* or *prevent* collection of information. In an e-commerce context, the terms are applied primarily to:

(a) **email marketing**, specifically **email lists** (and whether people agree to be on them or not, and so either agree or not, to accept emails from an organization); and

(b) data collection for **database marketing**. Note that not only are the following aspects of business practice, but in some parts, they are a legal requirement; see **EU Directive on Privacy and Electronic Communications**.

Adaptations of *opt-out* include:

- Users are added to the list without their express permission. They remain there until they request to be removed. It is not considered 'ethical' practice to simply keep sending emails until the recipient finally loses patience and takes action to opt-out. More ethical practice is to communicate the situation to the user, with an option to opt-in or out included in that message.
- Users are propositioned with joining a mailing list – perhaps as part of an online purchase procedure. There are two routes for the marketer to take: (a) the user must **check a box** to agree, or (b) they must check a box to decline. In the latter, no action equals tacit agreement, and so is questionable from an ethical standpoint.

Adaptations of *opt-in* include:

- Single opt-in – where recipients are added to a list through a single subscription-type act (e.g. sending an email to a specific address). Subsequently, no confirmation is sent, or the subscription verified. Potential problems with this model include that it can be (a) open to abuse in that third parties can subscribe innocent users – either as a joke or with malicious intent; (b) subject to false subscription, where users feel they are being coerced into giving an email address – so they simply enter a false one; or (c) used in list poisoning, where a **trap address** is deliberately subscribed – the intention being to have the senders (those gathering emails for the opt-in list) penalized as **spammers**.
- Notified opt-in – an extension of the single opt-in, this is where recipients are added to a list through a single subscription-type act, then an email is sent to notify them of their addition and to enable them to opt-out if they wish. Note that action needs to be taken to opt-out, inertia results in the recipient staying on the list. All of the potential problems raised above still stand, though the notified opt-in can mitigate against them to a degree.
- Confirmed, or *double*, opt-in – after recipients are added to a list through a subscription-type act, a confirmation message is sent to the address and an affirmative action must be taken to activate the subscription, e.g. a positive response to that email, or clicking on a 'confirm subscription' link. The confirmed opt-in is the preferred model of the anti-spam community. Because recipients have to perform two actions to join a list, false or mistaken subscription is virtually impossible. For marketers the ethically sound double opt-in method produces the most robust email lists, but they will,

inevitably, be smaller. Unethical practice – like opt-out – might bring short-term success, but will ultimately damage the reputation of the organization.

There is a third option that falls somewhere between opt-in and opt-out, and it is identified in the **EU Directive on Privacy and Electronic Communications** as a 'soft opt-in'. This is where emails are sent 'in the course of a sale or negotiations for the sale of a product or service' and so can be deemed to have 'actively expressed an interest in purchasing a company's product and services'. If this is the case, unsolicited emails can be sent until such a time that receiver opts-out of receiving more. However, good practice would suggest that after the immediate sale or negotiation the receiver should be offered a single opt-in (as above).

Opt-in list

See **email list (1)**.

Opt-out

See **opt-in/opt-out**.

Order acquisition ratio

A **metric** used in **web site analytics**, this is the **cost per order** divided by the **cost per visit**.

Order confirmation

In e-commerce terms this is an email message notifying a customer that an order has been received and will be processed. Rather than a bland statement, this email should be considered as an element of marketing communication and be treated as part of a **CRM** programme.

Organic listings

Listings that appear in a **search engine results page** based purely on the content of that web site – and not because a payment has been made for that site to appear in the listing. Hence they are organic (natural) rather than manufactured (paid for). To achieve organic listing is the objective of **search engine optimization**.

See also **search engine marketing, paid placement, paid search** and **paid inclusion**.

Organic search

The use of a search engine purely for **organic listings**.

Orphan page

A page that (a) does not link back to the main site of which it is a part, (b) has no content, or (c) that no longer exists – a page at the end of a **broken link**.

Outbound link

See **link**.

Overture

See **paid search**.

O

P2P (people-to-people or peer-to-peer trading)

See **C2C**.

P4P (pay for performance)

See **pay per click**.

Packet

The name given to a bundle of data that travels the Internet. Effectively, the division of data into packets and their transfer from sender to receiver is the basis of the Internet. At the time of the Cold War the US military wanted to develop a system of communication that would still work in the event of a nuclear attack. Normal methods of communication rely on a single line, and if that is broken, communication ceases. The **ARPANET** system broke up the data into multiple bundles and dispatched it on multiple lines to its destination – if one or more lines were broken the packets sought out other unbroken paths. When the various packets reached their destination they were 'reassembled' to make up the complete message. This practice of moving packets around the web is called packet switching. An additional advantage of the system – for contemporary Internet users – is that many people can use the same lines at the same time, and if one line gets overloaded the packet is switched to a different one.

Packet filters

Applications that can accept or reject incoming *packets*. Any rejection or decision to accept the packet can be made based on the **IP addresses** of the source and destination of the packets.

Packet Internet Gopher

See **PING**.

Packet switching

See packet.

Page counters

Software applications that count the **visitors** or **hits** on the web site on which they are placed. Widely available online at no charge, page counters were ubiquitous in the early days of the web, but are now rare. They will normally sit at the bottom of a site's **homepage**, and might identify themselves as such, or simply be a box containing a series of numbers. Early expectations were that visitors would read that 'thousands' of users had visited the site and so perceive it to contain valuable information. Users are now more educated in the way that the web works and pay little, or no, notice to these counters. Note that commercial sites should employ more accurate methods of collecting **metrics** for any **web site analytics**.

Page impression

The downloading of one web page, also known as a *page view*. Normally single **impression** counts are irrelevant without that count being over a specific time period.

See also **ad impression**.

Page jacking

Where **content** (text or images) or **source code** from a web site are taken and used on another site by someone who does not have permission to do so. The practice would normally be an offence against the laws of **copyright**.

See also **siphoning**.

PageRank

An element of the Google **algorithm**, a site's PageRank is assigned based on the number of incoming links pointing to that site. The more links to the site, the more 'valuable' it is assumed to be, and so the higher the rating. The intention [of the algorithm] is to reward sites that generate genuine, generic links to them. PageRank is named after its founder, Larry Page, one of the co-founders of Google, and was developed from Page's **BackRub** project. Like other elements of **search**

engine ranking, however, the system is open to abuse, with **black-hat SEO**s manufacturing links to increase a site's rank. An attempt to address this is **TrustRank** which assesses the quality (rather than just quantity) of links going into a web site. Hence only sites considered authoritative and/or relevant to the linked site are used in assigning PageRank. Google's **Jagger** update went a stage further by devaluing some sites where there is obvious reciprocal linking. Note that the patent for PageRank is owned Stanford University, where Page was studying when he developed the algorithm.

See also **link popularity** and **reciprocal link.**

Page request

When a user selects – clicks on – a **link,** or they type a **URL** into a web **browser**, that user is requesting the page that is the target of that link – they are making a *page request.*

Page view

A metric used in **web site analytics**, a page view is – as the name suggests – a count of how many times a page has been viewed by a user. A more accurate term that is used more often to describe the same thing is **page impression**, which refers to how many times a page has been **downloaded**. This is because *view* projects the notion that the page content has been read by the user who has downloaded it, which is not always the case.

See also **visitor.**

Paid-for emails

See **sender certification.**

Paid inclusion (or pay *for* inclusion)

Where web site pages are guaranteed to be included in a search engine or directory's index in exchange for payment. Note the guarantee is only for inclusion in the index, not a guarantee of a high **search engine ranking**, which is based on **organic listing**. Organizations pay for their pages to be included on a **CPC** basis or per-**URL** fee basis, with no guarantee of specific placement.

P

Paid links (1)

This is where a web site's publishers offer to add an outgoing **link** to non-affiliated sites for a fee. This service can only be successfully offered by web sites that are recognized by the search engines as being reputable – making links from them to be deemed **trusted links**, so making them useful to the web site that is buying the link. The practice is rare in that it might be considered unethical by the search engines (and humans) and so penalize the selling site in their **algorithms**. A notable example of the practice is that of Harvard University, who have offered paid links from their site.

Paid links (2)

An alternative term used to describe the practice of **paid placement** of ads on web pages other than search engine results pages.

Paid listings

See **paid placement.**

Paid placement

An ad program where listings are guaranteed to appear in a **search engine response page** (SERP) for particular search terms, with higher ranking obtained by paying more than other advertisers. Paid placement listings (identified on the SERP as sponsored links, sponsored matches or **sponsored listings** to differentiate them from the **organic listings**) are purchased from a portal or a search network (Overture and Google are the largest), with each **keyword** being auctioned to the bidder who offers the highest sum per click. The winning bidder will then pay that sum for each click on the listing. Because they react to **metadata**, ads placed on SERPs are sometimes known as meta ads. It is worth noting that the major search engines recognize that simply publishing the highest bidder's entry does not always best satisfy the individual searcher's needs. For example, an **adult site** might pitch the highest bid on an innocent, non-related term. To combat this, paid search ad placement also takes into account the relevance of both the web site and **landing pages** of organizations that bid for placement (Google's control mechanism for this is called *Quality Score* and Yahoo's, *Project Panama*). Sometimes called *paid links*, the same ad programs are used to place ads (text and banner) on web sites other than SERPs. Any **web publisher** can feature such ads on web pages where the products or services being advertised can be matched to the subject of the page's content.

See also **paid search.**

Paid search

In this case the 'pay' is on the part of the business which pays for their web site to be listed in search engine results. The concept is accredited to Bill Gross, who launched the first paid search engine in September 1998 – GoTo.com. At the time, search engines were inundated with **spam** – particularly from **adult web sites** (it is generally recognized that pornography and gambling sites have always been at the leading edge of any developments in search engine manipulation). Gross thought the only way to combat spam was to have businesses pay to have their sites listed. This would lead to users being more likely to use a spam-free engine and, more importantly for GoTo, far greater income from **pay per click** advertising – which would replace the **CPM** (cost per thousand impressions) method more common at the time. Gross realized that the inherent value of **intentional traffic** was far greater than that of **undifferentiated traffic**. He also realized that some **key words** and phrases were more valuable than others, so ad prices were not fixed, but varied depending on demand. GoTo's business model was a form of arbitrage – 'the purchase of currencies or commodities in one market for immediate resale in others in order to profit from unequal prices' (*Collins Dictionary*). In this online arbitrage, GoTo purchased links from other sites (Netscape, for example) for a flat rate per click in a CPM deal, and then resold those clicks on a PPC rate on its own site. For example, a link on Netscape for the key phrase 'domain name registration' might be purchased (as part of a much larger package) for 10 cents per click. This would take users to the GoTo **seach engine results page** (SERP) for 'domain name registration' that would list a number of advertisers who wished users to visit their web site in order to register a domain name. In order to drive **differentiated traffic** to their sites, the domain name registrars would attempt to outbid their rivals for the top spot (or higher listings) in the GoTo SERP – each of these advertisers paying far more than 10 cents for any **clickthrough**. The result was arbitrage-style profit for GoTo. Although the GoTo model of paid-only search still exists (GoTo became Overture in September 2001), the concept is now more common as part of a SERP, where organic search results are listed separately to those that have been paid for.

See also **paid placement.**

P

Paid to read rings

See **click fraud**.

Panel van web sites

See **white van web sites.**

Parallel browsing

A term used to describe the practice of having more than one browser window open on a user's screen, with multiple web sites being viewed at the same time. For example, one window for **surfing** and another that features updated sports scores, or viewing multiple sites at the same time to draw comparisons with their content – hotels or cars, perhaps. Larger computer screens better facilitate parallel browsing. Note that the same term can be applied to more general computer use; for example, using spreadsheet and word-processor windows simultaneously.

Pas 78 (Publicly Available Specification 78)

A set of guidelines for web site accessibility developed by the Disability Rights Commission (DRC) in collaboration with the British Standards Institute. Reviewed by accessibility experts and advocates, Pas 78 also has support from the RNIB and input from organizations such as the BBC, IBM and Tesco.

See also **bobby.**

Passing off

A legal term used when one individual or entity pretends to be – *passes itself off as* – another. In an e-commerce environment it is laws based on this principle that prevent individuals (or entities) registering the domain name of another company and using that name to host a web site selling similar products to those of the 'passed-off' organization.

See also **cybersquatting.**

Password

Something of a misnomer in that a password need not be a *word*, but a series of characters that allows a user to access a resource via a computer. This could be the computer system itself, a file, a program or a web site. Unlike a **login**, which may be public knowledge, a password should be confidential to the user.

Password dictionary attack

See **dictionary attack (1)**.

Patriot Act

An Act introduced into the US Congress shortly after the 11 September 2001 attacks. As a US law it has no direct effect on non-US citizens except that it allows officials to intercept communications from outside the USA addressed to anyone inside the country – including reading emails. The full application, and implications, of the Act are still being argued in the US courts and press and it is included here for its potential implications on **email marketing**.

Pay for performance

See **pay per click**.

Pay for placement

See **paid placement**.

Payment service provider (PSP)

A third-party service used predominantly by small businesses to allow them to offer customers online purchase facilities. The PSP would connect the trader's e-commerce system to appropriate banking service providers – with whom the PSP will be registered to ensure the integrity of the operation.

P

Pay per –

It is worth noting that in many elements of **e-metrics** *cost* per – and *pay* per – (for example cost per order, pay per click) are used almost at what seems like random. Effectively the two terms mean the same – that is, how much the advertiser pays per click or how much each click costs. Quite why *pay* or *cost* is applied to different terms can only be down to custom and practice. Perhaps the future will see finite definitions for these terms, but in the meantime they are interchangeable.

Pay per call

Where an online ad – or associated web site – features a freephone number, software tracks any contacts made through that number and a fee is paid for each call. The fee charged for pay per call is higher than other pay for performance models, but the advantage to the advertiser is that callers are more likely to be quality leads and so the chances of achieving a sale are also much greater. The model is enabled by **click to call** technology.

Pay per click (PPC)

A method paying for **online advertising** in which the advertiser pays on performance by paying for each **click** made on the ad; that is, no clicks, no fee. The system is also known as CPC (cost per click) and CPA (cost per action). The system works like this. An advertiser specifies the **keywords** that they wish to trigger their ads and the maximum amount (rate) they are willing to pay for each click that a user makes on that ad. The advertiser that puts forward the highest bid (in an auction-based system) for a specified keyword featured highest in the list of 'sponsored links' – that is, those links on the **search engine results page** (SERP) which are not **organic listings**. When a user puts a search term (keyword) into a search engine the SERP includes not only organic listings that match their search term, but also the PPC listings that are, in effect, ads. Note, however, that some search engines add to the basic premise of the highest bidder winning the highest ranking. Google's AdWords, for example, builds the relative clickthrough rates of the ads into the equation in order that well-targeted, relevant ads are listed higher.

The same scenario is repeated on web sites that feature PPC ads provided by an **online advertising network** as an element of a **paid placement** strategy. In these cases the delivered ads match keywords featured in the content of the web page; for example, vehicle insurance on a car-related web site.

Pay per click can give marketers better **metrics** on their advertising spend in that the consumer must take an action – the *click* – that indicates that they have read the ad. For example, a vendor selling designer handbags might pay around 30p for each user who clicks on an online ad. A full-page ad in a magazine like *Cosmopolitan* might cost around £50,000, but the magazine might have a circulation of half a million people – a cost of only 10p per reader, a third of the PPC cost. The difference, however, is that the 30p outlay on the click is more likely to produce a sale than the 10p 'exposure' in the magazine. Not only that, but the online marketer can count how many users have clicked on the link – the magazine advertiser (or publisher) has no idea of how many readers even noticed the ad, much less took heed of its message. The model is open to abuse, however, from **click fraud**.

The main players in PPC advertising are the foremost search engines who all have their own PPC ad networks. They are Google AdWords, Yahoo! search marketing and MSN AdCenter.

Pay per click scammers

See **click fraud**.

Pay per click search engines

See **paid placement**.

Pay per impression (PPI)

An **online advertising** model where the advertiser pays an agreed amount for the number of times their ad is downloaded on a web site, regardless of the user's subsequent action. Early online advertising used this method extensively, mainly due to its application in offline media. Like its offline cousin, the problem is that only the user knows whether or not they have actually seen the ad, let alone read it. This lack of accountability has seen PPI mainly replaced by the **pay per click** model. PPI, however, does still have viable applications. Raising brand awareness, for example, where the objective is to get the brand name, logo or message seen, and not necessarily having the viewer click on the **banner** is best suited to this method of advertising. Like pay per click, the model is open to abuse; see **spam web sites**.

Pay per review

A model adopted by *human-reviewed* directories and search engines that allows web site owners to 'jump the queue' for having their site reviewed. The practice dates back to the early days of the commercial web where directories such as Yahoo! (it was originally a directory, not a search engine) were inundated with submissions for sites to be reviewed – for free – and so be added to the directory. To overcome this, the directories offered to review sites on demand, but only for a fee. Note, however, that users pay for the review, and there is no guarantee of inclusion if the site does not meet the criteria of the directory.

P

PDA (personal digital assistant)

A hand-held personal computer. As technology evolves, many devices fall under this generic description, including **smartphones**.

PDF (portable document format)

A file format that reproduces documents in an electronic form so that they can be sent, viewed and printed exactly as they originally appeared. A significant advantage of PDF files is that they are difficult to change, and therefore reduce plagiarism of the content (users cannot easily cut and paste the content). Most web users will use the Adobe Acrobat reader to open PDF files.

Perfect search

The utopian ideal pursued by search engineers. The concept is that the searcher doesn't simply get *an* accurate answer to a search, they get *their* perfect answer to a search – one that matches the context and intent of the search.

See also **intelligent search**.

Permission-based email

Term used to describe email campaigns where mailings are sent only to those recipients who have given their permission for those mailings to be sent to them.

See also **opt-in/opt-out**.

Permission marketing

Another element of offline marketing that has transferred easily to the online environment. Traditionally, permission marketing referred to aspects of marketing that deviate from advertising (it being a **push medium** and therefore not permission-based); customers who request brochures, for example. While similar requests can be made online, it is with email marketing that *permission* is most closely associated. This is as a consequence of the **opt-in** aspect of **permission-based email**.

Personalization (1)

See **online personalization of products**.

Personalization (2)

See web site personalization.

Persuasion architecture

The notion that a web site can be constructed in such a way as to convince (persuade) visitors to take a series of desired actions – for example, to follow links from the home page through to placing an order for a product. The term has been popularized by Bryan Eisenburg, who advocates that sites should be developed using the perspective of the customer as the driving force. Persuasion architecture has close links with the **conversion funnel**, **usability**, **navigation**, and the **call to action**, and has its foundations in the **AIDA** concept. Note that the term *persuasion architecture* has been trademarked by Bryan Eisenburg.

Persuasive momentum

A close associate of **persuasion architecture**, persuasive momentum is the intangible influence that keeps customers moving forward through the web site in their buying process by the skilful use of well-crafted copy, trigger words, calls to action and the conversion funnel. As with many aspects of e-commerce, the concept of online persuasive momentum is based on tried and tested offline practice. In this case, that practice is a common sales tactic where momentum is created during personal sales – with the customer being almost obliged to say yes to the purchase as a result of being swept up in the momentum of the sales process. The online version has similar objectives.

PFI (pay for inclusion)

See paid inclusion.

Pharming

An extension of **phishing** that sends emails containing **malware** programs that redirect the user's browser to a fake web site. The sequence of events is this. The pharming software recognizes a specific URL, normally of a bank, and when it is typed in to the browser the user is redirected (see **domain name pointing**) to the fake site, which is designed to look like the genuine site. The user is then tricked into logging into their bank account – so revealing their security details to the fraudsters.

P

Phishing

A type of scam that uses bogus emails designed to deceive customers into revealing personal financial data. The email will normally purport to be from the user's bank and report a security breach or problem with the bank's database that requires the user to re-enter their security details by following a link on the email to a bogus web site. Although the original concept of phishing was to direct users to a fraudulent web site, the term has been extended to include all email-derived swindles, including those like the **419 scam**. Spear-phishing is highly targeted phishing. The same concept is also applied to **VIOP** (voice over Internet) phone calls where the bogus message is delivered by a person via a phone call – this has been dubbed *vishing*.

Phrase search

A search for documents containing an exact sentence or phrase specified by a user.

> *See also* **Boolean search** – the antithesis of a phrase search.

Piggyback email

A practice from **email marketing**, a piggyback email is something of a misnomer in that the term is used to describe an *ad* that piggybacks *on* an email. The concept is that emails sent to **opt-in** subscribers include ads from a third-party advertiser. As the practice can damage the email sender's credibility (and may lead to the receiver cancelling a subscription), ads must be carefully screened and should be for products or services that complement those of the email sender.

PING

A facility used primarily to determine if a computer is connected to the Internet. **Packets** of information with an 'echo' command are sent to a computer (or **server**) and a response tracked. No response means the target computer is not connected to the network. Hence the term to 'ping' a web site to see if it is live. Note that the term PING was applied by its founder, Michael Muus, because the program is an online equivalent of a sonar – which makes a 'ping' sound when an object is detected. Subsequently, others have 'converted' it into an acronym for *packet internet gopher*. More recently – because the practice has the same technological basis – the term has gained a common application when used to describe the notification of updated content sent out by blogs. For example, a blog will PING a search engine in the hope that the search engine will **spider** the new content and so update its **index**.

Pixel

The individual dots used to display images on computer monitors. The number of pixels per inch (PPI) determines the resolution of an image.

See also **dot pitch.**

PKI

See **public key infrastructure.**

Platform

In IT terms, a platform describes a framework on which **programs** can run, in other words, the hardware and software of the system. Windows XP, for example, is a platform. Cross-platform refers to applications that will run on different platforms.

Plog

A personalized log (hence P-log) that appears on the customer home page of Amazon.com. While Amazon might hope the concept is a success for the online store, the term is unlikely to spread beyond Amazon – they have trademarked it (Plog™).

Plug-in

A (usually small) piece of software that adds features to a larger piece of software. Plug-ins are often created by people other than the publishers of the software with which the plug-in will work.

Podcast (podcasting)

A term that has its origins in a combination of 'broadcasting' and '**iPod**' – making it something of a misnomer, as neither an *iPod* nor a *broadcast* is necessary. The concept is that audio versions of web site content (e.g. music, interviews, blogs or seminars) can be downloaded as an **MP3** file and replayed on any suitable personal audio (MP3) player. That iPods were fashionable at the time explains why 'pod' became part of the

P

descriptive term. Not only is Podcasting a new tool for the online marker to add to their communications toolbox, but it also offers the opportunities targeted for advertising – though obviously without the aid of any images. A video distributed using the same concept is known as a **vodcast**.

Pogo sticking

A term from search engine use, this describes how searchers bounce back forth from a **search engine results page (SERP)** to the various sites listed – clicking on sites in sequence – in an effort to find what they are looking for. The better the search results, the fewer bounces ther will be – with searchers sticking with the first (or early) listings if those sites satisfy their search needs.

Point of presence

See **POP**.

POP (point of presence)

Usually a city or location where a network can be connected to, often with dial-up phone lines. If an Internet company says they have a POP in Sunderland, it means that they have a local telephone number in Sunderland and/or a place where leased lines can connect to their network.

POP3 (Post Office Protocol version 3)

A **protocol** by which the majority of subscribers to individual **Internet service providers'** email accounts can access their email from a remote **server** over a **TCP/IP** connection – essentially, they can access their email from any Internet-connected computer.

Pop-under ad

A type of **pop-up** ad that loads *behind* a web page and so is not seen until the browser is closed. A pop-under ad is also known as a Superstitual™ – a brand name for the product. Although pop-unders are common on sites that seek to generate income through advertising, multiple pop-under ads are normally the province of **adult web sites**.

See also **pop-up ad** and **superstitual™**.

Pop-up ad

Although its actual name is an interstitial (meaning *in between*), this form of **banner** advertising is universally recognized, and usually derided, by the common term *pop-up*. An interstitial is an advertisement that appears in a separate web **browser** window while a web page loads. The pop-up appears over the top of the loading page, so making it visible immediately. Although consistently voted the second most annoying element of the Internet (after spam email), the ubiquitous pop-up is still an effective mode of **online advertising** if it is practised judiciously. Pop-ups are also called window ads they open a new window in the browser – though this term usually emanates from ad agencies who appreciate how negatively the term 'pop-up' is normally perceived.

See also **superstitual**.

Pop-up blocker

Software that can be downloaded on to a user's browser so that any **pop-up** ads on sites they might visit are disabled. Because it is pop-up *ads* that users wish to block, the software is also known as an ad-blocker.

Pop-up page

See **pop-up window**.

Pop-up window

Although the term pop-up is normally associated with **pop-up ads**, it has also become common practice to call any small browser window that opens over an already opened full-size browser window a *pop-up*. As the small browser window has content, it is also known as a pop-up *page*. The pop-up window can be made to open when a user *clicks* on a text or image, or simply when the mouse pointer hovers over it. **Frequently asked questions** pages can use this technique, the answers appearing in the pop-up window. They can also be used to good effect when moving away from a page would break the flow of **persuasive momentum** of a site. For example, if a user is completing a form, elements of that form might need some explanation to make questions clear – the link being perhaps a question-mark icon or text saying 'help' or 'more information'. Rather than forcing the user away from the partially completed form to another (full-size) page, a pop-up page can be used to clarify any issues, and the customer simply closes the pop-up page and continues with the form.

P

Portal

What is recognized as a portal has changed over the years. In the early days of the Internet, portals were seen as the *home* or *entry* page for users; that is, the page that first appears when the user opens a **browser** on their PC. In its truest sense, this page then becomes the user's portal (dictionary definition: entrance, gateway or access to a place) to the world wide web. As the web has developed, however, the term portal has come to be used in more wide-meaning contexts. Although still acting as portals, many web sites act as gateways to *limited* information rather than the whole of the web. Because the subject content of these *sub*-portals is finite, they attract only users who have an interest in those subjects (a sport or hobby, for example), and so often develop into an online – or 'virtual' – community. Organizations quickly realized that creating a direct dialogue with customers by making use of **virtual communities** could not only help maintain loyalty, but that commercial portal/community providers could create a club mentality amongst customers which might become a new source of competitive advantage. The two most common types of portal are those of **Internet service providers** and shopping (see also **shopping search engines**). These types of portals are businesses in their own right, but there are other categories that organizations can develop to attract potential customers to their products or services. These include:

- Geographical portals – where the product or service has a geographical association.
- Special interest portals – normally associated with a sport, hobby or pastime. Such sites could also be product-related. A grass-seed vendor might, for example, host a web site on lawn care that could develop into an online community, with users (or members) asking questions, raising issues or providing solutions to others' problems. Such is the nature of these sites that their users have been described as partaking in the practice of **social networking**. Note that it is common practice for the product seller to appear as sponsor of the site in order to distance themselves from their commercial interests behind the site (see also **sponsorship**).
- Information portals – commonly used in B2B trading, such portals attract workers in specific industries or users of certain products. Taken out of a directly competitive environment, it is not unusual for business owners and/or managers to be willing to offer help to other businesses, forming a **commercial network**.
- Exchange portals – another B2B application of the model, where portals are normally designed to appeal to a targeted audience. This

narrow targeting has led to many B2B portals being referred to as *vertical*, suggesting that the content runs *deep* rather than *wide*. The objective of exchange portals is to bring businesses together and so promote commercial exchanges, again, encouraging commercial networking. Exchange portals can be divided into five main types: (a) **catalogue services**, (b) searchable directories – where approved suppliers have been pre-vetted by the directory publishers, frequently industry bodies such as trade associations or Chambers of Commerce, (c) **forward auction**, and (d) **reverse auction**. B2B portals are sometimes referred to as hubs.

- Functional – where the focus is on providing the same functions or business processes across different industries.

Note that B2B portals and **e-marketplaces** are often difficult to differentiate – with a B2B portal and e-marketplace often being integrated on the same web site.

This definition is based on, or cites, content by the author in R. Gay, A. Charlesworth and R. Esen, *Online Marketing: A Customer-Led Approach*. Oxford: Oxford University Press, 2007.

Position

In an e-commerce environment, *position* is generally used in the context of search engines; see **search engine rank**. Note, however, that the term could be used in its wider marketing role – product or brand positioning – when referring to the *positioning* of a web site in relation to other sites in the minds of the target market.

Posting

A single message entered – *posted* – on a network communications system – a **newsgroup**, for example. The first *post* will start a **thread**.

Post Office Protocol

See **POP3**.

PPI

Pixels per inch – a metric used to measure the size and clarity of electronic images.

Premium content

Offline, premium suggests excellence. When used online *uniqueness* is added – premium content being that quality content which cannot be found elsewhere on the web. Premium content could be used as a **unique value proposition** for the web site that carries it.

Pre-moderation

Term used to describe the vetting of comments made by visitors to web sites, **blogs** or forums. Many web sites and blogs invite readers to leave their own comments online – a major problem of an interactive medium being that it is open to abuse. For this reason many sites have a pre-moderation facility, where visitor's comments are checked before publication. This can be automatic – software identifying and rejecting certain words, terms or phrases – or manual. Human intervention is more effective, but very time-consuming.

Pre-selling page

Web content writer, Nick Usborne, suggests that content writers need to be aware of three sequential stages of pages on an e-commerce site. They are:

1 the *home* page – with just enough information on a topic to interest the visitor;
2 the *pre-selling* page, where people arrive after reading the short text on the home page – this page gives the visitor all the information they need in order to feel comfortable about making a purchase;
3 the *sales* page – the page that visitors are guided to next: the product having been pre-sold, this page is where a 'maybe' is turned into a 'yes'.

His notion conforms to the concept of **persuasive architecture** and has it roots in the **AIDA** model.

See also **content (2)**.

Price comparison site

See **shopping comparison site**.

Privacy policy

A declaration on a web site that states clearly what the organization will or will not do with any personal information disclosed by a customer in the course of their dealings with that organization. Like **disclaimers** and **terms and conditions**, any privacy policy should be written by a qualified person – normally a lawyer. It should be noted that, given the public's concerns over identity theft and spamming, a sound privacy policy (that is well promoted on the web site) is as much a marketing essential as it is a legal necessity.

See also **online credibility**.

Prompted search

An addition to any search facility that suggests likely search terms that use those words (or letters) typed into the search box. Any suggestions – *prompts* – are based on previous searches. The user can then select the most appropriate search term. For example, typing in 'New Y' might bring the prompt 'New York City'. The 'Google Suggest' facility works on this principle.

Program

The **software** instructions and directions for computers, without which they are useless. There are a number of programming *languages* (the way in which they are written); the program for developing basic web sites is called **HTML**. Those people who develop or write programs are called programmers.

A note on the spelling of program. Program is the American spelling of *programme*. In the UK this spelling is used when referring to any programme not in a computing context. For example, a TV programme and university postgraduate programmes. However – even in the UK – when referring to *computer programs* the US spelling is used.

Prospect

A term that refers to a member of the public who, by word or action, has shown themselves to be a potential customer rather than, for example, being a window shopper. In a sales environment, particularly **B2B**, prospects are referred to as *leads* – see **lead generation**. For many web sites (being part of a **pull media**), the fact that a user has chosen to look at content on that site would suggest they are a prospect.

Prospect acquisition

See **lead generation**.

Protocol

The rules, conventions or standards that make possible the exchange of data between two computers on the Internet, or within any given **network**.

Provider portal

See **portal.**

Proximity search

A type of search where the user specifies words or phrases that should appear near each other on the pages that are returned in the search results. In practice, search engine algorithms do this as a matter of course.

Proxy server

A **server** that sits between the web **browser** and a *real* server, and is normally operated by **ISP**s or large organizations that have their own **firewalls** (universities, for example). A proxy server intercepts all requests to the *real* server to see if it can fulfil the requests itself, acting as a kind of **cache**. For example, if two users in the same city in Europe use the same ISP to access a web site hosted in the USA, the pages of the first visit will be held in the ISP's proxy server. When the second user requests the same pages, rather than requesting them from the American host, the ISP simply delivers them from its own proxy server. The system relieves traffic on Internet **backbones** and gives faster downloads for the user.

Public comment sites

See **consumer-generated media.**

Public key infrastructure (PKI)

A method of online authentication, and kind of **digital certification**, in which each user is issued a public *key* and a private *key*. Messages intended for particular recipients are encrypted with their public keys. The message recipient is then able to decrypt the message using their private key. Similarly, messages sent by one party are signed by a private key and may be decrypted by any party with access to the corresponding public key. A PKI system might be used, for example, by a large organization that has some information it likes to keep private from all but those to whom it wishes to have access.

Farhoomand, A., *Managing (e)Business Transformation*. Basingstoke: Palgrave Macmillan, 2005.

Publisher

See **web publisher**.

Pull-down menu

See **drop-down menu**.

Pull media/medium

This term is included here because the web is a *pull* medium. That is, the user *pulls* the information to them on a voluntary basis. If the user – the customer – chooses not to seek out a web site, or even access the web, there will be no (online) communication with the organization. Push media (e.g. TV advertising) is intrusive to the individual; it is *pushed* at the public whether they want it or not. Note, however, that a more pragmatic view of push media that the e-commerce practitioner should consider is that if the web site does not meet the needs of the potential customer – that is, it is badly designed and/or the information is poorly presented – it will *push* the user *away*.

Purchase behaviour matrix

See **online purchase behaviour matrix**.

Purchase funnel

The buyer-side view of the **sales funnel** and the online **conversion funnel.** As with those two models, the purchase – or buyer – funnel owes much to the **AIDA** model and can be used by marketers to as part of an analysis of **online buyer behaviour**. For example, if a potential customer stepped out of the conversion funnel at a certain stage then vendors could look at how they could prevent that happening. The funnel analogy comes from the notion that potential buyers are many, all of them seeking generic product information to help them make a purchase decision (the top, or widest part, of the funnel). As their search for information gets more specific – the funnel narrows – the number of potential customers reduces, until finally only a few are left – and they require explicit information. Any purchase-funnel analysis would look more specifically at what the user *expected* at each stage of the funnel and why their needs were not met. Naturally, the answers to those issues would help come up with a solution of how to make the sales or conversion funnel better. It is worth noting that research into online buyer behaviour suggests that the purchase funnel is being changed by the way contemporary buyers use the web in their purchase decisions; see **purchase tumbler**. In an online context, the purchase funnel has links with **online buyer behaviour** and the **online purchase behaviour matrix**. Considering the buying process from the point of view of the customer will also help develop successful **persuasion architecture** for e-commerce web sites.

Purchase tumbler

A study commissioned by Yahoo! (www.yahoo.com) and OMD (www.omd.com) called the 'Long and Winding Road: The Route to the Cash Register' (published in May 2006) suggests that Internet technology is changing the way that buyers seek and collect purchase information. Touted as 'the first research study to examine how cultural shifts brought about by the proliferation of technology have radically altered the way consumers make purchasing decisions', the study proposes that the traditional purchase funnel has been replaced by a *purchase tumbler*. The demand on information being (almost) constant as the buyer narrows their options (that is, travels from top to bottom of the funnel/tumbler). The consequence for e-marketers of this phenomenon is that they have a much longer (wider) opportunity to reach the potential customer rather than any opportunity being restricted as the buyer descends to the narrower end of the funnel.

P

Pure online brands

See **online branding**.

Pure online business (or pure-play)

Businesses that trade online only; that is, have no offline trading presence. Such businesses are rare, the majority operating in niche segments – obvious exceptions including Amazon and eBay. It should be noted that the pure online business will have a physical presence of some kind, administrative centre, warehouse and distribution depots, for example. A trader with no physical presence is known as a **virtual business**.

Push media

See **pull media**.

P

Quaero

One of a number of projects announced in April 2006 by the French government aimed at stimulating local technological, industrial and economic development, Quaero (*I search for* in Latin) is a Franco-German search engine intended to rival Google.

Qualified traffic

Users who have arrived at a site after having searched for the site's offering on a search engine. Such visitors are deemed to be *qualified* because they are thought to be more likely to interact with the web site.

> *See also* **prospect, intentional traffic, differentiated traffic** and **undifferentiated traffic**.

Query term

> *See* **keyword**.

Radio Frequency Identification

See RFID.

RAD Lab (Reliable, Adaptive and Distributed Systems Laboratory)

An internet research laboratory, located at the University of California, that helps entrepreneurs develop web-based software services. Opened in December 2005, and backed by Google, Microsoft and Sun Microsystems, the lab gives away any products and services developed there.

RAM (random access memory)

See memory.

Rank/ranking

See search engine rank.

Rappa's online trading business models

In 1998 David Rappa suggested that there were a limited number of ways in which an online-only business could make money. It is a reflection of his foresight that the list is still valid, and that no others have been added since. It should be noted that the models do not have to run in isolation; several of the models could be used to generate income from one web site. Rappa's nine online trading business models are:

- The Brokerage Model – where brokers bring buyers and sellers together and facilitate transactions. The broker makes money by charging a fee for each transaction enabled.
- The Advertising Model – an extension of the traditional broadcasting-media model where the broadcaster, in this case a web site, provides content and services and sells space for advertising messages.

- The Infomediary Model – this capitalizes on the value of data about consumers and their buying habits by collecting such data and selling it on to third parties.
- The Merchant Model – the classic wholesaler or retailer of goods and services.
- The Manufacturer Model – where manufacturers reach buyers directly and so compress the distribution channel.
- The Affiliate Model – where purchase opportunities are provided wherever people may be surfing by offering financial incentives to affiliated web sites.
- The Community Model – this relies on visitors to community web sites having a high investment in both time and emotion in the site's subject, so making such sites ideal for targeted advertising, affiliate or infomediary opportunities, as well as the potential for subscription fees.
- The Subscription Model – depends on users paying for access to the site, meaning that high value-added content is essential.
- The Utility Model – has users paying for services that they might access from the site.

Rappa, D., *Managing the Digital Enterprise*. 1998. Available online at www.digitalenterprise.org.

RDF (Resource Description Framework)

A coding language used by those working towards the **semantic web**.

RDNS (Reverse DNS)

A method of name resolution in which an **IP address** is resolved into a domain name.

See also **DNS**.

R

Reach

More commonly used in offline **push media** than in relation to **online advertising**, *reach* refers to the number of unique individuals who view an ad, no matter how many times they might see it.

See also **ad impression**.

RealAudio

A format developed by Real Networks, RealAudio is a popular **plug-in** for **streaming audio** used to listen to sound recordings on the web.

Streaming audio allows for more immediate playback of music, news, sports, etc., on the site visitor's computer.

RealNames

An online service that that matches company and brand names with their web site address. At one time this was a popular service, but has now been largely superseded by search engines and the public's better understanding of domain names.

Reboot

See **boot**.

Reciprocal link

An exchange of **links** between two sites. This can be a good thing – sites linking to others is the basis of the world wide web and both parties might benefit – a small, family-run hotel and a tourist information site, for example. However, search engines can use inbound and outbound links as part of their **algorithm** to **rank** web sites in their **listings**, and this is often the reason site owners exchange links. This, too, can be beneficial to both sites, but excessive reciprocal links might be considered by search engines to be **link farming** and they would penalize them accordingly.

See also **PageRank** and **TrustRank**.

Recovery search

See **discovery-based search**.

Redirect

See **email redirect** and **web site redirect**.

Referrer

The term used, in a **log file**, to identify from where the user came immediately before they arrived on the site. Although the referrer in a web log is normally a **referring site**, it could be the user themself if they have typed the URL of the web site directly into their browser. Referrer data is useful in **web site analytics**.

R

Referring site/page

A web site that sends a user to another site via a **link** from that site. A **search engine results page** is normally considered to be the referring page. Details of referring pages appear on a web site's **log files**.

Registration

See **web site registration.**

Reinclusion request

Sites that have been added to a **search engine blacklist** will – if they are legitimate – seek to be reinstated on that engine's listings. To achieve this, the site's publishers must file a reinclusion request. The search engine will want to be assured of two things: (1) that the problem – whatever that is – has been corrected, and (2) that it won't happen again. Details of actions taken will strengthen the case. Of course, this assumes that the site's publisher knows why it was excluded in the first place. Those who practise **black-hat search engine optimization** will know what they have done to be blacklisted, but for many web site publishers the reason might be a mystery. This could be for a number of reasons, not least that they may have employed a **search engine optimization** agency that has used black-hat methods without the site publisher's knowledge or permission. It is also possible that the site is the innocent victim of a change in a **search engine algorithm** (see **Google dance**).

Relationship marketing

Whereas *traditional* methods of selling and negotiation are *transaction*-oriented because their purpose is to close a sale, *relationship* marketing looks beyond the immediate sale and seeks to build a long-term supplier–customer relationship. Its relevance to e-commerce is that 'e' technology can be used as part of the communications mix used in developing and maintaining a relationship with customers.

Relevancy

In e-commerce terms this is how well the results of a search request are matched to the intentions of that search. In essence, the ultimate goal of all search engines is to return only results that have 100 per cent relevancy to the individual's search.

Reliable, Adaptive and Distributed Systems Laboratory

See RAD lab.

Re-marketing

See re-targeting.

Re-messaging

See re-targeting.

Repeat order rate

An element of **web site analytics**, repeat order rate calculates the ratio of orders placed by existing customers (those who have purchased from the organization in the past) and total orders placed.

Repeat visitor

A **unique visitor** who has visited a web site on a previous occasion. This **metric** is useful in **web site analytics**.

Report spam button

See spam button.

Reputation scores

See email accreditation.

R

Request

See browser (1).

Resizable text

Depending on the design, the text on a web page can be of a fixed size (e.g. it is part of an **image**), or it can be *resizable*. Standard **HTML** can normally be resized by the user (control and + or -), or an application can be put on the web page by the designer where the user simply clicks on an icon to increase or decrease the text size.

Resolution

The clarity and sharpness of an **image**, expressed in **pixels per inch** for monitors, scanners or image files. High-resolution images require more **memory** or **bandwidth** and so take longer to **download** on to a **browser**.

Re-targeting

Also known as *re-marketing* or *re-messaging*, this is an aspect of **behavioral targeting** where e-commerce traders **cookie** visitors and then track significant activity and (even better) interactions on the site. Using an **online advertising network**, ads are then served to those visitors based on those interactions – they are *re-targeted* after having been first targeted when they visited the web site. For example, a visitor to a travel web site might go to a number of pages that describe a particular resort. They may also go to a 'review' page where several 5-star hotels are reviewed, check out **faq** answers for that resort, search on car-hire prices and seek temperatures in June for that geographic region. Although that user might not make any effort to purchase a holiday on that visit, they would be prime candidates for ads that feature 5-star hotels in that resort in June with special offers on car hire if booked before a certain date.

Return bidding

A tactic from the management of advertisers' ad listings on PPC search engines, return bidding tracks enquiries from bids for specific keywords to see if they produce sales (or whatever the objective of the ad is). By doing this, bids can be adjusted automatically to reflect the **cost per acquisition** – that is, bids should not exceed a breakeven figure for acquisition. Similarly, an e-commerce site which offers a wide range of products could calculate the average profit of each order and create rules to adjust bids on this basis, for example, more aggressive bidding for high-profit products than that on low-profit ones. Return bidding is not something that can be done manually, utilization of **bid management software** being necessary.

Reverse auction

Sometimes referred to as an online event, this is where the buyers put their requirements on a web site and invite interested parties to bid for the business. This is an extension of the traditional (offline) practice of tendering, used extensively by local and national governments. The auction is often part of the services offered by a B2B **portal**.

See also **forward auction** and **online tender**.

Reverse logistics

The management of goods being returned from a buyer to the vendor. The practice is important to any distance-seller as it contributes towards credibility and so loyalty.

See also **e-logistics**.

Rewrite engine

See **URL rewriter**.

RFID (Radio Frequency Identification)

A method of automatically identifying products using data stored on small objects – known as RFID tags – that can be attached to or incorporated in a product, animal or person. The data on the tags will include the **electronic product code**. The system allows goods to be accurately tracked in a logistics environment. A wider marketing application is to use RFID tags to electronically track when, how long and where displays (of tagged goods) are placed in stores and how successful they have been. Critics of the RFID tags refer to them as 'spy chips'.

RFM (recency, frequency and monetary *value*)

A term used in **web site analytics** that has been adopted from offline practice. Essentially, customers are assessed by three key criteria: (1) how long is it since a customer made a purchase (or visited a site), (2) how often do they make a purchase (or visit a site), and (3) how much do they spend? Any targeted marketing efforts can be tailored to suit the outcome of a RFM test. For example, a regular visitor who does not spend would be encouraged to make a purchase while they are there (by limited-period promotional offers, perhaps), or big spenders encouraged to visit the site more often.

R

Rich media

A term used mainly in **online advertising** that is still to settle on a precise definition. Broadly speaking, *rich media* describes a range of technologies and implementations within digital media that result in some kind of dynamic motion and an element of interaction. For some this means the use of technology such as **Flash**™ or the inclusion of video, audio, animation or any combination of these. For others, a relatively simple **animated GIF** is classed as rich media.

Ripping

The term used for transferring CDs on to a computer as compressed audio files, most frequently **MP3**s.

ROAS (return on advertising spend)

An analytic that assesses sales revenue generated for each unit of currency (pound/euro/dollar, etc.) spent on either an online ad campaign or a specific ad. Online advertising using **pay-per-click** arrangements provides greater scope for accurate ROAS than that using offline media.

Robots.txt (Robots Exclusion Protocol)

An exclusion file included on web pages to prevent them from being indexed by search engines. Although most publishers want their sites to be listed on search engines, for some anonymity is preferred. This would normally be for reasons of personal privacy – a family site, perhaps – commercial sites that require confidentiality should not rely on excluding search engines as a mode of security. The *noindex* (do not index this page) tag serves a similar function; however the **nofollow** tag – though frequently used in this context – actually serves a different purpose.

Router

A computer (or software package) that handles the connection between two or more **networks**. Routers spend all their time looking at the destination addresses of the **packets** passing through them and deciding which *route* to send them on – hence the name.

RSS (RDF site summary, rich site summary or really simple syndication)

A format for syndicating web content. Syndicated content includes such data as news feeds, events listings, news stories, headlines, project updates or excerpts from discussion forums and blogs. In short, a way for site owners to let others know what new content is available within their web site. Unlike web sites, which are a **pull media**, RSS *pushes* content to the user – albeit because they have requested it. Note that the first two abbreviation descriptions are from the technical environment; the latter has become popular because it is closer to being a description of what the format actually does.

RSS search engine

A search engine that accepts content not only by sending **spiders** around the web, but by receiving **RSS** feeds of new pages or sites. In reality, the main search engines accept RSS feeds and the best **search engine marketing** companies will run their own RSS feeds into the search engines to maintain the search engine ranking of their customers' sites. Note that the search engines will normally charge a fee for accepting RSS feeds.

RSS tracker

Also known as a *blog reader*, this software application tracks key words, phrases or terms that appear on **blogs** (which use **RSS** for their trans-mission). This type of application should be an essential part of any organization's **online reputation management** or public relations (PR) efforts. The RSS tracker will alert the PR team any time the key phrase appears in any blog, anywhere. Positive comments can be noted (perhaps for future use as endorsements), but negative remarks should be responded to immediately. For example, a blogger might have had a specific problem with a retail outlet that is one of the brand's chain of stores. Within minutes of the blog being posted (probably before many, if any, people have read it) the company can contact the store concerned to verify the complaint. If the complaint is justified (as well as internal action instigated) an online response can be posted, or direct email/phone contact made with the blogger. Done properly, this will defuse the situation and no damage will ensue. Similarly, if the complaint is not justified a direct response can be offered (which is unlikely to satisfy the complainant) and online posts can be made that clearly set out the company's point of view. Again, if this is done prop-erly, reasonable people will see the complaint for what it is and no great damage will result. Anyone who doubts the damage that bad service plus bad response can bring is advised to read up on the case of PriceRitePhoto.com. The case is well covered online: just put the name in any search engine.

See also **consumer-generated media.**

Rule of one

It is generally accepted by online marketers that if more than one per cent of a web site's visitors share a certain technological trait – for example, **browser** type or **monitor** resolution – then that group should be considered in the design of the web site. Although marketers appreciate the reasoning behind this *rule* – that no potential customers should be ignored for any reason – many web site designers do not, and still develop web sites that some potential customers cannot use because their hardware or software does not conform with that of the web site.

R

Safelist

A list of email addresses, the holders of which have agreed (**opt**ed-**in**) to receive email messages from a specific organization. So called because it is *safe* to send emails to those on such a list without upsetting the receivers or invoking any kind of anti-spam action. Those on a safelist are considered to be on an organization's email **white list**.

See also **CAN-SPAM Act**.

Sales copy

See **content (2)**.

Sales page

See **pre-selling page**.

Sales funnel

The offline concept from which the online **conversion funnel** originates and which also has a close relationship with the **purchase funnel** – all of which owe a debt to the **AIDA** model. Just as sales is an element of the marketing discipline, so the sales funnel is also one element of the **marketing funnel**. The funnel model is used to represent the fact that the organization starts with many **prospects** (represented by the wide end of the funnel), but few will become customers (the narrow end). Rather than being a smooth flow, each potential customer passes through a number of stages as they progress down the funnel, and at each stage they can either leave the process or progress to the next. The funnel is used by marketers to identify problems within the sales process, for example at which stage prospects leave, and so address related issues. For a **bricks-and-mortar** business, the Internet could represent an element of the overall sales funnel. In a wider marketing context, a successful **segmentation** strategy would help to (a) reduce the stages in the funnel, and (b) increase the ratio of buyers to prospects – effectively putting only *real* prospects in the top of the funnel.

Sandbox

In computing terms a sandbox is a security device for running programs safely – somewhere a new program could be tested away from the public, for example. In e-commerce terms, however, the term is used in association with search engines, Google in particular. **Search engine marketers (SEM)** speculate that Google puts all new sites into a 'sandbox' for a set period of time, so preventing them from **ranking** well until that period has passed. The theory is that the search engine filters the sites until such time as the **algorithm** deems the site to be what it purports to be. The speculation is that **trusted links** into such sites can help them escape those filters.

SAW (single-action web site)

A concept championed by direct marketing expert Bob Serling, where a web site has only one objective – to sell a (single) product, for example. Serling argues that too many web sites offer the visitor too much choice of what to do or what to buy – which results in confusion and, ultimately, no purchase at all. This notion comes from Serling's direct marketing background, but single action is also common in traditional sales training and practice.

Scientific content management

A concept put forward by web site content expert, Gerry McGovern (www.gerrymcgovern.com). He argues that as more and more of an organization's output is content (that is, information), then that content must be managed. He says that 'within the next fifteen years, organizations will become far more rigorous in how they manage email, web pages, presentations and reports. It will be discovered that there is a science to content; a best way to write a heading or summary, for example.' Hence, *scientific content management*.

Scrapers

A description used for software tools designed to create masses of textual content for **spam web sites** by touring the web and stealing (*scaping*) content that is relevant to a given subject.

Screendump

See **screenshots**.

Screensaver

Once considered essential to protect live but inactive monitor screens, but now largely outdated by the technology used in modern screens, screensavers are software programs that prevent images becoming permanently 'burned' on to the screen. Identified in the early days of the web as an excellent promotional tool, and still used as such today, screensavers are an integral element of many **viral marketing** campaigns.

Screenshots

Also known as screen*dumps*, these are images – pictures – of a web page as it is presented in a browser's window – that is, as the user sees it. They can be captured by specialized software or simply pressing the *print screen* button on the keyboard. Screenshots can be reproduced as an image on a web site or in other visual media – a magazine, for example.

Screen size

See **viewable area**.

Screensucking

A term used to describe what someone is doing when wasting time on the web while they should be doing something else. Although that something could be work, screensucking in a work environment is popularly known as **cyberloafing**.

See also **meanderthal**.

Script (scripting)

A term used to describe the computer language in which a program is written. For example, a web site's scripting could be **HTML**.

Scrolling (to scroll)

The movement of page content up or down (vertical scrolling) or across (horizontal scrolling) a computer screen in order that all the content may be seen by the user. Typically, a web site visitor will start at the top of the web page and *scroll* down the contents. Having a user scroll across a page to read content is considered bad web design practice.

S

Scrub rates

A term used to describe how email addresses are removed from a database as a result of emails to those addresses bouncing (see **email bounce**). Such action would be data cleansing. Higher scrub rates would be expected from opt-out addresses and double opt-in addresses should return virtually zero scrub rates (*see* **Opt-in/opt-out**).

Search&Display (all one word)

An interactive **banner** ad that allows users to search within that banner and then access content without ever clicking through to another site. For example, the banner could promote a retail outlet, and the user *searches* the ad to locate the nearest store within the Search&Display banner.

Search box

The box into which keywords are typed in order to conduct an online search. It is most commonly a white box with the word 'search' next to it – that word acting as the button to be clicked in order for the search to be performed.

Search-driven marketing

See search engine marketing.

Search-informed marketing

See search engine marketing.

Search engine

A tool or program which allows users to search for relevant web sites or information on the Internet. This is achieved by conducting a search on a **keyword** or phrase. A search engine is, essentially, made up of three elements: the **spider**, the **index** and the analysis. The spider gathers data on the web (not just web sites but such things as PDF files, images and audio/video files as well), which is then categorized in the *index*. When a searcher types in a search word or phrase, the index is analysed for content that matches that search. Those *matches* are then presented to the user on the **search engine results page** (SERP). Note that this description is somewhat basic and perusal of the following *search* terms listed in this glossary will add to the reader's understanding of the subject.

See also **directory**.

Search engine advertising

See **paid placement**.

Search engine algorithm

The rules by which a search engine ranks the web sites listed in its **index** in relation to a particular query. How their algorithm works is a carefully guarded secret of each search engine. The reasoning behind this is twofold. First, in a business context they want to keep the information from competitors, but more importantly, they need to keep the specific details from the general public. If details of the algorithm were freely available then it would be relatively easy to develop web sites so that they top the **search engine results pages** (SERP). While this is not a problem for the search engines with regard to genuine web sites, it would be easy for the less scrupulous ones (**adult web sites**, for example) to **spam** the search engines and so reduce the validity of search results. Each algorithm is technical and complex, but in simplistic terms high listing is a competition where each entrant (web site) is judged on a number of criteria, the algorithm calculating each site's total score. The one with the most points comes top of the SERP. To extend this analogy still further, it is like the decathlon, where it is the best *overall* athlete that wins the event. It is no good being the best sprinter if you are poor at the other nine elements. Unlike the decathlon, however, each element in the algorithm is not created equal. Each criterion is graded, so a site might actually score highly in a number of criteria, but if there are low-scoring elements the overall score will be low. The situation is complicated still further in that the search engines do not state which elements score what points and periodically they change all the rules (*see* **Google dance**).

S

Search engine blacklist

As the title suggests, this is where a web site is *blacklisted* by a search engine and, as a result, none of its pages will appear in **a search engine results page** (SERP). While for some **bricks-and-mortar** businesses this may not be a major problem, for pure online players this would be a disaster. Blacklisting would normally be the result of **black-hat search engine**

optimization practices, but it is also possible for a server or service provider to be blacklisted, so affecting all sites hosted on that service.

See also **reinclusion request.**

Search engine cloaking

The practice of getting a search engine to record content for a **URL** that is different to what a user will ultimately see. Although some aspects can be approved by search engines, this is rare and the vast majority of cloaking is disapproved of and guilty sites are blacklisted by the search engines when caught. As with **search engine spamming**, the practice should be shunned by all legitimate businesses, with any short-term benefits being outweighed by long-term damage to the organization's brand, as well as the problem of having any web pages on the domain name **delisted** by search engines.

See also **IP delivery.**

Search engine demographics

As the search industry moves towards maturity, more and more information is being made available to improve online marketing efforts. Search engine demographics refers to the demographics of those people who use search engines, and which ones they favour. For example, a March 2006 report from Hitwise (www.hitwise.com) found that Yahoo! users tend to be younger, MSN users tend to be older and Google users tend to be more affluent. Such information could influence the e-marketer in deciding which search engine they should invest their **pay per click** ad budget.

Search engine listings

The generic term used to describe the information that appears on a **search engine's results page** (SERP) in response to a search – the *list* of links to web sites. To be listed on the SERP is the objective of the online marketer. The **search engine optimizer** seeks to be listed by using **organic listing** and the **search engine marketer** by using **paid placement** and **ad listing**.

Search engine marketing (SEM), or search marketing (SM)

The practice of marketing on the web using search engines. This can be achieved by improving the site's **rank** in **organic listings**, by purchasing **paid listings**, or by a combination of the two. It is not to be confused with **search engine optimization**, which is an *element of* SEM. Despite the term being relatively new, practitioners in the field are already mooting other phrases to supersede it. One of the leading proponents of SEM, Mike Grehan, argues that the practice is now so important that it should be considered as an element of the organization's marketing mix, hence his suggestion of **marketing-led SEO**, which he describes as 'the application of marketing communications to **information retrieval** (IR) on the web'. Other terms being put forward include 'search-driven marketing' and 'search-informed marketing', both intending to reflect more that search has an integral role in marketing rather than being a stand-alone discipline.

See also **consumer-controlled advertising**.

Search engine optimization (SEO)

Although the phrase is now common, it is something of a misnomer. Search engine optimization gives the impression that it is the search engines themselves that are being *optimized*, when in reality it is the web site that undergoes *optimization*. A term that better fits the function it describes would be *optimization for search engines*. In essence, **search engine algorithms** set out to provide the searcher with web pages that best match the keyword or phrase on which the search is based. In a perfect world, the web pages which best match the keyword do so because their content is pertinent to the search, the match-up being more natural than contrived, hence the term **organic listings**, that describes these *natural* match-ups, as opposed to listings that are part of **paid placement**. In real life, however, these *organic* results need help if they are to realize their full potential in **search engine listings**. It is this *help* that is search engine optimization. Numerous methods exist, though none are absolute as no-one really knows fully just how the individual search engine algorithms work – and they change frequently (see **Google dance**). There is, however, much good practice that the search engines themselves advise web site designers to use. Needless to say, where competitive advantage means greater income, there are those who look to gain higher placing on the organic listings by using less than honest methods, effectively trying to fool the search engines into delivering content that doesn't actually match up with the search term. So named because of early movie portrayals of the Wild West where the good guys wore white hats and the villains, black, those who seek to outwit the search engines using nefarious means are referred to as 'black-hat' operators (naturally those who follow the rules are 'white hats'). These villains of the search engine peace use methods such as **search engine cloaking**, web site spam (see **spam 2**) and **IP delivery**. It is now generally recognized that search engine optimization refers only to organic listings, and that seeking to be at the top of any paid listings is part of **search engine marketing**.

Search engine position

See **search engine rank**.

Search engine rank (ranking)

Also known as search engine position or positioning, this is how highly a web page appears in the **organic listings** on a **search engine results page** (SERP). If it is at the top of the list, for example, it is ranked number one, twenty-first on the list has a rank of twenty-one, and so on. To say a web site is listed on a search engine return is of little value to the publisher of that web site unless it has a *high* rank on that list. Ideally a site should be ranked in the top ten, putting it on the first page of the results listings – searchers rarely going beyond the first page.

Search engine results – or returns – page (SERP)

The web page that appears as the result of a request on a search engine which shows the results of that search. On the major search engines the results will be in two columns. On the left will be the **organic listings** and on the right the **sponsored listings**, which are part of **paid placement** campaigns. Some search engines also include sponsored listings above the organic list.

Search engine spamming

An element of the manipulation of search engine results by nefarious means, such practice would include **spam web sites** and **link spamming**, the objective being to artificially raise a web site's **search engine rank**.

See also **black-hat search engine optimization**.

Search facility

A small-scale **search engine** that conducts a limited-range search. The most common application is on a web site. Normally using a **search**

box, users might search the site for a product (e.g. on a shopping site) or information (e.g. on a university site).

Searching page

The page that is presented to a user while a search is being made. For the major search engine whose searches take only seconds – or even fractions of a second – this is not an issue, but for other sites a search can take much longer. On sites where a complex search has been initiated, the searching page will normally show a message saying that the search is being performed, often with some form of apology or reason for the delay. An example would be a holiday-search web site where it is not unreasonable for the user to wait for a search of numerous holiday companies to produce comprehensive results. The searching page can also be used to host targeted ads, perhaps for other products available on the host web site (in the holiday-search example, perhaps travel insurance), or the space could be sold to third-party advertisers.

Search marketing

See **search engine marketing**.

Search-plus

Search engine advertising (see **paid placement**) that is synthesized with other forms of promotion. The notion is that when, for example, an ad runs on TV then users might go online to investigate further the product, offer or company. While the advertiser *might* have featured a **URL** on the ad, it is more likely that the user will go to a search engine to find the relevant web site – and so the appropriate key terms should be purchased for the period of time that the TV ads are aired. Search-plus includes paid placement being integrated with a number of other marketing tactics, including:

- Search-plus television – perhaps the best-practised application of the concept, where research has proved that not only ads, but product placement, can cause **search spikes** for relevant key phrases.
- Search-plus outdoor – both pedestrians and commuters often see only a fleeting glimpse of an outdoor ad, and so may search for details online when they reach their home or work.

S

- Search-plus word of mouth – in this instance, *word of mouth* refers to both the offline and online applications of this traditional method of marketing, though the e-marketer will take more note of that appearing online (see also **consumer-generated media**). Search advertising can be used to reinforce the positive, and respond to the negative, word-of-mouth message.
- Search-plus public relations – while search-plus word of mouth is often reactive, public relations (PR) efforts are normally proactive – and so paid placement can be arranged in advance as part of a co-ordinated venture. The PR message can drive people to the search engines, and the results of those searches can be manipulated to the organization's benefit.
- Search-plus direct mail – perhaps the most obvious application of search-plus, where direct mailings – both offline and online – promote a product or service. Although URLs can be included in the mailing, prospects are likely to seek 'independent' information on that being promoted – and use search engines to that end.

Note that **organic listing** can also be part of search-plus; however, it is more of a long-term strategy than **paid placement**, and is difficult to synchronize with other forms of marketing, particularly at short notice.

Search release

A press release whose structure is such that it is optimized for search engines. The concept is that press releases aimed purely at the *press* are becoming increasingly rare as public relations (PR) departments use press releases to reach the organization's stakeholders (such as current or future customers, investors or trading partners) through the Internet. The intention is that the target audiences will discover the release via search engines or **content aggregation services**.

Search spikes

Where searches on specific **keywords** increase significantly over a short period of time – showing as spikes on a performance graph. For example, when the devastating hurricane hit New Orleans in 2005, there was a search spike on the word 'Katrina'.

See also **search-plus**.

Search term

See **keyword**.

Second life

See **metaverse**.

Secure browser

A web browser that uses a secure protocol, like **SSL**, to access a secure server. The secure browser enables visitors to web sites to conduct secure transactions, like the transmission of credit-card numbers. When a browser connection is secure, the **URL** of the web page will start with 'https' and in the bottom corner of the browser window a closed padlock is displayed.

Security Certificate

A piece of information (often stored as a text file) used by a **SSL** protocol to establish a secure connection. Security Certificates contain information covering who it belongs to, who it was issued by, a unique serial number or other unique identification, valid dates and an encrypted 'fingerprint' that can be used to verify the contents of the certificate.

Segmentation

A key element of contemporary marketing strategy, segmentation is included here because many online applications are based on the concept. Segmentation is the process of dividing the market into groups (segments) according to their needs and wants. Each segment of customers (or potential customers) can then be the target of specific marketing efforts (so-called target marketing). For example, academic texts are marketed at the student segment. As a segment, students might also be targeted by alcohol vendors or local accommodation providers. However, few segments are completely homogeneous in their needs; for example, not all students will drink alcohol and some may live with their parents. Note that it might be argued that online marketing (being a **pull medium**) is self-segmenting because the potential customer seeks out only the web sites that they think will satisfy their needs best; that is, by choosing to visit a web site they place themselves in the segment of the product or service being promoted on that site.

S

Self-hosting

Where a business hosts its own web site. Although the cost of **web servers** has plummeted in recent years, this requires not only the appropriate hardware but also software, staff skills and telecommunications facilities. For this reason self-hosting is a rare practice with some, or all, of the operation normally being outsourced to specialist organizations such as an **application service provider**.

SEM

See **search engine marketing**.

Semantic mapping

See **latent semantic indexing**.

Semantic search

See **latent semantic indexing**.

Semantic Web

A project that is intended to create a universal medium for information exchange by giving meaning – *semantics* – to the content of documents on the web in such a way that it can be understood by machines rather than only by humans. Ultimately, the aim of the semantic project is for computers to be able to harness the enormous quantity of information and services on the web, for example, perhaps allowing a user's PC to automatically seek out local services for its owner – and book an appointment that suits their diary.

See also **web 2.0**.

Sender certification

The concept of having *sender-certified* email is where a trusted third party investigates the email practices of senders before certifying them as legitimate – or not. Certified emails are guaranteed progress past participating **Internet service provider's** (ISP) spam filters, those rejected having their emails bounced. The third party continues to monitor members of the scheme, investigating complaints where necessary. The latest sender certification technology uses encrypted tokens in each email that is unique to each email – participating ISPs are able to detect and decrypt the token. Mailers pay on a per-delivered-email basis, causing the concept to be dubbed *paid-for email*. Industry insiders predict that sender certification could, ultimately, be the key to eradicating **spam**.

SenderID

See SPF.

Send-to-a-Friend (STAF)

A form of **viral marketing** where email or web page readers are prompted to send the message/article to someone they know who they think will be interested in the content. In a B2C environment this is likely to be a joke, game, or similar. In B2B it is more probably some kind of industry-related article, tip or advice.

SEO

See **search engine optimization**.

Sequential advertising

A model of online ad presentation where the advertiser controls the sequence in which ads are shown to the site visitor, no matter what pages, or *sequence* of pages, a user visits on a site. A series of ads will normally build a message and usually lead to an ad that contains a **call to action**. It is necessary to have ads on a single page change over a set period of time to pre-empt the possibility of the visitor only visiting a small number of pages.

SERP

See **search engine results page**.

S

Server

A computer, or a software package, that provides a specific kind of service to client software running on other computers. The term can refer to a particular piece of software or to the machine on which the software is running. The most common servers in the e-commerce environment are those for email (**email servers**) and web sites (**web servers**).

Server farm

Also known as server *cluster*, this is a number of networked servers sited in one location with the purpose of distributing the workload between the servers in the group. This farm could be owned and operated by an organization for its own web sites or as an **application service provider** for other publishers.

Server log

The server log is more commonly referred to as the **log file**.

Service provider

See **Internet service provider**.

Shareware

Copyrighted software available for personal use for a small fee – often downloadable from the Internet.

Shell web sites

See **domain name parking (2)**.

Shilling (to shill)

In an online environment, to shill is to place fake bids on online auctions in order to raise the price – a practice that is considered to be at best unethical, and at worst, fraudulent. Note that the origin of the term comes from the practice of having a partner of a street vendor pretend to be unassociated with the seller and act as an enthusiastic customer, so encouraging others to make a purchase.

Shipping calculator

See **shipping costs**.

Shipping costs

Although in Europe it is more usual to refer to cost of *delivery*, online the US term *shipping* is more commonly used, and so it has become the accepted term in an e-commerce environment. Shipping costs are important to both parties in any online transaction. To the vendor the decision must be made on whether delivery is to be *free* to the customer, with any costs built into the selling price (common in B2B; not so in B2C) or whether the customer will be charged the carriage and any *packing* costs associated with the purchase. For the customer, the shipping costs are additional to the purchase price and so carry physiological as well as actual influence. Best-practice e-commerce sites will include details of shipping costs. This could be as simple as a chart listing the product (or product category) and potential destinations, or a more complex shipping calculator which requires departure and destination addresses as well as the package's weight and full dimensions.

Shockwave

A **plug-in**, developed by the Macromedia company, used in presenting interactive animation on web sites.

Shopbot

See **shopping comparison site.**

Shoposphere

Introduced by Yahoo at the end of 2005, like the **blogosphere,** the shoposphere is intended to be a world where like-minded users connect and link in what Yahoo terms 'social commerce'. In the shoposphere users can rate products, write reviews, create *best of* lists and search for other people's recommendations.

See also **consumer-generated media.**

Shopping agent

See **shopping comparison site.**

Shopping basket

See **shopping cart.**

Shopping cart

Also known as a shopping basket in parts of Europe and sometimes under the generic title of checkout, online this is a software application that facilitates online order taking and processing. All three terms are now commonly recognized by users as being the means of confirming orders and paying for goods – so much so that cart or basket images are used on a retail web site without additional text. It is also something of a quirk that all three terms are accepted in their online manifestation without an 'e' prefix. The application allows customers to accumulate items in a virtual basket, keeping a running total cost for the purchases. In best practice shipping costs are also included in the total cost, and items can be extracted as well as put in. Poor shopping cart design is often cited as the reason for intended purchases not being completed (see **shopping cart abandonment**).

Shopping cart abandonment

The term used when a visitor to an e-commerce site starts the online purchase procedure (i.e. puts a product in the cart/basket), but does not complete the purchase – that is, they *abandon* the cart with goods still in it. Shopping cart abandonment is the ultimate failure in the **conversion funnel**.

Shopping comparison site

Although known by a number of other terms, most notably 'shopping search engine' and 'price comparison sites', these are sites that will search for specific products, or categories of products, that are available from online traders. Although they act as a search engine, to call them search engines can mislead users. Generic search engines (Google, Yahoo!, etc.) will include all web sites in their **organic listings**. The 'shopping' search engine, on the other hand, is limited to those sites that have not only agreed to be listed, but reward the search engines if users follow links from the listings to the store (normally in a **pay per click** business model). The shopping search engines look not only at the sites of individual sellers, but also at those sites which conduct their own searches. Popular in the latter category are airline flights, holidays and car insurance, where the searcher need only enter purchase details once. For example, on a comparison site the user enters the date and destination of a flight and the search checks multiple airline sites using those details – so saving the user from entering the same details on a number of individual airline's sites.

For the online trader, using comparison sites as part of their online marketing mix can be a sound business model, and sites can be optimized so as to appeal to the comparison search engines. Although the comparison sites' 'commission' must be accounted for in any product pricing policy, the fees can be offset as *marketing* costs as the comparison site is, in effect, doing the online marketing for the vendor. Some comparison sites go further than simply listing results and offer review facilities for products listed. In these cases the site becomes an amalgam of a **portal** and a **search engine**.

While a number of shopping comparison sites are popular with users for the service they provide, there is a drawback to the concept. A number of faux-comparison sites have sprung up that seek to take advantage of pay per click agreements with little or no commitment to consumer satisfaction. Often hosted on **intuitive domain names**, such sites will concentrate their efforts on gaining high **search engine rankings**, often by using **black-hat search engine optimization** methods. These pseudo-comparison sites can be frustrating to search engine users (and the search engines), because they can fill **search engine results pages** in detriment to the **organic listings** of genuine retail web sites.

Shopping engine

See shopping comparison site.

Shopping portal

See portal.

Shopping robot

See shopping comparison site.

Shopping search engine

See shopping comparison site.

Short codes

See common short codes.

Shoshkele™

A type of **floating ad** that is similar to a **pop-up** in that it opens in the user's browser. Whereas a normal pop-up is a solid form, the shoshkele™ features free-moving forms, e.g. a bird *flying* across the screen.

Shrink wrap

See click-wrap.

Signature file

A predetermined message automatically added to the end of an outgoing email. Although the original idea was for the signature file to be details of the sender – contact details, for example – it has become common for it to be used to present a marketing message. At its most basic this might simply be the **URL** of the sender's organization's web site, or the **domain name** of a particular promotion. Having a marketing message as a signature file is an element of **viral marketing** – indeed, it is such practice from which the term viral marketing originated. Although signature files were originally text only – and most still are – sometimes images are used, though they are subject to the vagaries of the receiver's email system (see **email specification**). Note that the sending organization's physical address is required on the bottom of direct-marketing emails in order to comply with the **CAN-SPAM Act**.

Single access

A **metric** used in **web site analytics**, this is when a visitor accesses only one page of a web site – normally the **homepage**.

Siphoning

While **page jacking** involves the copying of a web site's content for that content's value (or because the developers of the copy-site are lazy), siphoning is a little more devious. It is the act of taking a web site's entire content – including text, **tags** and trademarked names and phrases – and then putting it on the *siphoner's* own site in an attempt to *steal* visitors from the original site via **search engine rankings** – with the search engines confusing the *copy* site with that which has been copied.

Site map

A plan of the pages that make up a web site presented as a hierarchical model. As a site map is, in effect, an aid to web site **navigation**, only large sites need them; for smaller sites their own navigational features serve the same purpose. A site map can also help in **search engine optimization** in that it makes it easier for the **spider** to find all of the site's pages.

Site session

See daypart session.

Skunkworks

An American term (taken from a comic strip) which describes a small group of people who are given *carte blanche* in the way that they research and develop a project. This means that skunkworks normally operate independently of an organization's research and development operations and so outside the usual rules and management constraints. Typically the term is used in regard to technology projects that are conducted in secret – hence its common military associations.

Slivercasting

Aimed at niche markets that take advantage of the **long tail** concept, slivercasting is the practice of showing TV-style content on the web – and nowhere else. The content comes from two primary sources: (a) developed purely for the medium, and (b) from the vaults of TV production companies. In the case of the latter, this could be material too specialized to have a large enough audience to merit putting it on TV, or compilations of material on minority-interest subjects. The end result is, effectively, TV on the web, but with the advantage of costs being significantly lower, even if the audience is small. Note that although the practice was already in existence, the term *slivercasting* is attributed to a *New York Times* article of March 2006.

Slow tail

The time-lag between a user first visiting a web site and making a purchase on it. Research by Dr Alan Rimm-Kaufman (2005) suggests that 75 per cent of online conversions take place within 24 hours of a customer starting an online search that features the selling web site in the **search engine results page**. The remaining 25 per cent is the slow tail – with the sales-cycle delay being up to three months. Rimm-Kaufman's research also found that the slow tail is more prominent in large-value purchases. Tracking of the slow tail is important for accurate **web site analytics**.

Rimm-Kaufman, A., *The Click-To-Order Interval Study*. San Jose, CA: Search Engine Strategies, 2005.

S

SMART (Salton's Magical Automatic Retriever of Text)

Developed by mathematician Gerard Salton in the late 1960s, this was the first digital search engine, incorporating many of the features – such as relevance **algorithms** – of web-based search engines.

Smartphone

A mobile (cell) phone that has Internet capabilities.

See also **m-marketing**.

SMB (small to medium-sized business)

See SME.

SME (small to medium enterprise)

A generic description for a small business. Definitions vary, but are usually based on those put forward by the Bolton Committee in its 1971 Report on Small Firms. This states that a small firm is 'an independent business, managed by its owner or part-owners and having a small market share'. The report goes on to give more specific descriptions of SMEs in different industries. Note, however, that outside Europe the term used is small to medium-sized businesses (SMBs).

See also **microbusiness**.

SMTP (Simple Mail Transfer Protocol)

The main **protocol** used to send email on the Internet. SMTP consists of a set of rules for how a program sending mail and a program receiving mail should interact.

Snail mail

A rather dismissive description of tradition postal systems from early email users. As email has become more common – and accepted – the phrase has become less commonly used.

Sniping

An online auctioning practice made popular by its use on eBay – so much so that software is available to aid users in its exercise – sniping is the term used when a higher bid is entered in the last seconds of an auction, so winning that auction.

Social bookmarking

A concept that, like some others in the e-commerce environment, periodically rises to be *flavour of the month* with commentators and investors, but has yet to reach universal appeal. Unlike browser bookmarks that remain personal to the user, social bookmarks are made available on the web for others to access. Multiple users' bookmark lists are combined to produce an information source for others who search the 'master' bookmark list using keywords that match **tags** on the bookmarks. While advocates of social bookmarks see them as an alternative to search engines, there is a certain irony in that **search engine optimizers** seek to have their web site listed in such social bookmarks as they create links to the site which count in their favour in **search engine algorithms.**

Social computing

See **networks (commercial and social).**

Social network

See **networks (commercial and social).**

Social proof

A concept originally outlined by Robert Cialdini (2000), the premise being that people are more likely to purchase something that others have commended. Online this can be practised through such content as **testimonials**, best-seller lists, product awards, reviews or case studies. Although Cialdini penned the term quite recently, **direct marketers** have long since learned the value of testimonials and the like.

See also **consumer-generated media** and **customer evangelists.**

Cialdini, R. B., *Influence: Science and Practice* (4th edition). London and Boston: Allyn & Bacon, 2000.

Social shopping

See **online social shopping.**

Soft bounce

See **email bounce**.

Soft opt-in

See **opt-in/opt-out**.

Software

Intrinsically linked with **hardware** – and synonymously with **program** – software is the element of a computer system that makes the computer work. More generic than *program*, the term software is used to describe anything that can be stored electronically as well as any non-physical entity that has any part in a computer's operation. For example, if a computer is not working and all the physical – that is mechanical, electrical or technical – elements are functioning, then it would be described as *a software problem*.

SOHO (small office/home office)

Normally a reference to business computer users as a segment of that market, though the term is also used to describe a **microbusiness** run from home.

See also **mom and pop operation**.

Solus email

A practice from **email marketing**, a solus email is one that is sent by an advertiser to subscribers to an opt-in list of a third party – with that third party's permission. The practice is a risky one for the owner of the list in that it can damage their credibility and may lead to the receivers cancelling a subscription. Any ads must be carefully screened and should be for products or services that complement those of the email-list owner. The reasoning behind the allotment of *solus* in this term is questionable. Solus advertising refers to ads that are separated from competing ads – solus means separate – therefore that *solus* emails are separate from those of the list owners would seem something of a stretch. Though it does make a little more sense if solus emails and **piggyback email** are considered to be stablemates – where one includes ads on third-party emails, and the other keeps them separate.

Source code

The original code (or *language*) used to write computer programs. Source code is normally a collection of files presented in a format readable by humans that can be converted to a computer-executable form. Note that in a technical environment, source code and computer script (or source script/script language) are distinct – to the non-technical user, however, the terms can be taken to mean the same thing.

Spam (1) emails

The online equivalent of offline *junk mail* that arrives in the post, spam is frequently cited as one of the worst things about the Internet (**pop-up ads** run a close second). Nor is it a new phenomenon, the first spam being sent by a marketing rep to every **ARPANET** address on the West Coast of America in 1978 – though it hadn't yet been dubbed *spam*. The term was being used in other connotations from the late 1980s before it was commonly applied to emails, it being a generic term to describe any kind of Internet abuse. Even the origins of the term are unclear. Many observers apparently related the flooding of a **chat** room or computer with a nonsensical repetitive text to the Monty Python sketch, the spam song. Others argue that it is an acronym of either Single Post to All Message-bases or Simultaneously Posted Advertising Message – although both of these seem to have appeared *after* the term was in common use. While a multitude of definitions for *spam* exist, there is (to date) no finite definition of spam that is accepted, or recognized, by everyone.

Definitions in legal documents offer little help towards clarity. The **CAN-SPAM Act** defines spam as 'any electronic mail message the primary purpose of which is the commercial advertisement or promotion of a commercial product or service (including content on an Internet website operated for a commercial purpose)'. The Act exempts *transactional* or *relationship* messages.

Article 13 of the European Union Directive on Privacy and Electronic Communications (2002/58/EC) refers to 'unsolicited communications for the purposes of direct marketing ... without the consent of the subscribers concerned or in respect of subscribers who do not wish to receive these communications'.

Disputes over the definition revolve around a number of words or phrases that most frequently appear in definitions. With examples of arguments raised, they are:

- *Unwanted, irrelevant or inappropriate*. Each of these is subjective; the spam sender might argue it is all of these, the receiver none.

S

- *Unsolicited, meaning without permission or request.* Although recipients can **opt-in** (or **opt-out**) of receiving emails from specific organizations, does opting-in mean the receiver agrees to all emails, even if they consider them irrelevant or inappropriate?
- *Bulk or mass.* Certainly much of what is generally perceived as spam is where an identical message is sent in bulk to multiple email addresses, but what is bulk? A million, a thousand, one hundred, ten?

While few argue against the millions of unrequested emails selling unwanted products being *spam*, the case is not always so clear. Take the following case as an example. Suppose that the manufacturer of a new type of safety valve for scuba-diving air bottles trawls the web looking for scuba-diving clubs all over the world. He then sends a polite email to each club's email address pointing out the potentially life-saving advantages of using the valve, with a link to the company web site. Is this spam – or is it good business practice?

Historical elements of the above were gleaned from Brad Templeton's history of spam, available on http://www.templetons.com/brad/spamterm.html#surf.

Spam (2) web sites

Web sites, including **blog** pages, that are filled with nonsensical content that has been harvested (by **scrapers**) from other sites purely to appeal to search engines – and advertisers. The concept is this. **Online advertising networks** place targeted ads on web pages where the content of the web page and the ads have some synthesis – hotels, car hire or airlines on a portal for Athens, for example. The scammers apply this model, but instead of going to the effort of creating – and maintaining – a genuine web site, they develop web pages full of relevant content gathered for other web sites. This content could be an article, a paragraph or just a sentence. It is all shuffled (to avoid search engines spotting it as duplicate material) and dumped on a page. To the human visitor it makes no sense, but they do not know that when they see the page listed on a **search engine results page** and click on to it. Naturally, they leave immediately, but not before the ads have registered as being downloaded – so returning an income for the page's publisher on a **pay per impression** advertising agreement.

See also **click fraud.**

Spam (3) blogs

See splog.

SpamAssassin

An **open source** project from the Apache Software Foundation, SpamAssassin is a software programme that filters emails for **spam**. The program runs each email message through hundreds of tests analysing such things as text and **HTML** coding as well as checking **domain names** and **IP addresses** against **DNS blocklists** and **filtering databases**. Each of the tests it performs is graded, so failing any test results in a score of anything from a fraction of a point to multiple points. If an email scores too many points, SpamAssassin rejects it. Rather like **search engine algorithms**, the actual scoring system is a secret, though most checkers agree that a score of 5 or more will see an email rejected. The email marketer should be aware of the SpamAssassin tests in order to not only comply with them, but also use them as a benchmark for good practice.

Spam button

In an attempt to cut down spam some **Internet service providers** (ISPs) and **email service providers** (ESPs) provide users with a simple and easy to use system of reporting a spam email, a *this is* spam – or *report* spam – button featured prominently in the user's email window. Clicking on the button alerts the ISP that the receiver considers the email to be spam. The ISP records such reports and, if the same sender appears frequently, they are blacklisted, with all emails from that sender being filtered out (see **spam filter**). While noble in its intentions, the use of spam buttons can be a major problem to genuine email marketers. Users' ignorance of the potential damage to reputable senders of using the spam button can cause a sender to have all their emails to any user of that ISP blocked – a significant number if the ISP is, for example, AOL. Various research has shown that around a third of users click their spam button when they do not find an email interesting – even though they have previously agreed (**opted in**) to receive emails from that sender.

Spam filter

Also known as a mail filter, this is a piece of software that takes in email messages and makes a decision, based on preselected criteria, whether or not to forward it to its addressee. Normally operated by **Internet**

S

service providers (ISPs), **email service providers** (ESPs) or IT departments for organizations with their own mail **servers**, the filters are designed to block **spam**. Although they are becoming increasingly complex (in order to address equally complex technology used by spammers), a basic filter would be to block any email with words like 'free' or 'sex' in an email's subject line.

> *See also* **filtering database, DNS blocklist, email bounce, email accreditation** and **do not use words.**

Spammer

Someone who sends **spam**.

Spam trigger

Any element of an email that attracts the notice of a **spam filter.**

Spam web sites

> *See* **spam (2) web sites.**

Spear-phishing

> *See* **phishing.**

Special-interest portal

> *See* **portals.**

Specific offline advertising

Unlike **incidental offline advertising**, where encouraging users to visit a web site is not the primary objective of the ad, its *specific* relative has the sole objective of driving people to a site. Although it is used mainly by pure online businesses, the tactic can be employed by offline organizations that are using the web as the medium for carrying extended information on the promotion, brand or product as part of an integrated marketing strategy.

> *See also* **traffic-building campaign.**

SPF (sender policy framework)

The standard Internet **protocol** for transmitting email (**SMTP**) allows any computer to send email claiming to be from anyone – so making it easy for **spammers** to send emails from forged addresses. An extension to SMTP, SPF makes it easier to track forged 'from' addresses in emails, so helping to counter spam. SenderID is Microsoft's model of SPF.

Sphere of influence

Although the term has much wider applications in environmental or political terms, in e-commerce the sphere of influence applies to elements of the Internet where the organization has (a) control of the content, and so (b) can exert an influence on the user – complete an online sale, for example – effectively, this is any aspect of the organization's web presence.

Spider

Also known as a *bot* (short for robot) or *crawler*, a spider is a software application used by search engines to *crawl* around the web and gather information about web pages for their **index**. Although the inference is that the spider actually wanders around the web gathering data, it actually goes nowhere. It resides on its own **server** and sends out **requests** to web sites in the same way as a **browser** does, but instead of downloading pages for viewing, it indexes the content.

Spikes

See **search spikes**.

Spinning logo

In the early days of the web, if a designer wanted to show off their skills they most commonly used **animated gifs** – so much so that it became almost obligatory to have a spinning logo on every web site. That is, the organization's logo would spin or rotate rather than remaining static on the page. The best web sites saw beyond the novelty and the fashion soon died. Since then, any inappropriate design that pampers to the vanity of the designer rather than the satisfaction of customers is given the derogatory description of being a *spinning logo*. The same description can be used for the phrase *flaming logo* – something IBM parodied in a TV ad campaign in the late 1990s. Spinning logos were early incarnations of **whistles and bells**.

S

Spiral of prosperity

A model from **direct marketing**, based on **database marketing**, that presumes that the more that is known about a customer, the better their needs can be satisfied – the spiral representing the increase in knowledge about the customer.

Splash page

A term used to describe the first page of a web site that uses **Flash**™-type technology. A splash page appears before the site's **home page**, and is normally used to give visitors instructions or advice on how to use the web site. For example, if the site requires the user to have specific software installed to open it, the splash page could simply contain a message telling the user that they need to download or update their software and/or browser before they can enter the site. Splash pages are generally frowned on by marketers as they contravene the **rule of one**, and many see the splash page as the contemporary version of the **spinning logo**.

Splog

A term used to describe **spam** on **blogs**. The blog spammer – *splogger* – uses automated tools to create thousands of fake blogs from content stolen from legitimate blogs or web sites. Splogs tend to fall into one of two categories:

1 The most common is to create a type of **link farm** of blogs with the intent of manipulating search results. This would increase traffic to those sites by fooling search engines (which look for frequently linked-to sites) into thinking that the sites are popular and so increase their **search engine ranking**.
2 The second application is to produce blogs that simply recycle content and then run **AdSense** or other advertising on them in the hope of making money from users clicking on the ads.

Although the technology battle goes on (as antidotes are developed, the sploggers develop newer software applications), blogging services find it difficult to detect and filter out this kind of spam completely.

Splogger

Someone who perpetrates **splogs**.

Sponsored ad

See **sponsored listing**.

Sponsored listing

When a user inputs a query to a search engine, the results page may include ads that have been purchased based on the **keywords** used in the search. These ads are described by the search engines as *sponsored listings* or *sponsored matches* – as opposed to **organic listings** – though in essence, they are ads.

See also **pay per click**.

Sponsorship

Online sponsorship follows the same basic model as that offline. However, there are other interpretations that are unique to the web. These include:

- The most common interpretation is for an organization to sponsor an entire web site, a sports equipment manufacturer sponsoring the web site of a sporting event, for example. As with its offline relative, sponsorship of web sites treads a fine line between sponsorship and advertising.
- Common practice, particularly in the early days of the web, was for Internet-development companies (web designers, for example) to build, host and maintain web sites for charities, clubs and other non-profit organizations. These *sponsored* sites served as examples of their work in the developer's portfolio.
- Sponsorship is used to describe advertising on search engines (*see* **sponsored listing)**.

Sporn

A term used to describe email **spam** made up of adult or pornographic content.

Spy chip

See **RFID**.

Spyware

The generic title given to software that covertly gathers user information through the user's Internet connection without their knowledge. Although the term originally referred to malicious use of such software – its association with theft of personal information, for example – its use

S

in advertising (see **adware**) and **e-metrics** has seen public attitude towards the concept soften.

SQL (Structured Query Language)

A specialized programming language which is used for sending queries to databases.

SSL (Secure Sockets Layer)

A protocol designed by Netscape Communications which enables **encrypted**, authenticated communications across the Internet. SSL is used mostly (but not exclusively) in communications between web **browsers** and web **servers**. One of the first, and so most popular systems for making secure online purchases, SSL is often used as a generic term for the practice.

STAF

See **send-to-a-friend**.

Status bar

The bar at the bottom of a web browser window which provides information on the status of the web page which is loading. This would include the URL of the web site being accessed, plus that of the **Ad server** if there are ads on the page. When the page is fully downloaded the bar simply says 'done'. Users of **broadband** would normally only see the URL(s) briefly as the page downloads; sometimes the download is so fast that users see only the 'done' message. If a web page is *hanging* without downloading fully, the status bar will show the URL of the page (or ad) that is causing the problem.

Stemming

The ability of search engines to recognize the stem of words and return derivatives in searches. For example, stemming allows a user to enter 'hunter' and receive results that include *hunt* and *hunting*.

Stickiness

Popular in the early days of the commercial web, use of this term has faded in recent years. It describes the ability of a web site to retain the attention and presence of a visitor – that is, how long they *stick* on the site. A *sticky* site will keep visitors on it for longer than a *non-sticky* site. The term has mostly been superseded by such phrases – and practices – as **persuasion architecture** and **usability**.

Stop words

Also known as filter words, these are words that because they add little semantic value, are ignored by search engines when used in a **search term** – it is, therefore, a waste of time for a searcher to type such words into a search box. Common stop words include 'and', 'to', 'or' and 'the'.

Storefront

In an e-commerce context, this term mirrors its offline equivalent, describing that part of a web site where goods are displayed and offered for online sale.

See also **back office** and **virtual mall**.

Storyboarding

A practice in web site development that was adopted from the TV advertising industry, this is the use of drawings or **screenshots** of partially complete, or mocked-up, web pages to review the design with customers (external) or stakeholders (internal). Storyboarding might be used as an element of a **wireframe**.

Strap line

See **tag line**.

Streaming (audio/video)

A technique for transferring data such that it can be processed as a steady and continuous stream so that the recipient of a file does not have to wait for a whole file to download before listening or viewing. Effectively, the user can be watching and/or listening to the content while it is still actually arriving – *streaming* – on their computer.

Style guide

Although even the smallest web site should follow a predetermined style guide, this is something found more commonly in larger organizations where there may be a number of people and/or departments responsible for the organization's web pages. This is particularly true of international companies who have different web sites for each country in which they trade. Similarly, a university might have a number of schools, all of which have responsibility for their own web presence. A style guide helps to convey a consistent, accurate message and image of the organization – in marketing terms, this would be an element of branding. Considerations for a style guide might include:

- **Content** – norms for grammar, spelling and syntax.
- **Creative** – maximum **pixel** and **byte** size for images.
- Corporate – colours, fonts, logos.
- Technical – **source code**, **meta tags**.
- Legal – **disclaimers**, **copyright**.

Subject line

The part of an incoming email which (should) tell the receiver what the email is about. In **email marketing**, it is an essential – if not *the* essential – aspect of the textual content of the message. If the subject line does not appeal to, or attract, the attention of the receiver they are likely to delete the email without even opening, let alone reading, it.

Submission

In an e-commerce environment the term submission refers to the act of submitting a **URL** for inclusion in a search engine's **index**. Unless done through **paid inclusion**, simply submitting web pages to a search engine does not guarantee **listing**. Submission can be done manually by completing and submitting the online form featured on all search engines, or by using a software program that makes the submissions automatically.

See also **RSS feed**.

Sub-viral

See **viral marketing**.

Superstitual™

See **pop-under ad**.

Surfer (surfing)

Someone who spends time travelling – *surfing* – around the web. To surf suggests a lack of direction or objective for being online, while a **user** is online for a purpose – though this is a somewhat pedantic distinction and the two terms are often interchanged.

See also **meanderthals**.

Surround sessions

A form of ad presentation in which a visitor to a web site sees only ads for one product, brand or organization. First introduced by the *New York Times* online edition (www.nytimes.com) in 2001, the format can incorporate **sequential advertising**.

S

T-1

A leased-line connection capable of carrying data at 1,544,000 bits per second. At maximum theoretical capacity, a T-1 line could move a megabyte in less than 10 seconds. That is still not fast enough for full-screen, full-motion video, for which you need at least 10,000,000 bits per second. T-1 is the fastest speed commonly used to connect networks to the Internet.

T-3

A leased-line connection capable of carrying data at 44,736,000 bits per second. This is more than enough to do full-screen, full-motion video. T-3 lines are used mainly by Internet service providers connecting to the Internet **backbone** and for the backbone itself.

Tabbed browsing

A relatively new feature in some **browsers**, tabbed browsing allows users to visit multiple pages by loading the web sites into *tabbed* sections of one page, rather than opening multiple pages. The advantage for users is that they can jump between sites quickly and easily, perhaps to follow a link from a news story without losing their place in the original text.

Tag

An instruction inserted in a document that identifies how the document, or a portion of that document, should be read by a software application. For wider applications of tags, tagging and tagged see **folksonomy**.

Tag line

Also known as a *strap* line, this is a slogan or phrase used to promote a product, service or brand. It may express a particular attribute of the product, or be more generic. In print media the tag line might be the only text used; in TV ads it might be the last spoken content – it is *tagged on* to the ad. Often it will be a theme to a campaign, particularly in brand advertising – Nike's 'Just do it', for example. Online, a tag line can be used as the page header or footer, particularly if it is descriptive.

Targeted advertising

See **contextual targeting.**

Target marketing

See **segmentation.**

Target page

The page to which a user is taken when they click on a **link**, the source of the link being the **anchor tag**. Target page is the term normally used by web designers, with **destination site** – which is effectively the same thing – being used by web surfers.

TCP/IP (Transmission Control Protocol/Internet Protocol)

A group of **protocols** that specify how computers communicate over the Internet. All computers on the Internet need TCP/IP software.

Techies

A non-abusive term bestowed on people whose work is primarily the development, or operation, of technical aspects of the Internet in particular or computing in general. In America – at the likes of Google and Yahoo, where such people all have PhDs – they are *engineers*.

See also **creatives** and **geek.**

Technorati.com

The web site that is the **blogging** equivalent of Google. It is a search engine for blogs, and so popular that its name is synonymous with anything to do with data on blogs and blogging. For example, the site includes statistics on blogs (such as how many blogs link to a particular web site) and, when quoting such data, it is common practice to simply refer to *Technorati stats.*

Template

See **web site template**.

Terabyte

See **byte**.

Terms and conditions

Conditions or stipulations limiting what is proposed to be granted or done, or something demanded or required as a prerequisite. In e-commerce terms this is a legal statement that should be included on all web sites to make clear to the user the *terms and conditions* that apply when dealing with that organization. Like **disclaimers** and a **privacy policy**, any terms and conditions should be written by a qualified person.

Test big (verb)

A slang term meaning to carry out a test that uses, or presents, something radically different to that used previously. An element of risk is normally associated with such an undertaking.

Testimonials

Popular for many years in **direct marketing**, customer testimonials are recommendations from satisfied users of a product or service. Unlike **consumer-generated media**, however, testimonials will have been communicated directly to the selling organization rather than being posted on third-party web sites. Testimonials' popularity with direct marketers reflects that they are an established method of gaining trust with potential customers and are an element of the concept of **social proof**.

Text file

A file whose data are set down as words, sentences and paragraphs that are readable by humans. Microsoft Word documents are text files.

Text-only email

See **email specification**.

Third-party ad server

See ad server.

Third-party logistics (3PL) supplier

See fulfilment house.

Third screen

A term attributed to Chris Galvin, chairman and chief executive officer of Motorola, which refers to a mobile (cell)-phone screen. The notion is that people use three screens in their daily life. The mobile-phone screen is preceded in use by first, the television screen and second the computer screen – though in some demographic groups, particularly 18–25-year-olds, the rankings are not so clear-cut.

Thread

The original **posting** and a series of follow-up related messages in an Internet discussion forum. For example, on a car-related forum the thread might be started by a posting asking for advice on a particular mechanical problem, with subsequent postings of advice being continuations of the thread.

Tiered web delivery

See net (network) neutrality.

TIFF (Tag Image File Format)

A **defacto standard** format for image files, TIFF is a popular format for transmitting high-colour depth images. It is rarely used on the Internet because a TIFF image, owing to its clarity, is too large a file and so would **download** slowly.

Tilde search

See Boolean search.

Tiling

The term used to describe what the user sees when a web site causes multiple browser windows – **pop-unders** – to be opened. This is considered to be bad practice, and rarely seen away from **adult web sites**.

T

Time-based bidding

A tactic from the management of advertisers' ad listings on **search engines**, time-based bidding takes into account that in some industries **conversion rates** can vary by time of day and day of the week. The use of **bid-management software** permits online advertisers to control bids and campaigns on a time and day basis – lowering bids on days that are notoriously poor for conversation, for example.

TLD (top level domain)

See **dns.**

Toolbar

That part of a software or browser window that includes **icons** or textual descriptions for specific commands or actions. The toolbar on a web browser would include, for example, icons for the back button (an arrow) or the browser's homepage (a house). The actual contents of a toolbar can be set by the user and are significant in determining the **viewable area** of a computer screen.

Traceroutes

A program that traces a **packet** from a user's computer to an Internet host, showing how many stages (hops) the packet requires – generally, the more hops, the slower the download. Such a facility is normally used to check difficulties with downloading to find where the problem lies.

Trackback

Also known as a *trackback* **PING**, a reference to the original technology that was designed to track updates between web sites, it is now more commonly recognized as the the **blogging** equivalent of a **backlink**. This is where one blogger wishes to comment on, compliment, or raise issues about the comments made by another blogger. The responding blogger would put a link in his/her reply to original comments, so allowing the reader to *trackback* to the original, so putting the reply in context. As with web sites, the more more links going into a blog the more credibility that blog has with search engines.

See also **PageRank.**

Trade mark

A trade mark is any sign which can distinguish the goods and services of one trader from those of another. A *sign* includes, for example, words, logos, pictures, or a combination of these. Basically, a trade mark is a badge of origin, used so that customers can recognize the product of a particular trader. To be registrable, a trade mark must be:

- distinctive for the goods or services which you are applying to register it for;
- not deceptive, or contrary to law or morality; and
- not similar or identical to any earlier marks for the same or similar goods or services. (www.patent.gov.uk)

While any organization that uses the Internet in the course of its operations has the same considerations of trade mark as those offline, there is one issue that is unique to e-commerce. The problem centres around the way search engine algorithms work – in that they seek to match a searcher's **keywords** with web sites on which those keywords appear. Therefore, company 'A' might include on its web site's **tags** the trademark name of company 'B', the idea being that when a user searches on the (trademark) name of company 'B', the **search engine results page** will feature company 'A'. The practice has been outlawed in the US courts, but is still carried out by some less scrupulous operators. The same issue arises with the purchase of keywords in **paid placement**, though most search engines – as a result of legal action in the USA – now refuse bids on trademarked words.

Traffic

In an e-commerce environment, traffic is the body of **visitors** to a web site, normally expressed as visitors within a stipulated period of time. Traffic is the online equivalent of the offline retail outlet's footfall. As with footfall, high volumes of traffic do not automatically equal high volumes of sales. Also, as with offline trading, acceptable profits can be made from low traffic – so long as it is the *right* traffic.

See also **niche marketing** and **long tail**.

Traffic-building campaign

A time-specific promotional effort with the sole objective of driving traffic to a web site. Promotions could be online (e.g. banner ads or search engine paid placement) and/or offline (e.g. TV or press ads).

T

Specific offline advertising might be part of a traffic-building campaign. Online marketers should have distinct objectives for the web site once users arrive at it as a response to the traffic-building campaign. A traffic-building strategy is, by definition, a longer-term undertaking than a single campaign, and strategic in nature.

Traffic splitter code/traffic splitting

This is software that is used to divide traffic from links to or from a web site. It is used in **A/B testing**, where it is desirable for a single link to take every other user to a different web page (A or B) in order to access the performance of that page.

Transaction costs

A **metric** that can be greatly reduced by the use of the Internet as a medium for sales – and in limited circumstances – delivery. A transaction cost is the total cost of marketing, sales and distribution of a product. Online, the entire marketing effort could be conducted at a much reduced cost to that offline. In some circumstances – that of a **niche product**, for example – where **organic listing** on search engines is enough to generate business, the marketing costs are limited to those of the development, hosting and maintenance of the web site. Similarly, those costs are the only ones involved in running the online retail outlet, and stock holding can be minimal as products can be ordered only in response to online orders. Also, no goods are required for display purposes. An obvious added cost to the online retailer is that of delivery – unless it is an electronic product – though this can be either (a) included within a pricing policy, or (b) charged to the customer.

Trap address

See **honeypot email address** and **opt-in**.

Trigger words

Words, terms or phrases that indicate to people that they are on the right web page (or email) and so give them confidence and encouragement to take the next step – or click. Trigger words should be part of the web site's **copy** and should trigger a response from the reader. For example, if the customer is seeking information on a particular product, say a 'red

yagahit mark4', then they will scan the page for that term. If it is there, it will be the *trigger* for them to read more or follow the link (trigger words are well suited to be **links**). **Hit bolding** works on the trigger-word concept.

See also **persuasion architecture, persuasive momentum** and **call to action.**

Trojan horse (Trojan)

A destructive program installed on a computer that masquerades as a benign application to encourage a user to execute a specific action. A Trojan horse is used for nefarious purposes, usually to compromise the security of a computer, so allowing remote access by unauthorized people. Unlike a **virus**, however, a Trojan horse does not replicate itself, but it can be just as destructive.

Trusted link

In this case the *trust* is on the part of the search engines. The idea is that when a new web site comes into the index of a search engine, part of its **algorithm** has to decide whether the site is what the keywords suggest it is. One of the methods used is to consider the links going into the new site. If any of those links are from what the search engine judges to be reputable sites – they are *trusted* links – the search engine will include the new site in its listings. For example, the BBC would be unlikely to have a link from its gardening pages to a site that wasn't relevant to gardening in some way, and certainly not an **adult web site**.

TrustRank

See **PageRank.**

Turing test

Named after its inventor, British mathematician Alan Turing, the test is a model to prove whether or not a machine (computer) can be considered to be intelligent. To date, no machine has passed the test, but research into artificial intelligence (AI) continues. To achieve AI the machine must have all the knowledge of a human so that it can make logical decisions. In e-commerce, while **intelligent search** is no where near being AI, it follows the concept.

Typosquatting

The practice of registering a domain name that is a variation on a popular domain name with a view to taking advantage of the general population's poor typing ability (see **fat-finger typos**) by registering domain names of common misspellings of companies, brands or products. Although the name might be offered for sale by the organization that has *squatted* the name, the more common use is to host a web site on the typo with the expectation that the site will get **traffic** because of users' misspelling of the name.

See also **domain name parking (2)** and **cybersquatter**.

T

UI (user interface)

A close relative of **usability**, UI is a term used to describe the meeting of user and computer programs and the *interface* between the two. The issue of UI is how easy – or hard – it is for the user to achieve their needs and wants when using the computer. In an e-commerce environment, the interaction is between the user and the web site – via their computer – with better UI meaning a greater chance of the site's objective being met. For e-commerce web sites a major issue in UI is consistency, which may refer to keeping the functionality of a site the same throughout the site and over periods of time, or making the site operate in the way that visitors would expect it to – that is, use accepted methods of practice that are common on the most visited sites on the web.

Undifferentiated traffic

Users who (a) visit a web site by accident, or (b) are misled into visiting it (generally) by spam or poor search engine results. While such visitors do no actual harm to a web site (other than taking up **bandwidth**), they bring no benefits to the site's publishers. Their main disturbance is in the site's **metrics**, where visitor numbers are inflated.

See also **differentiated traffic**.

Undirected information seeker

Unlike the **directed information seeker**, this is the individual who goes online with no particular aim or purpose.

See also **surfer**.

Unique visitor

Also known as *distinct* **visitor**, this is a **metric** used in **web site analytics**. A unique visitor to a web site is one who has been identified, and so is included only once in a count of total visitors to that site.

Upload

To transfer a file or files from a user's computer to a remote computer. In e-commerce, a web site designer would *upload* web page files to the Internet using **FTP** software.

UPS (uninterruptible power supply)

A device that provides battery backup when mains electrical power fails. In an e-commerce environment the UPS would be installed to keep computers of all kinds – **servers**, for example – running for a period of time until full power can be restored.

Up-selling

A close relative of **cross-selling**, up-selling is where the salesperson offers an upgraded or higher-specification product to increase sales value. As with cross-selling, done properly, up-selling is perceived by the buyer as being part of good service. For example, a customer chooses their own PC *off the shelf*, but when the salesperson asks pertinent questions they discover that the buyer needs a higher-specification machine to handle the uses for which they are buying the PC, and so advises one with a higher spec. Naturally, any up-selling that exceeds the buyer's needs has the reverse effect. While online cross-selling is relatively straightforward, up-selling is a more difficult transition. Offline the salesperson can ask the purchaser direct questions as part of a point-of-sale conversation. Online, having clicked on the *buy now* button it is (a) difficult to ask questions, and (b) risky, as the customer may be put off their purchase (see **persuasive architecture**). However, a carefully worded prompt (see **content 2**) at the point of purchase might meet up-selling objectives.

URI (Uniform Resource Identifier)

A generic term for all types of Internet names and addresses. A **URL** is one kind of URI.

URL (Uniform Resource Locator)

A series of characters that identifies a web page. Note that it is a common error to identify the first word as *universal* or even *unified*, rather than uniform. In simple terms, a web page's URL is its address on

U

the web. To access the required page the URL must be entered into the **browser** *exactly*. A URL is made up of several parts. For example, the URL

http://www.yagahit.com/UK/welcome.html

consists of: the protocol (http), the domain name (www. yagahit.com), the path within the domain – in this case, a directory (UK) and the file (welcome), and the programming language (html).

See also **domain names, protocol, HTML** and **HTTP.**

URL rewriter (also known as **rewrite engine)**

A software application that rewrites a site's **URL**s if they are extremely long or contain multiple variables. Such URLs are common in **dynamic web pages**, resulting in them not being indexed by search engines. In order to gain search engine **rankings**, URLs are rewritten in a more search engine-friendly fashion. For example, a dynamic page of an online store containing product information on a digital radio might have the URL

http://www.sitedomainname.com/info/%20?894573959brief~?567.asp.

The URL rewriter would change the product page to something like

http://www.sitedomainname.com/info/digitalradio.

Usability

Web usability has its origins in the sciences of graphical user interface (GUI, pronounced *gooey*) and human–computer interface (HCI) and it is, effectively, all about making a web site *user friendly*. Although proponents of usability argue that it is the most important element of web site design, this often runs contrary to the views of some designers, particularly those from a **graphic design** background. Most outspoken in its favour is usability guru Jacob Nielsen – whose background is in HCI. In defence of his views on the importance of usability, he says: 'If a web site is difficult to use, people leave. If the homepage fails to clearly state what a company offers and what users can do on the site, people leave. If users get lost on a web site, they leave. If a web site's information is hard to read or doesn't answer users' key questions, they leave.' While Nielsen uses the term usability to encompass all aspects of web site design, it can be difficult to identify where usability starts and other elements of web site design begin. Good **navigation**, for example, is an

U

integral part of good usability and yet it is normally discussed as a separate issue.

> *See also* **usability testing** and **UI**.

> This definition is based on, or cites, content by the author in R. Gay, A. Charlesworth and R. Esen, *Online Marketing: A Customer-Led Approach*. Oxford: Oxford University Press, 2007.

Usability testing

Unlike aesthetical elements of a web site – for which any test is subjective – the **usability** of a web site can be objectively assessed. Good practice in usability testing involves asking people who have no connection with the site's design to visit the web site and perform certain tasks. Ideally the participants will be from the target market for the site and any tasks asked of the participants should be essential to meeting the objectives of the web site – for example, buying a product, paying a bill or simply finding a contact phone number.

USENET

An online system of discussion groups, with comments passed among hundreds of thousands of machines. USENET is completely decentralized, with over 10,000 discussion areas, called **newsgroups**.

User

Generally speaking, in an online context the three terms *user*, *surfer* and *browser* mean the same thing – a person who accesses the web. However, in e-commerce the three terms can be differentiated. Hofacker (1999), for example, subdivides *surfers* into two groups:

1 *hedonistic* surfers who use the web as an escapist pastime, rather like some people might use films or sports events; and
2 *utilitarian* surfers who are on a mission, the web being a tool they use to search for and gather information.

The notion can be taken a stage further, using Hofacker's distinction as a basis to discriminate user, surfer and browser. The description *utilitarian* can be applied to *user* – an e-commerce web site *user* being someone who interacts with the site, or has the potential to be a customer. A *surfer* complies with Hofacker's hedonistic concept. Surfers are on the web as a hobby; they have no specific interest in e-commerce. Online *browsers* are the same as their offline equivalent – they might visit an e-commerce site, but are just looking and have little or no intention to purchase. Note, however: (a) good content, copy and navigation can convert a surfer or browser to being a buyer, and (b) the same individual could, on different occasions, go online as a user, surfer or browser. They might even switch from one to the other in a single online session.

Hofacker, C. F., *Internet Marketing*, 2nd edition. Dripping Springs: Digital Springs, Inc., 1999.

User-centric (centred) design

A *buzz-phrase* description of web sites that are designed with the user's on-site experience as the paramount consideration. In essence, the phrase describes the concept of web site **usability**.

User-generated content (UGC)

A more informal term for **consumer-generated media (GCM)**.

Username

See **log in.**

User session

A phrase that is somewhat confusing in that it applies an unconventional meaning for session – that of *repetition*. The term user session is used to describe the frequency of visits to a site over a specified period of time and not a single site visit – as a more common interpretation might be. The time period is variable based on the objectives of gathering the data. For example, on sites that offer independent reviews of hotels, a user might *revisit* the site a dozen times over an hour as they switch back and forth from travel sites offering deals on hotels to the review site to check reviews. In this case the dozen visits are classed as one user session.

USP (unique selling proposition)

Although the concept has evolved over time to include other elements of the marketing mix, it originally applied only to advertising. In his book *Reality in Advertising*, Rosser Reeves, the concept's author, gave the following definition of a unique selling proposition. He said that:

1 Each advertisement must make a proposition to the customer: 'buy this product, and you will get *this specific benefit*'.

2 The proposition itself must be unique – something that competitors do not, or will not, offer.

3 The proposition must be strong enough to pull new customers to the product.

Although some web sites, or elements of them, could be described as advertising (and so qualify as being a USP), the concept of the **unique value proposition (UVP)** is more pertinent to the online marketer.

Reeves, R., *Reality in Advertising*. New York: Knopf, 1961.

Utility computing

Dubbed a *utility* because the supply flows on demand (rather like gas, water and electricity), this is a service that offers computing resources when requested from around the world. The user accesses only the software that they require. Before the price of computers – and associated software – fell to current levels, some pundits predicted that utility computing would be the future of computer access. Though it was never widely accepted for generic software, more specialized services are made available in a similar way (*see* **application service provider**).

UVP (unique value proposition)

A direct descendant of the **unique selling proposition (USP)**, the unique value proposition is the more appropriate of the two for the online marketer. While the USP is associated with the product or its promotion, the UVP should answer the **prospect**'s question: 'Why should I do business with you and not your competitor?' Online, the web site – primarily its textual content – must answer that question. Also, while the USP is related to the uniqueness of the offering from the point of view of the selling company, the UVP is all about the value of the offering from the perspective of the **visitor**.

See also **you are your web site**.

U

Validation

The online context of this term refers to checking – *validating* – a web site's **source code** for errors that might cause problems for **users** when they visit the site. The procedure is software-driven, and so can be purchased as a software package or as a service by a firm that will conduct the validation remotely.

Vanity search

Also known as an *ego* search, this is the act of using a search engine to search on your own name. Anyone doing so should be prepared for indifferent or bad results as well as complimentary. There is a serious business application, however. For someone whose reputation is an important aspect of the business they practise – a financial consultant, perhaps – it is well worth while checking up on what people are saying about you online.

VAR (value-added reseller)

Common in the electronics and computing industries, a VAR is an orga-nization that that takes an existing product (or combination of products), adds some feature and then sells it – usually directly to end-users – as a new package. The added value will normally come from the professional services in which the VAR specializes. This could be training, customiz-ing, consulting or implementation. Online it is possible for the VAR to be a **virtual business**, using the web as the hub of its business model.

VDR

See **virtual data room**.

Vertical e-marketplace

See **e-marketplace**.

Vertical hub

See hub.

Vertical portal

See vortal.

Vertical search

A type of search that drills deep into a specific subject area to facilitate more specific searches. Some commentators predict that vertical search represents the future of online search; certainly Google appears to believe this is so with its basic *all web* search plus *vertical* searches options of Images, Groups, Froogle (shops), Local, Print, Catalogs and Scholar. At the time of writing the introduction of two additional applications (Google Base and Google Sitemaps) had prompted conjecture that Google would soon be in a position to offer even more vertical searches, including many commercial categories such as: Car Search, Job Search, House Search, Holiday Search, and so on.

Video-hyperlink ads

A conceptual technology that will allow a TV or DVD viewer to click on a product in the programme/film and so find out about that product. So if the viewer likes the shoes that a character is wearing, they can select the product and get information on price, styles and colours – and then be taken to a web site where the shoes can be purchased. The concept is included here as an example of what e-commerce practitioners might have available to them in the future. Note that *clickable video* technology already exists, but it is mainly limited to specific elements of video ads. For example, on an online video ad for a car the user might be able to click on an image of the estate version for more details of that variation of the car.

Viewable area

The area of a user's computer screen which is available for a web site to be displayed. Fundamentally this will depend on the size of the user's **monitor** (PC) or screen (laptop or PDA-type device). There are a number of screen sizes available, including 640 × 480, 800 × 600, 1024 × 768, 1152 × 864 and 1280 × 1024 (measured in **pixels**). Although monitor sizes have increased (as prices have come down), so too has the use of laptops, meaning that the most common size is still 800 × 600. However, the physical size is not the only consideration as the user's own toolbar preferences will reduce the actual viewable space. The issue of viewable area is important for web site developers as they need to determine how big to make each web page. Too small, and screen space is wasted, too large, and users will spend more time scrolling down, and worse, having to scroll across the page to read the content. It is possible for developers to design a fixed-size page (where all users see the same size) or flexible width, where pages resize themselves to suit each user's screen (so called *fluid* or *liquid* design). Either option means sacrifices in other design elements and so the trade-offs should be considered carefully.

See also **above the fold.**

View-based conversions

These are **conversions** which are judged on whether a user has seen – but not necessarily clicked on – a particular ad banner before going to the web site promoted on that banner. This is made possible by having the **ad server** track if there is an **impression** of an ad on a web page that the user has downloaded, then record the fact to check if that user subsequently visits the target web site. Although the model has flaws – the user may have been prompted to visit the site based on seeing ads in other media, for example – it can be useful for assessing ads that might have the objective of branding, rather than direct sales.

View page info

A facility available on most browsers (though not Internet Explorer). By right-clicking the mouse while on a web page, and selecting *view page info* from the resulting menu, a new window is opened which presents information such as the page's size and when it was last modified.

View page source (view source)

A facility available on most browsers. By right-clicking the mouse while on a web page, and selecting *view page source* from the resulting menu, a new window is opened which presents the **source code** of that page.

Viral marketing

Although the term was coined in the late 1990s by Steve Jurvetson (the venture capitalist behind Hotmail.com), the practice has existed for as long as trade itself – though viral marketing is accepted as the *online* version. Jurvetson's own definition – *network-enhanced word of mouth* – betrays the origin of the concept, that is, that a marketing message can be passed from individual to individual by *word of mouth*. However, for a viral campaign to be successful, the marketer must offer some motivation for the customer to pass the message on, not least that some kudos or reward comes from forwarding the message. The concept has also become commonly known as *buzz marketing* because a carefully crafted message can create a *buzz* in the market-place. A variation on the viral theme which depends on an element of controversy is the *sub-viral*. This involves advertisers deliberately releasing spoofs of their own (offline) ads to the web in an effort to generate online buzz. For the idea to really work they will normally – initially at least – deny responsibility for the spoof, so increasing the controversy element of the tactic.

Virtual (as a prefix)

Rather like the ubiquitous 'e' (for electronic) and **cyber** prefixes, *virtual* has been added to numerous offline terms to describe their online application. It has generally come to be accepted that the prefix *virtual* means that whatever it precedes does not have a tangible form.

Virtual business

A business that trades only online, with no physical presence. While it is impossible to have *literally* no physical presence, the true virtual business has *practically* none. An example might be a business that sells promotional mugs. The product is available only online, where customers select style, colour, message and quantity from options listed on the web site. The order is then placed, and payment arranged. The owner of the business receives the order and passes it on to a manufacturer who sends the mugs to the customer and an invoice to the seller. The virtual business has never stocked, or even taken ownership of the product – but has made a profit from the transaction. The ultimate virtual business would actually have the customer's online order processed and forwarded to the mug manufacturer by computer, with the virtual business owner having no input or involvement in individual transactions. While such automation is possible, true virtual applications are rare. In the early days of the Internet, businesses like Amazon were erroneously described as virtual – this is not the case, as Amazon (even in its early days) has physical distribution and administrative centres.

It should also be noted that although the phrase has been popularized by its association with online businesses, the concept of the virtual business has long existed in the offline environment – though like the online version, the virtual business must have at least minimal physical presence. Examples include the agent who facilitates purchase, transport, logistics and sale of goods without ever taking possession of them and the business that facilitates projects by managing the outsourcing of tasks necessary to complete that project.

See also **drop shipping** and **fulfilment house**.

Virtual community

A phrase attributed to Howard Rheingold (author and founding executive editor of Hotwired), which refers to the way in which people can interact with each other using information technologies (rather than face-to-face contact). Although Rheingold's comments came before common public use of the Internet, it is the Internet that embraced the concept and made the virtual community what we know it as today. As with an offline community, the virtual – or *online* – community can have many attributes, such as shared interests, common traditions, common ownership and mutual advantage. Virtual community web sites are now commonly referred to as **portals**; indeed, it is often difficult to differentiate between the two. For the online marketer the virtual community should be considered as an element of **consumer-generated media**. Of particular relevance in this context is that virtual communities, by their very nature, are supported by people who are outgoing, vociferous even – sometimes to the point of being evangelical – about their chosen interests. In marketing terms, these people are not only early adopters of new products, but are referred to as *influencers* – that is, those individuals whose opinions others, both in and outside that community, listen to and follow.

See also **customer evangelists** and **networks**.

V

Virtual data room (VDR)

Also known as virtual *deal* room, this is a series of **extranets** that provide a secure online repository of data available to authorized users and a confidential virtual meeting room for professionals and their clients.

Virtual learning environment (VLE)

A term used to describe a type of **intranet** that makes available online teaching and learning facilities. Most universities (if not all) will have a

VLE, as will distance-learning educators and the training departments of large organizations. Although a VLE could be bespoke, the market is dominated by a small number of companies who offer a personalized version of their standard product. At their most basic level, a VLE will facilitate contact between staff and students, though this would be to vastly under-use the services on offer, which might include such things as online assessment.

Virtual mall

Taken from the American term for shopping centres – malls – a virtual mall is a web site that features a number of different shops. In the early days of the commercial web many offline retailers mistrusted the Internet and didn't have web sites hosted on their own domain names, so they sold goods on the web site of a third party. The falling cost of the design, maintenance and hosting of an e-commerce web site has seen even the smallest companies be able to afford their own online shop, resulting in a fall in demand for virtual malls. However, the concept does still exist in a different guise. Perhaps the most well-known manifestations are those of Yahoo! – which hosts online stores as part of its *Merchant Solutions* service – and eBay which encourages its *trade* sellers to have their own storefront on the auction site. It should be noted, however, that many of the Yahoo! and eBay traders also have a web site on their own domain name. In these cases the small business traders receive three significant benefits from being part of the Yahoo! or eBay set-up: (a) the marketing efforts of the online giants, (b) online purchase facilities which might not exist on the home site, and (c) the credibility that is associated with the Yahoo! and eBay brands.

Virtual marketplace

See **e-marketplace** and **butterfly model**.

Virtual press kit

See **electronic press room**.

Virtual private network (VPN)

This term usually refers to a network in which some of the parts are connected using the public Internet, but the data sent across the Internet is encrypted – so making the entire network *virtually* private. A typical example would be a company network where there are two offices in different cities. Using the Internet, the two offices merge their networks into one network, but encrypt traffic that uses the Internet link.

Virus

In a computing environment, this is a program that, when executed, attaches itself to other programs on a computer which then transfer that virus to other programs or users. A virus will normally cause damage to any program it comes into contact with. Part of the function of a **firewall** is to block viruses before they reach users' computers.

See also **worm**.

Vishing

See **phishing**.

Visit

When someone downloads a web site onto their browser, they are deemed to have made a visit to that web site, making them a **visitor** to that site.

See also **unique visitor**.

Visit duration

A **metric** used in **web site analytics**, this is the length of a **visit** to a web site measured in time. Note that *visit duration* is the time spent on the site without leaving. For short-time repeat visits, see **user session**.

Visit frequency

A **metric** used in **web site analytics**, this is how often a user visits a specific web site.

See also **RFM**.

Visitor

In an online environment this is something of a misnomer in that while the visitor is tangible, the place they visit exists only on the Internet – and so is not visited in physical terms. In e-commerce, a visitor is an individual who downloads a web site on to their **browser** – that is, they

V

visit it. For purposes of **web site analytics**, some sites will count someone as a visitor only if they stay on the site for a given period of time (**visit duration**) or move deeper into the site than the **home page**. A visitor session is a visitor's time and activity on a web site in one distinct visit (session) on the site.

Bryan Eisenberg at Future Now Inc (www.futurenowinc.com) proposes that there are four different categories of visitors that might land on a web site:

- Those who know exactly what they want, and if presented with it, will make a purchase.
- Those who have a pretty good idea of what they want and would buy if presented with the right item, but are still in the process of narrowing down their final decision.
- Those who don't have anything specific in mind, but would buy if they came across something of interest (think window-shopper).
- Those who have landed on the site by mistake.

He argues that all web sites should cater to all of these groups and so are significant in his concept of **persuasion architecture**.

See also **unique visitor**.

Visitor session

See **visit**.

Visit tenure

A **metric** used in **web site analytics**, this is the time that has elapsed since a **visitor's** first visit to a specific web site. It is valuable in assessing customer loyalty.

Visual rendering tool (VRT)

Software tools designed to assist online marketers with **email specification**. The basic problem is that the **email clients** of different **Internet service providers** (ISPs) do not deliver emails in a uniform format. For example, an image that is an important part of an email marketing message might download perfectly on one email system, but not appear at all on another. Rather than test an email by sending it to addresses on all the possible systems, the VRT will show the email as it is presented by different ISPs, so performing not only an aid to email creation and design, but also quality assurance checks.

Vlog

A combination of *video* and *log*, this is a **blog** delivered on video rather than text or voice only.

Vodcast

Although video has been available online for some years, the practice of presenting a specific piece of information in a video – a speech to shareholders, for example– has been dubbed a vodcast, the term being an adaptation of **podcast**.

See also **webcast**.

VOIP (voice over Internet protocol)

The technical name for the **protocol** used in **e-telephony**.

Voken

See **floating ads**.

Vortal (vertical industry portal)

A term used to describe a **portal** web site that provides information and resources for a specific business sector or industry, that is, the focus is narrow but deep (vertical), rather than wide and shallow (horizontal).

See also **e-marketplace**.

VPN

See **virtual private network**.

V

W3C

See **World Wide Web Consortium.**

Walled garden

The description given to online services that are deliberately limited, or reduced, in some way. Walled garden has been adopted to describe a number of diverse limitations on services available or accessible, from mobile platforms that do not have full web capacity to password-protected environments provided by **Internet service providers** (with moderated content for children, for example). A less common use of the term is where it is used to suggest limited thinking with regard to how the Internet is used or applied. For example, to encourage more imaginative ideas about e-commerce strategies, a manager might suggest that staff 'think outside the walled garden'.

WAN (wide area network)

Any internet or network that covers an area larger than a single building. A university, for example, might use a WAN to network the PCs on its campus.

WAP (Wireless Application Protocol)

The most popular **protocol** for applications that use wireless communication – Internet access from a mobile device, for example – WAP helps address the limitations of small devices. Devices with such facilities are deemed to be WAP-enabled.

WAV (WAVEform audio format)

An audio file format used for storing audio on computers. Though largely superseded by **MP3** files, WAV files can still be found on the web, usually containing short soundbites taken from other media – catchphrases or short quotes from TV characters, for example.

WCR

See whitelist challenge and response.

Web

See www.

Web 2.0

A title originally coined by O'Reilly Media in 2004 to promote a series of conferences, web 2.0 refers to the second generation of the Internet. Unfortunately, its subsequent proponents have not yet determined when this will happen or how it will be different from version 1.0. Some argue that because it changed the fundamental way in which web pages refresh, **Flash**™-type technology heralded the introduction of web 2.0, while others link its development to the **semantic web** concept. It is not unusual for commentators – and some academics – to reference web 2.0 to convey that they are thinking at the leading edge of Internet development, while some companies use the term in their marketing as a buzzword to infer that the company incorporates all the latest Internet technologies and techniques into the services it offers.

Web address

This term is employed in two related, though different, ways. Marketers use *web address* in a literal manner by associating the term with the organization's **domain name**. While this is a reasonable description, it is more accurate when referring to the online *presence* of the organization. An offline analogy would be to say that a domain name is the name of the building in which the organization resides, but it does not state on which floor and in which office the CEO can be found. The more specific interpretation comes from the technical department, where the **URL** is considered to be the web address as it gives details of a specific web *page*, rather than simply the web *site*. To continue the offline analogy, the directory and file – added to the domain name – in the URL give the floor and office numbers.

W

Web beacon

See web bug.

Web billboards

See domain name parking (2).

Web browser

Someone who *browses* the web (see **user**), or a computer program that facilitates access to the web (see **browser (1)**).

Web bug

Also known as a clear **GIF**, this is a graphic **image** – often transparent – embedded in web pages. Too small for the human eye to detect, the image is placed on a web site for the purpose of collecting information about visitors to the site. It will normally be used in combination with a **cookie**. When included in an email, a web bug can be used to tell if the receiver has opened the email (though note this only works if the email system does not block **HTML** images, as does that of Gmail, for example).

Webcast

A video or audio broadcast transmitted over the world wide web. Originally the webcast would be available only as the broadcast went out live – though now webcasts are routinely made available as a **podcast** (audio) or **vodcast** (video).

Web constellation

A collection of web sites that are all part of one organization, parent company or brand but are developed for different audiences or market segments. Procter & Gamble, for example, has its corporate site on pg.com and different sites for products in its portfolio such as pgpharma.com (pharmaceuticals), olay.co.uk (cosmetics), headand-shoulders.co.uk (hair care), ariel.co.uk (laundry), fairy-dish.co.uk (household cleaners) and gillette.com (male grooming).

W

Web content

See **content**.

Web crawler

See **spider**.

Web feed

See **content aggregator**.

WebFountain

A project at IBM that has been dubbed an *analytics engine*. The project aims to address the problem that a computer can match search terms, but it has no idea what those terms mean. Essentially, WebFountain aims to be the online equivalent of the librarian who takes your initial enquiry and points you towards the right section of books based on her prior knowledge of the subject and the information available.

Webinar

A seminar held on the web. A seminar has two primary definitions. Both involve people discussing a subject, but one is tutor–student oriented and the other more inclined towards the exchange of information. The webinar is more popular in as the latter. While **virtual learning environments** normally include online seminars where a teacher can facilitate and control discussion between students in a **chat room** scenario, the webinar lends itself better to discussion groups, where all parties bring equal knowledge and experience and, through the discussion, disseminate it among other participants.

Webisode

Derived from *web-only episode*, webisodes are a series of short films or sketches that appear only online. They follow a similar format to TV ads of the same nature – usually a famous personality playing a character in a series of (often comic) situations. While the webisodes appear only on the web, they will normally be one element of an **integrated marketing** campaign, often with an element of **viral marketing**.

Weblogging

See **blogging**.

Web logs

See **log files**.

Webmail

The interface that allows users to access an email account through a web browser. Webmail services are provided by **Internet service providers** or dedicated email services (e.g. Google, Yahoo!, or perhaps

W

the most popular, Hotmail). The advantage of using webmail is that by entering their **username** and **password**, email can be accessed by users from any Internet-connected computer anywhere in the world.

Webmaster

The name sometimes given to the person in charge of, or responsible for, maintaining the technical aspects of a web site. The term owes its status to the early days of the Internet, where it was not unusual for the web site to be the domain of one person – the webmaster. As the web has evolved it is now rarely the case that one person has responsibility for an organization's **web presence** (though it is still possible in micro businesses), so the singular title is somewhat redundant. However, the term is still usefully employed as a generic contact email address for people reporting faults on a web site, or querying use and/or operating procedures on it. When employed as the *technical* person in a team of people responsible for a web presence it has become common practice for the term *web site administrator* to replace webmaster.

Web presence

Although an organization's web *site* could be described as its web presence, the term web presence is normally used where the organization might have more than one web site, or even an extensive site. It might also mean that the organization has some content on the sites of others, or that it advertises on the web (an *advertising* presence).

Web publisher

Someone who publishes on the world wide web. The actual definition can vary depending on the environment in which it is used. There are four common interpretations:

1 As with the offline newspaper or book, where the author writes the content, etc., but it is *published* by a controlling organization.
2 In a more generic sense, that all sites on the web have been *published* on the web.
3 That an organization *publishes* its own web site – or at least the content contained in it. This reflects offline practice where a business might say it *publishes* its own product catalogue.
4 That a web design and hosting company *publishes* a web site for its client.

All of these have an element of reason to them – making it hard to argue against, or in favour of, any. As with many Internet-related terms, this is another that might become more finite as the years pass.

Web ring

Once very popular with non-commercial sites, but with the ascendancy of search engines the practice has all but disappeared. The idea is for groups of individual web sites that have a mutual subject to link to each other in a chain – or *ring*. That is, A links to B, which links to C, and so on, until the last member links back to A. This means that whichever site the user lands on first, they can visit each by following the links on each site around the ring.

Web server

A **server** that hosts a web site (or sites). Most web servers are operated by companies that sell **web space** on them as a business model, although large businesses and organizations may have their own – as will larger e-commerce operators. However, technology has driven the cost of servers down and it is now feasible for even small companies to have their own web server – though maintenance is an issue.

   See also **dedicated server.**

Web site

Technically, a collection of appropriate files that are presented on the world wide web by means of **FTP** transfer. More generically, however, it is the name given to a collection of web pages that are associated with a particular person, organization, entity or brand – for example 'it is the company's web site'. In business terms, a web site could be described as an organization's premises, or *presence*, on the web. Note that *web site* can be presented as two words or one – *website*. As there is no absolute rendition based on any objective consideration, whether it is presented as one or two words is left to the personal preference of the person doing the writing.

W

Web site accessibility

Although accessibility is important for all web site users, for most it is addressed generically under the headings of **navigation** and **usability**. More specific issues of accessibility are associated with those users who have certain disabilities. As more countries pass laws stating that web sites must be accessible to disabled people, the issue of making a web site accessible to *all* Internet users has moved from one of business and ethical grounds, to legal grounds. However, to address accessibility issues to indulge social pressure or respond to legal enforcement would suggest that the organization's web site development has not followed best business practice in the first place. The **World Wide Web Consortium**, under the auspices of its Web Accessibility Initiative, has produced a comprehensive set of guidelines for the creation of accessible web sites – the guidelines are organized to allow for three levels of compliance and have been widely adopted. As the need for web sites to be built with accessibility as a consideration has become more widely accepted, so there has been an increase in the number of tools and resources available to help organizations ensure that their sites follow relevant accessibility guidelines. The most popular of these – perhaps because it is free – is the '**Bobby**' verification service.

See also **Pas 78** and **Disability Discrimination Act.**

Web site administrator

See **webmaster.**

Web site analytics

As with all business expenditures, web sites must be able to show a return on investment (ROI). To help assess any return, metrics of the web site – e-metrics – can be gathered and analysed. The actual e-metrics harvested for a site will depend on the objectives of that site. For example, if the objective is to increase sales, metrics harvested might include such things as sales volume and average order size. An objective of improving after-sales service would require such metrics as page-download numbers or the length of time a user spends on the site (where long stays might be bad, an indication that the information sought is hard or impossible to find). On the other hand, if the goal of the web site is to develop the brand, long stays might be considered a good thing. Analysis of such metrics will provide information on which the marketer can act both tactically and strategically.

See also **key performance indicator.**

Web site availability

A figure – expressed as a percentage – that is of great interest to the e-commerce trader as it signifies how often a web site is available to the user. While 100 per cent is preferable, even the best in the business will suffer the occasional *downtime* – possibly through no fault of their own – therefore the high nineties is the norm; less than 97 per cent is problematic.

Web site bounce

An element of **web site analytics**, this refers to a web site visitor who either (a) gets no further than the page on which they enter the site, or (b) stays on the site for less than five seconds – effectively, they *bounce* straight off to another site. Too many visitors bouncing would indicate there is an issue with either the web site content – it doesn't appeal to the visitor – or the places from which they are referred – for example, poor **keyword** selection for search engine **paid placement**.

Web site navigation

See **navigation**.

Web site personalization

Once predicted to be the **killer application** of the Internet, personalized web sites have never quite lived up to that billing. The theory was that using the personal details and demographics of an individual, a web site could be personalized for each customer as they arrive at it. Personalization would then create a one-to-one sales situation for every sale. While proponents continue to argue that the concept still has potential, in reality the marketing Holy Grail of one-to-one online-sales scenarios still seems a way off – not least because users are reluctant to reveal the personal details necessary for the concept to truly succeed. To date there are three main types of web site personalization being practised:

- Ad personalization. The type made popular by Amazon, where ads are delivered based on the user's purchase history. Such applications rely on the visitor having previously registered with the site – perhaps when making a purchase.
- Content personalization. Similar to the previous model, but with personalized content being delivered. For example, Yahoo!'s homepage allows users to pick and choose the news and entertainment content relevant to them.
- Segment personalization. This is where the home page of the web site requests users to identify their basic demographics. This, in turn, changes the presentation of the site, perhaps its content, and

W

certainly any ads it carries will be changed. The most basic demographic for this type of personalization is male or female.

It should be noted that while **B2C** sites generate the most publicity, **B2B** sites can offer better opportunities for personalization because of the potential for closer relationships between vendors and customers.

Web site redirect

Sometimes known as **domain name redirection** – for the user the result is the same – and a close relative of the **meta refresh**, the web site redirect is most commonly used when a domain name has been withdrawn or made redundant – if a company moves its web site from one domain name to another, for example. There are a number of **HTTP** response codes that can be used on the domain name's **server**, including:

301 A permanent redirect status indicating that the resource has moved permanently.
302 A temporary redirect status.
303 A 'See Other' status that indicates that the resource (web site) has been replaced.

Selection of which to use is important for **search engine optimization**, as some **search engine algorithms** might see the redirection as a **black-hat search engine optimization** tactic.

Web site registration

In order to restrict users to all or some of a web site's content and/or facilities, they are required to register their details with the publishers of that site. Registration details can be used for **database-marketing** purposes. Once registered, users would normally need to **username** and/or **password** to access the site.

Web site template

Rather than starting with a blank screen for every web page, a format is developed which can then be used as a template for all the pages on that web site. Templates have been largely replaced by **cascading style sheets**.

Web site visitor

See **visitor**.

W

Webspace

The amount of space on a web **server** allocated to a live domain name (**IP address**) by its host. Webspace is normally measured in megabytes, and is charged for by the web site hosting company – usually in megabyte-sized chunks.

Web spam

See spam web sites.

Web surfer

See user.

Web user

See user.

Webvert/webvertising

It is perhaps the confusing way in which these terms were used in the early days of the commercial Internet that is the reason for the decline in their use. Webverts were those web sites that offered nothing (or little) more than would be presented in an ad in printed media. At the same time, banner ads placed on web sites by third parties was called webvertising. The terms were popular in the legal community, but used little in the general commercial environment.

WEEE (Waste Electrical and Electronic Equipment)

Implemented in 2006, the European Union's WEEE directive applies stringent controls to the disposal of electrical equipment – including all computers – and so impacts on e-commerce.

W

Welcome screen

Originally this was a term used for the first page of a web site, so called because many web sites started by welcoming visitors to the web site of the organization. As the welcome-message practice has dwindled so has the use of the welcome screen. A more unusual use of the term is for a welcome page to be developed for a particular purpose – an offline promotion, for example – though it is common practice for these to be called **landing pages**.

What You See Is What You Get

See WYSIWYG.

Whistles and bells

A term used to describe those elements of a web site that demonstrate leading-edge technology. Although the term is generally used in a positive sense – describing a site to be 'complete with all the whistles and bells' as being one that incorporates all that technology has to offer, for example – it can also be used in an ironic, if not outright negative, manner. The inference in this case being that some, if not all, of the technology being applied on the site is superflous to the site's primary business objectives, and is included as a showcase of the designer's abilities.

See also **eye candy web site** and **spinning logo**.

White-hat hacker

See **hacker**.

White-hat search engine optimization

See **search engine optimization**.

Whitelist

So named because it serves the opposite purpose to a *blacklist*, more accurately this is an *email* whitelist, but in an e-commerce environment *email* is omitted. A whitelist is a list of email addresses from which an Internet user is always willing to receive email. Whitelists are registered with the user's **Internet service provider** (ISP) and override any **spam filters** the ISP might operate. It is common for the terms whitelist and **safelist** to be interchanged – the difference is, however, that the organization has a whitelist while individual users form their own safelists.

See also **whitelist challenge and response** and **spam button**.

Whitelist building strategy

Where email marketers have a policy of encouraging new subscribers and so avoid having any subsequent emails being rejected as **spam** by the subscriber's **Internet service provider**. This is achieved by having a clear message on the subscription form asking the subscriber to add the company's email address to their address book, or **safelist**.

Whitelist challenge and response (WCR)

Anti-spamming software where the sender's email address must be on an approved **whitelist**. Emails from senders not on the whitelist are sent a *challenge* that the sender's system must respond to. Because many spammers do not use *live* email addresses, this challenge would receive no response and so the original email would be rejected. While such a system reduces spam in the user's mailbox it can also block genuine emails from friends and/or business associates because (a) the sender does not have the friend on their **whitelist**, or (b) the friend is not on the receiver's **safelist**.

White paper

A piece of literature that is a hybrid of an article and a sales brochure. Its purpose is to promote a product by providing the reader with useful information about a problem that is solved by the product the publishing organization is selling. The practice is known offline as a **bait piece**, and historically is closer to a sales brochure in its presentation. Online – to give the concept more credibility – the term white paper has been adopted. The white papers are more formal, often resembling an academic paper which presents the results of research or case study the *baiting* company has undertaken. Although its use is limited in a business context, the practice is very popular in both technical and marketing aspects of e-commerce. Its popularity has led to the concept of *white-paper marketing*.

White-paper marketing

See **white paper**.

White space

A term commonly used by proponents of web site **usability**, this refers to a web page that has limited content presented on a white (or near-white) background. The idea is that text is easier to read if it is surrounded by plenty of *white space*. The notion comes from the print media (consider the page you are reading now) and is practised by many of the web's most visited sites – Google, eBay and AOL, for example.

W

White van web sites

Also known in the USA as *panel van* web sites, these are commercial sites of limited content and functionality, but which meet the objectives of the business they represent – **lead generation**, for example. The term comes from the ubiquitous vans that are a staple of businesses around the world that need to transport goods from A to B with the least fuss and best return on investment. Like their namesake web sites, white vans are not a glamorous aspect of business, but they get the job done – hence the analogy. The opposite of such a site would be an **eye candy web site** that looks good but does not meet any business objectives.

See also **brochureware**.

WHOIS

A query-and-response database used for determining the owner of a US-registered **domain name** (.com, for example) or **IP address**. While the concept was developed with the best of altruistic intentions (such as allowing system administrators to look up and contact other domain name administrators in order to address problems), the system can have nefarious uses – like building email lists for **SPAM** campaigns. Online marketers might use a WHOIS database for a number of legitimate reasons, such as (a) checking who owns a domain that is inactive, perhaps with a view to purchasing it, or (b) as part of a competitor analysis – the registration of particular names might betray future business plans. Note that there is no WHOIS facility available for .uk and other EU domain names as the information is protected by the **Data Protection Act** in the UK and similar legislation in other EU countries.

Wi-Fi (wireless fidelity)

Although the term can apply to physical connections, it is most commonly used to indicate that a product can connect to another using radio frequency – a PC and printer, for example. Any products tested and approved as *Wi-Fi certified* are interoperable with each other, even if they are from different manufacturers. In an e-commerce context, Wi-Fi is most commonly associated with wireless connection to the Internet, usually in private homes or large buildings – university libraries, for example. However, Wi-Fi access can be over a wider area, a public outdoor space, for example (so-called **hot spots**). New technology – Wi-Max – is expected to provide much wider areas of access to Wi-Fi Internet connection – up to 30 miles, so covering entire areas of towns or cities with broadband access in so-called Wi-fi *clouds*.

Wi-Fi cloud

See **Wi-Fi**.

Wiki

A web site that is not only a collaboration of numerous authors, but is permanently a work in progress. Wikis allow anyone to edit, delete or modify their content. The most famous web site of this kind perpetrates the term in its domain name – wikipedia.org, the online encyclopedia. The origin of the term is the Hawaiian *wiki*, meaning quick. The concept's founder Ward Cunningham (www.c2.com) originally used the term WikiWikiWeb – meaning double-quick web, but the abbreviated version proved more popular.

Wi-Max

See **Wi-Fi**.

Window ad

Another name for a **pop-up ad**.

WIPO

See **World Intellectual Property Organization**.

Wireframe

A term used in web site development to describe the planned hierarchical structure of the functional elements of a proposed web site – that is, without the **graphics**. Wireframes are used not only as a development aid, but also to explain to other stakeholders how (eventual) users will interact with the site.

Within-page link

Also known as a *jump* link, this is a **link** that, when clicked on, takes the user to a different location in the open document – online, this normally means further down the same web page. They are frequently used in **FAQ**-type pages where questions can be listed at the top of the page, and clicking on the question takes the user to the answer – rather than scrolling down the page for all the questions and answers. Within-page links are considered to have poor **usability** traits because they contravene the user's mental model of what links are expected to deliver.

WOMMA (The Word of Mouth Marketing Association)

Of particular value to the e-commerce trader is WOMMA's-best practice guidelines that address critical issues of word-of-mouth transparency and ethics (www.womma.org).

World Intellectual Property Organization (WIPO)

The purpose of WIPO is to promote the protection of intellectual property throughout the world through cooperation between countries. Although it does have influence over issues of online intellectual property, it is most commonly recognized in the field of e-commerce through its involvement with the Internet Corporation for Assigned Names and Numbers **(ICANN)** in the arbitration system for resolving disputes over **domain names**.

World wide web (WWW)

Frequently, and incorrectly, used to describe the **Internet**, the world wide web – or simply *the web* – has two interpretations. They are (a) the whole constellation of resources that can be accessed using tools such as **Gopher**, **FTP**, **HTTP** and **USENET**, and (b) the universe of **hypertext** servers which are the **servers** that allow text, graphics, sound files and so on to be delivered to **browsers**. While the web as we know it now came into being in the mid-1990s, the concept can be traced as far back as 1980, when Tim Berners-Lee built what he called ENQUIRE. Although different from the web used today, ENQUIRE was made up of many of the same key ideas. At the end of the decade, Berners-Lee (with Robert Cailliau) published his formal proposal for the world wide web. August 1991 saw the debut of the web as a publicly available service on the Internet. In April 1993, CERN (for whom Berners-Lee worked) announced that the world wide web would be free to anyone, with no fee. Critical mass was achieved with the 1993 release of Mosaic, a web-based browser, which added graphics to the web – prior to this it had been text only. It is generally accepted that the launch of Mosaic signified the birth of the web as it is now recognized – though the *actual* birthday is debated (*see* **Mosaic**).

World Wide Web Consortium (W3C)

According to the W3C's web site front page, this organization 'Develops interoperable technologies (specifications, guidelines, software, and tools) to lead the Web to its full potential. W3C is a forum for information, commerce, communication, and collective understanding.' While it does serve an important purpose, it should be noted that acceptance of any and all of W3C's input is voluntary – that is, it offers guidelines, not rules.

Worm

A type of **virus** that replicates itself across a computer network, usually performing malicious actions, such as using up the computer's resources and so shutting the system down.

WPA (WiFi Protected Access)

Wireless access to the Internet that is encrypted for security. An enhanced version, WPA2, is now common.

WWW

See **world wide web.**

WWW Wanderer

The first web-based search engine. Developed by researcher Matthew Gray at the Massachusetts Institute of Technology, Wanderer collected web sites into its index and provided a search facility for users to search that index.

See also **Archie** and **SMART.**

WYSIWYG (What You See Is What You Get)

The description given to design or editing tools that show the exact appearance of the desired output while the user is creating a document. It is commonly used for word processors, but has other applications, notably web-page authoring. The phrase originated during the late 1970s when the first WYSIWYG editor – Bravo – was created. It is said that the team of researchers who developed the Bravo software adopted the term from a catchphrase used by a character in a TV comedy popular at the time.

W

XML (Extensible Markup Language)

A specification enabling the definition, transmission, validation and interpretation of data between applications. In layperson's terms, XML allows computers to communicate with each other and so has played a significant role in the ascent of e-commerce.

XML Feeds

A form of search engine **paid inclusion**. Rather than paying to have search engines crawl web sites, the online marketer pays for the search engine to be *fed* web pages via **XML**, so facilitating the search engine's gathering of information.

Yagahit

The online equivalent of the once ubiquitous widget – a generic, nonexistent product used in examples where a specific product might bias the example.

Yahoo! search marketing

Yahoo's **pay per click** advertising system.

See also **AdWords**.

You are your web site

Phrase often used to convince business owners/managers that skimping on web site development is a false economy. The notion is that in the online environment, the web site is the only thing that a customer – or *potential* customer – knows about the organization, the perception being that bad **web presence** equals bad organization.

See also **online credibility**.

Zip file

A file that has been compressed to preserve **memory** and facilitate easier transfer, this is particularly useful for email attachments where the email system has limits to its capacity.

Zone batching

The practice of sending out emails in batches to suit the time zones of the recipients. For example, a company might have research that suggests that users tend to read their personal email around lunchtime, and so want emails to arrive between 9 a.m. and noon. If those users are in different geographic locations and in different time zones, the emails need to be dispatched at staggered times so that they are delivered during the required period in the user's local time.

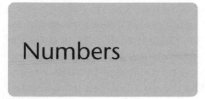

Numbers

1G/2G/2.5G/3G/4G

The series of generations of wireless technology. 4G is still awaited. 1G was analogue-only and the latest – 3G – supports **rich media**. It was the launch of 3G that brought these *generations* to the notice of the general public when a number of mobile phone companies bidding for the licenses to broadcast the technology in the UK became national news. Despite their efforts, the phone companies are yet come up with the **killer application** for 3G technology.

3PAS

See **adserver**.

40/40/20 Rule

Created in the 1960s by Ed Mayer – who many consider to have been the leading light in modern **direct marketing** – the 40/40/20 Rule is the formula that still guides many of the world's direct marketing campaigns. The Rule states that direct marketing campaigns should be built by focusing attention on (a) the audience, (b) the offer and (c) the **creative** in the following percentages: 40 per cent audience, 40 per cent offer, 20 per cent creative. More recently, however, it has been suggested that the rule needs to be updated to address direct marketing using the Internet by adding a fourth element – technology. This would give a revised rule of the 4-Way Split – 25 per cent audience, 25 per cent offer, 25 per cent creative, 25 per cent technology. Whether or not this revision stands the test of time in the same way as Mayer's original remains to be seen.

404 File not found message

An HTML **error code**, probably the most common encountered by users online. The 404 error message indicates that the server went looking for a requested web page but found only a dead link. Likely causes for the message being displayed fall into one of two camps: (a) the web site's fault, or (b) the user's fault. The most common reasons for these are (a) if there is a problem with the **server** on which the site is hosted, (b) the web site might no longer exist – perhaps because the organization it represented no longer exists, (c) the web site address – the **URL** – typed into the **browser** is incorrect, or (d) the URL in a **link** has been entered into the **source code** incorrectly.

In the USA *moved to Atlanta* is a colloquial term for the 404 message, originating from the telephone area code for Atlanta, Georgia – 404.

404 trapping

A term used to describe the application of a custom-made page to host a **404 file not found message**. The practice is normally used by sites with extensive content where site updates, changes or reorganization can result in content being moved from one **URL** to another. Although internal links to that content will be amended, external links (those held on **search engine listings**, for example) will still refer users to the *old* page – where they get the 404 message. With 404 trapping, rather than seeing a *standard* file not found page from their browser or service provider, users see a message from the site publisher advising them why the page has moved and a link to either the new URL of the content or the site's **homepage**.

419 scam

A form of advance-fee fraud, perpetrated online, in which the *target* receives an email that promises fabulous rewards – the drawback being that some kind of advance payment is required. Although many exist, the most popular are the next-of-kin scam (tempting targets to claim an inheritance of millions of dollars in a foreign bank belonging to a long-lost relative, then collecting money for bank and transfer fees) and the laundering crooked money scam (in which targets are promised a commission on a multibillion-dollar fortune). This type of scam originates in Nigeria, where 419 is the criminal statute against fraud – hence the name. It is estimated that 419 scams net hundreds of millions of dollars annually worldwide, with most victims too afraid or embarrassed to report their losses.

Further reading

While a multitude of sources, not least the author's own experience, have been used in compiling this book, a number of web sites have proved particularly useful. These include:

Clickz Network (www.clickz.com). A whole host of articles from experts in various e-commerce-related fields.

e-Consultancy (www.e-consultancy.com). Research and information on best practice for online marketing and e-commerce.

Excess Voice (www.excessvoice.com). Articles and advice from Nick Usborne, a leader in the field of online copywriting.

Gerry McGovern (www.gerrymcgovern.com). Although focussing on web content development and management, McGovern works at the leading edge of e-commerce.

Internet.com (www.internet.com). Some 160 Internet-related web sites organized into 16 channels.

Marketing Profs (www.marketingprofs.com). Some excellent e-marketing content, though the terminology used and models/theories quoted mean that the articles are mainly for readers with a background in marketing.

Market position (www.marketposition.com). News and views from search engine marketing.

Mediapost (www.mediapost.com). A provider of numerous newsletters on the media, marketing and advertising that keep the reader abreast of developments in those environments.

Webopedia (http://e-comm.webopedia.com). An online e-commerce glossary.

Wikipedia (www.wikipedia.org). As a **wiki**, the content of this web site has issues with reliability and objectivism – it is, however, an excellent starting point for research into the term.

Index

Note: page numbers in **bold type** indicate main definitions.